3rd Edition
Ventures 1

STUDENT'S BOOK

Gretchen Bitterlin ▪ **Dennis Johnson** ▪ **Donna Price** ▪ **Sylvia Ramirez**
K. Lynn Savage (Series Editor)

CAMBRIDGE
UNIVERSITY PRESS

CAMBRIDGE
UNIVERSITY PRESS

University Printing House, Cambridge CB2 8BS, United Kingdom

One Liberty Plaza, 20th Floor, New York, NY 10006, USA

477 Williamstown Road, Port Melbourne, VIC 3207, Australia

314–321, 3rd Floor, Plot 3, Splendor Forum, Jasola District Centre, New Delhi – 110025, India

103 Penang Road, #05-06/07, Visioncrest Commercial, Singapore 238467

Cambridge University Press is part of the University of Cambridge.

It furthers the University's mission by disseminating knowledge in the pursuit of education, learning and research at the highest international levels of excellence.

www.cambridge.org
Information on this title: www.cambridge.org/9781108449557

© Cambridge University Press 2018

First published 2008
Second edition 2014

20 19 18 17 16

Printed in Mexico by Litográfica Ingramex, S.A. de C.V.

A catalogue record for this publication is available from the British Library

ISBN 978-1-108-45053-9 Workbook
ISBN 978-1-108-44940-3 Online Workbook
ISBN 978-1-108-68985-4 Teacher's Edition
ISBN 978-1-108-44920-5 Class Audio CDs
ISBN 978-1-108-44909-0 Presentation Plus

Additional resources for this publication at www.cambridge.org/ventures

AUTHORS' ACKNOWLEDGMENTS

The authors would like to acknowledge and thank focus-group participants and reviewers for their insightful comments, as well as Cambridge University Press editorial, marketing, and production staffs, whose thorough research and attention to detail have resulted in a quality product.

The publishers would also like to extend their particular thanks to the following reviewers and consultants for their valuable insights and suggestions:

Barry Bakin, Instructional Technology, Los Angeles Unified School District, Los Angeles, CA;

Jim Brice, San Diego Community College District Continuing Education, San Diego, CA;

Diana Contreras, West Valley Occupational Center, Los Angeles, CA;

Druci J. Diaz, Hillsborough Country Public Schools, Tampa, FL;

Linda Foster, Instructor, Hillsborough County Schools Adult Education Department, Tampa, FL;

Margaret Geiger, M.Ed., Dallas, TX;

Ana L. Herrera, San Jacinto Adult Learning Center, El Paso, TX;

Cindi Hartmen, ESL Instructor, San Diego Continuing Education, San Diego, CA;

Patrick Jennings, Tomlinson Adult Learning Center, St. Petersburg, FL;

Lori Hess-Tolbert, Frisco, TX;

AnnMarie Kokash-Wood, Tomlinson Adult Learning Center, St. Petersburg, FL;

Linda P. Kozin, San Diego Continuing Ed, San Diego Community College District, San Diego, CA;

Caron Lieber, Palomar College, San Marcos, CA;

Reyna P. Lopez, Southwest College, Los Angeles, CA;

Rosemary Lubarov, Palo Alto Adult School, Palo Alto, CA;

Lori K. Markel, Plant City Adult and Community School, Plant City, FL;

Mary Spanarke, Center for Applied Linguistics / Washington English Center, Washington, DC;

Rosalie Tauscher, Fort Worth ISD Adult Ed, Ft. Worth, TX;

Timothy Wahl, Abram Friedman Occupation Center, Los Angeles, CA;

Delia Watley, Irving ISD Adult Education and Literacy, Irving, TX;

Andrea V. White, Tarrant County College, Arlington, TX;

Sandra Wilson, Fort Worth Adult Education, Ft. Worth, TX

SCOPE AND SEQUENCE

UNIT TITLE TOPIC	FUNCTIONS	LISTENING AND SPEAKING	VOCABULARY	GRAMMAR FOCUS
Welcome pages 2–5	■ Identifying the letters of the alphabet ■ Identifying numbers ■ Identifying days and months ■ Identifying abbreviations	■ Saying the alphabet and numbers ■ Spelling numbers and names ■ Saying days and months ■ Saying your birth month	■ The alphabet with capital and lowercase letters ■ Numbers ■ Months and days	
Unit 1 **Personal information** pages 6–17 Topic: **Introductions**	■ Identifying names ■ Identifying numbers ■ Using greetings ■ Identifying countries of origin ■ Exchanging personal information	■ Clarifying spelling ■ Using greetings ■ Using appropriate language to introduce self and others	■ Personal information ■ Countries and nationalities ■ Personal titles	■ Possessive adjectives ■ Subject pronouns ■ Simple present of *be* ■ Contractions
Unit 2 **At school** pages 18–29 Topic: **The classroom**	■ Describing location ■ Finding out location	■ Asking and giving location of things ■ Saying *excuse me*	■ Classroom furniture ■ Classroom objects	■ Prepositions of location (*in, on, under*) ■ *Where is?* ■ Singular and plural nouns ■ *Yes / No* questions ■ *this / that* and *these / those* ■ Contractions
Review: Units 1 and 2 pages 30–31		■ Understanding a conversation		
Unit 3 **Friends and family** pages 32–43 Topic: **Family**	■ Describing actions ■ Talking about family members	■ Asking and answering questions about current activities ■ Answering questions about your family	■ Family relationships ■ Daily activities ■ Descriptive adjectives	■ Present continuous ■ *Wh-* questions ■ *Yes / No* questions ■ Object pronouns (*him, her, it, them*)
Unit 4 **Health** pages 44–55 Topic: **Health problems**	■ Describing health problems and suggesting remedies ■ Expressing sympathy	■ Asking about someone's health ■ Expressing sympathy ■ Suggesting a remedy	■ Body parts ■ Health problems ■ Descriptive adjectives	■ Simple present of *have* ■ *Yes / No* questions with *have* ■ *have* and *need* ■ Contractions
Review: Units 3 and 4 pages 56–57		■ Understanding a narrative		
Unit 5 **Around town** pages 58–69 Topic: **Places and directions**	■ Describing location ■ Giving directions ■ Asking for directions ■ Confirming by repetition	■ Asking about a location ■ Describing your neighborhood ■ Clarifying directions	■ Building and place names ■ Imperatives for directions	■ Prepositions of location (*on, next to, across from, between, on the corner of*) ■ *Where* questions ■ Affirmative and negative imperatives

READING	WRITING	LIFE SKILLS	PRONUNCIATION
■ Reading the alphabet ■ Reading numbers ■ Reading months and days	■ Writing the alphabet ■ Writing names ■ Writing numbers ■ Writing days	■ Understanding dates	■ Pronouncing the alphabet ■ Pronouncing numbers ■ Pronouncing days and months
■ Reading a paragraph describing a student's personal information	■ Writing sentences giving personal information ■ Identifying and using capital letters	■ Reading a registration form ■ Understanding cultural differences in names ■ Using personal titles ■ Using a directory ■ Reading an ID card	■ Pronouncing key vocabulary ■ Saying telephone numbers ■ Saying addresses
■ Reading sentences describing a classroom ■ Using pictorial cues	■ Writing sentences about the location of items in the classroom ■ Using capitalization and periods	■ Reading an inventory list ■ Counting objects	■ Pronouncing key vocabulary
			■ Recognizing syllables
■ Reading a paragraph describing a family birthday party ■ Using a passage's title for comprehension	■ Writing sentences about your own family ■ Writing number words	■ Reading an insurance application form ■ Using family trees ■ Using formal and informal family titles	■ Pronouncing key vocabulary
■ Reading a paragraph describing a sick family's visit to a doctor's office ■ Interpreting exclamation points	■ Writing an absence note to a child's teacher ■ Writing dates	■ Using an appointment card ■ Matching remedies to ailments ■ Showing concern for someone's health	■ Pronouncing key vocabulary
			■ Pronouncing strong syllables
■ Reading an email describing a neighborhood ■ Interpreting pronoun referents	■ Writing a description of your neighborhood ■ Capitalizing proper nouns	■ Reading and drawing maps ■ Giving and getting directions ■ Understanding what a DMV is	■ Pronouncing key vocabulary

UNIT TITLE TOPIC	FUNCTIONS	LISTENING AND SPEAKING	VOCABULARY	GRAMMAR FOCUS
Unit 6 **Time** pages 70–81 Topic: **Daily activities and time**	■ Describing habitual activities ■ Asking for dates and times ■ Giving information about dates and times	■ Using *usually* vs. *always* ■ Using *has* vs. *goes to* for classes ■ Talking about daily schedules	■ Times of the day ■ Habitual activities	■ Simple present tense ■ *Wh-* questions ■ Prepositions of time (*at, in, on, from...to*) ■ *start / end* and *open / close*
Review: Units 5 and 6 pages 82–83		■ Understanding a conversation		
Unit 7 **Shopping** pages 84–95 Topic: **Food and money**	■ Asking about quantity ■ Reading prices ■ Asking the location of items	■ Asking and answering *How many?* and *How much?* ■ Talking about what there is and isn't ■ Using quantifiers	■ Grocery store items ■ U.S. currency	■ Count and non-count nouns ■ *How many? / How much?* ■ *There is / There are* ■ Quantifiers with non-count nouns ■ *some* and *any*
Unit 8 **Work** pages 96–107 Topic: **Jobs and skills**	■ Identifying past and present jobs ■ Describing skills	■ Talking about your job ■ Talking about skills	■ Occupations ■ Work locations	■ Simple past of *be* (statements and questions) ■ *can* ■ Contractions ■ *be* with *and* and *but*
Review: Units 7 and 8 pages 108–109		■ Understanding a narrative		
Unit 9 **Daily living** pages 110–121 Topic: **Home responsibilities**	■ Describing past actions ■ Discussing chores ■ Expressing appreciation	■ Talking about household activities	■ Chores ■ Household items ■ Time words	■ Simple past tense of regular and irregular verbs ■ *Or* questions
Unit 10 **Free time** pages 122–133 Topic: **Free-time activities**	■ Describing past actions ■ Describing future actions ■ Discussing plans	■ Talking about free-time activities	■ Free-time activities ■ Sports	■ Simple past of irregular verbs ■ Future with *be going to* ■ Contrasting past, present, and future
Review: Units 9 and 10 pages 134–135		■ Understanding a conversation		

College and Career Readiness section	pages 136–155
Audio script	pages 156–163
Photo / Art credits	pages 164

READING	WRITING	LIFE SKILLS	PRONUNCIATION
■ Reading a paragraph describing a person's schedule ■ Using *Wh-* questions to interpret a reading	■ Writing a description of your schedule ■ Using indents for paragraphs	■ Using class and other schedules ■ Understanding Parent-Teacher Associations ■ Understanding volunteerism ■ Using calendars ■ Reading clocks	■ Pronouncing key vocabulary
			■ Understanding intonation in questions
■ Reading a paragraph describing a shopping trip ■ Looking for clues to understand new words	■ Writing a note about a shopping list ■ Using commas in a list	■ Reading supermarket ads ■ Reading receipts and using basic consumer math ■ Using U.S. currency ■ Using multiple payment methods	■ Pronouncing key vocabulary
■ Reading a letter describing a person's job and work history ■ Interpreting narrative time through verb tense	■ Writing a paragraph about your skills ■ Checking spelling	■ Completing job applications ■ Identifying skills ■ Understanding job certification ■ Reading email	■ Pronouncing key vocabulary
			■ Pronouncing the -s ending with plural nouns
■ Reading a letter describing daily events ■ Interpreting the narrative voice	■ Writing an email describing household chores ■ Using the simple past in writing	■ Using a job-duties chart ■ Understanding household chores and the tools used for them	■ Pronouncing key vocabulary
■ Reading an email describing a vacation ■ Interpreting time words in a passage	■ Writing an email describing a past and future vacation ■ Creating new paragraphs as the tense changes	■ Reading a TV schedule ■ Using schedules ■ Understanding the cultural features of sports	■ Pronouncing key vocabulary
			■ Pronouncing the -ed ending in the simple past

TO THE TEACHER

What is *Ventures*?

Ventures is a six-level, four-skills, standards-based, integrated-skills series that empowers students to achieve their academic and career goals.

- Aligned to the new NRS descriptors while covering key English Language Proficiency, College and Career Readiness Standards, and WIOA requirements.
- A wealth of resources provide instructors with the tools for any teaching situation, making *Ventures* the most complete program.
- Promotes 21st century learning complemented by a suite of technology tools.

How Does the Third Edition Meet Today's Adult Education Needs?

- The third edition is aligned to the NRS' interpretive, productive, and interactive outcomes at each level.
- To help students develop the skills they need to succeed in college and the workplace, *Ventures* 3rd Edition offers a dedicated College and Career Readiness Section (CCRS) with 10 worksheets at each level, from Level 1 to Transitions (pages 136–155).
- Audio tracks and grammar presentations linked to QR codes can be accessed using smartphones (see page x), promoting mobile learning.
- Problem-solving activities added to each unit cover critical thinking and soft skills key to workplace readiness.
- More rigorous grammar practice has been added to Lessons B and C, and more evidence-based reading practice has been added to Lesson D.

What are the *Ventures* components?

Student's Book

Each of the core **Student's Books** contains ten topic-focused units, with five review units. The main units feature six skill-focused lessons.

- **Self-contained lessons** are perfectly paced for one-hour classes. For classes longer than 1 hour, additional resources are available via the Workbook and Online Teacher's Resources.
- **Review units** recycle and reinforce the listening, vocabulary, and grammar skills developed in the two prior units and include a pronunciation activity.

Teacher's Edition

The interleaved **Teacher's Edition** includes easy-to-follow lesson plans for every unit.

- Teaching tips address common problem areas for students and additional suggestions for expansion activities and building community.
- Additional practice material across all *Ventures* components is clearly organized in the *More Ventures* chart at the end of each lesson.
- Multiple opportunities for assessment such as unit, mid-term, and final tests are available in the Teacher's Edition. Customizable tests and test audio are also available online (www.cambridge.org/ventures/resources/).

Online Teacher's Resources
www.cambridge.org/ventures/resources/

Ventures Online Teacher's Resources offer hundreds of additional worksheets and classroom materials including:

- A *placement test* that helps accurately identify the appropriate level of *Ventures* for each student.
- *Career and Educational Pathways Worksheets* help students meet their post-exit employment goals.
- *Collaborative Worksheets* for each lesson develop cooperative learning and community building within the classroom.
- *Writing Worksheets* that help literacy-level students recognize shapes and write letters and numbers, while alphabet and number cards promote partner and group work.
- *Picture dictionary cards and Worksheets* that reinforce vocabulary learned in Levels Basic, 1, and 2.
- *Multilevel Worksheets* that are designed for use in multilevel classrooms and in leveled classes where the proficiency level of students differs.
- *Self-assessments* give students an opportunity to reflect on their learning. They support learner persistence and help determine whether students are ready for the unit test.

Workbook

The **Workbook** provides two pages of activities for each lesson in the Student's Book.

- If used in class, the Workbook can extend classroom instructional time by 30 minutes per lesson.
- The exercises are designed so learners can complete them in class or independently. Students can check their answers with the answer key in the back of the Workbook. Workbook exercises can be assigned in class, for homework, or as student support when a class is missed.
- Grammar charts at the back of the Workbook allow students to use the Workbook for self-study.

Online Workbooks

The self-grading **Online Workbooks** offer programs the flexibility of introducing blended learning.

- In addition to the same high-quality practice opportunities in the print workbooks, the online workbooks provide students instant feedback.
- Teachers and programs can track student progress and time on task.

Presentation Plus
www.esource.cambridge.org

Presentation Plus allows teachers to digitally project the contents of the Student's Books in front of the class for a livelier, interactive classroom. It is a complete solution for teachers because it includes the Class audio, answer keys, and the Ventures Arcade. Contact your Cambridge ESL Specialist (www.cambridge.org/cambridgeenglish/contact) to find out how to access it.

Ventures Arcade
www.cambridge.org/venturesarcade/

The Arcade is a free website where students can find additional practice for the listening, vocabulary, and grammar found in the Student's Books. There is also a Citizenship section that includes questions on civics, history, government, and the N-400 application.

Unit organization

LESSON A Listening focuses students on the unit topic. The initial exercise, **Before you listen**, creates student interest with visuals that help the teacher assess what learners already know and serves as a prompt for the unit's key vocabulary. Next is **Listen**, which is based on conversations. Students relate vocabulary to meaning and relate the spoken and written forms of new theme-related vocabulary. **After you listen** concludes the lesson by practicing language related to the theme in a communicative activity, either orally with a partner or individually in a writing activity.

LESSONS B AND C focus on grammar. The lessons move from a **Grammar focus** that presents the grammar point in chart form; to **Practice** exercises that check comprehension of the grammar point and provide guided practice; and, finally, to **Communicate** exercises that guide learners as

they generate original answers and conversations. These lessons often include a *Culture note*, which provides information directly related to the conversation practice (such as the use of titles with last names) or a *Useful language* note, which introduces useful expressions.

LESSON D Reading develops reading skills and expands vocabulary. The lesson opens with a **Before you read** exercise, designed to activate prior knowledge and encourage learners to make predictions. A *Reading tip*, which focuses on a specific reading skill, accompanies the **Read** exercise. The reading section of the lesson concludes with **After you read** exercises that check comprehension. In Levels Basic, 1, and 2, the vocabulary expansion portion of the lesson is a **Picture dictionary**. It includes a *word bank*, pictures to identify, and a conversation for practicing the new words. The words expand vocabulary related to the unit topic. In Books 3 and 4, the vocabulary expansion portion of the lesson uses new vocabulary from the reading to build skills such as recognizing word families, selecting definitions based on the context of the reading, and using clues in the reading to guess meaning.

LESSON E Writing provides practice with process writing within the context of the unit. **Before you write** exercises provide warm-up activities to activate the language needed for the writing assignment, followed by one or more exercises that provide a model for students to follow when they write. A *Writing tip* presents information about punctuation or paragraph organization directly related to the writing assignment. The **Write** exercise sets goals for the student writing. In the **After you write** exercise, students share with a partner.

LESSON F Another view brings the unit together with opportunities to review lesson content. **Life-skills reading** develops the scanning and skimming skills used with documents such as forms, charts, schedules, announcements, and ads. Multiple-choice questions (modeled on CASAS[1] and BEST[2]) develop test-taking skills. **Solve the problem** focuses on critical thinking, soft-skills, and workplace development. In Levels 1–4, **Grammar connections** contrasts grammar points and includes guided practice and communicative activities.

---

[1] The Comprehensive Adult Student Assessment System. For more information, see www.casas.org.
[2] The Basic English Skills Test. For more information, see www.cal.org/BEST.

UNIT TOUR

The Most Complete Course for Student Success

- Helps students develop the skills needed to be college and career ready and function successfully in their community
- Covers key NRS and WIOA requirements
- Aligned with the English Language Proficiency (ELP) and College and Career Readiness (CCR) standards

The Big Picture
- Introduces the unit topic and creates an opportunity for classroom discussion.
- Activates students' prior knowledge and previews the unit vocabulary.

Unit Goals
Introduces the competencies students will learn.

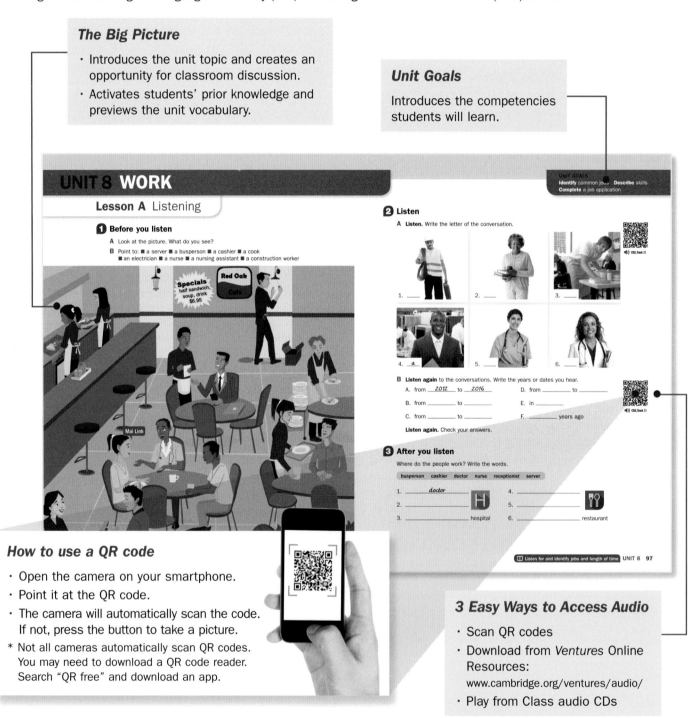

How to use a QR code
- Open the camera on your smartphone.
- Point it at the QR code.
- The camera will automatically scan the code. If not, press the button to take a picture.
- * Not all cameras automatically scan QR codes. You may need to download a QR code reader. Search "QR free" and download an app.

3 Easy Ways to Access Audio
- Scan QR codes
- Download from *Ventures* Online Resources: www.cambridge.org/ventures/audio/
- Play from Class audio CDs

Every unit has two grammar lessons taught using the same format.

Grammar Chart

- Presents and practices the grammar point.
- Extra grammar charts online can be used for reference and give additional support.

Grammar Presentation

Animated presentations to watch on mobile devices using QR codes allow for self-directed learning and develop digital literacy.

Additional Grammar Activities

Ensures students have the chance to practice more grammar to meet the rigor of CCRS.

Natural Progression

Moves from controlled to communicative activities for students to ask and answer questions about familiar text, topics, and experiences.

Real-life Practice

Engages students and provides meaningful application of the grammar.

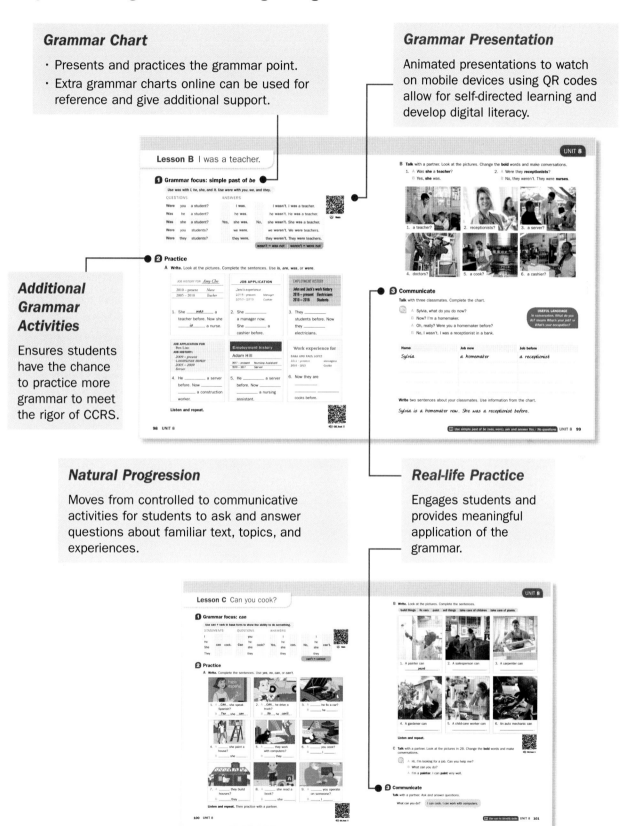

Reading

- Uses a 3-step reading approach to highlight the skills and strategies students need to succeed.
- Combines reading with writing and listening practice for an integrated approach to ensure better comprehension.
- Brings text complexity into the classroom to help students read independently and proficiently.

Picture dictionary

Expands unit vocabulary and practices pronunciation for deeper understanding of the topic.

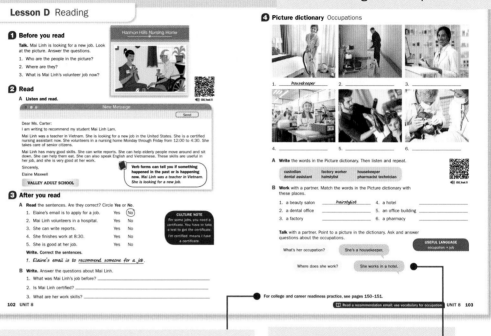

Writing

- Helps students develop a robust process-writing approach.
- Supports students to meet the challenges of work and the classroom through academic and purposeful writing practice.

College & Career Readiness Section

Builds critical-thinking skills and uses informative texts to help master the more complex CCR standards.

Speaking Practice

Helps students internalize the vocabulary and relate it to their lives.

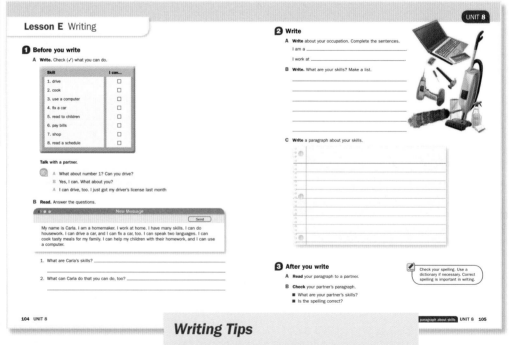

Writing Tips

Gives students confidence in writing with easy-to-follow writing tips and strategies.

Document Literacy

Builds real-life skills through explicit practice using authentic document types.

Grammar connections

Contrasts two grammar forms in a communicative way to help with grammar accuracy.

Test-taking Skills

Prepares students for standarized tests like the CASAS by familiarizing them with bubble answer format.

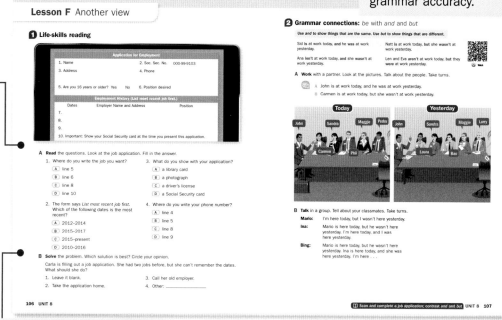

Problem-solving Activity

Covers critical thinking and soft skills – crucial for workplace readiness – and helps students meet WIOA requirements.

Review Pages

Allows students to review the vocabulary and grammar after every two units to confirm retention.

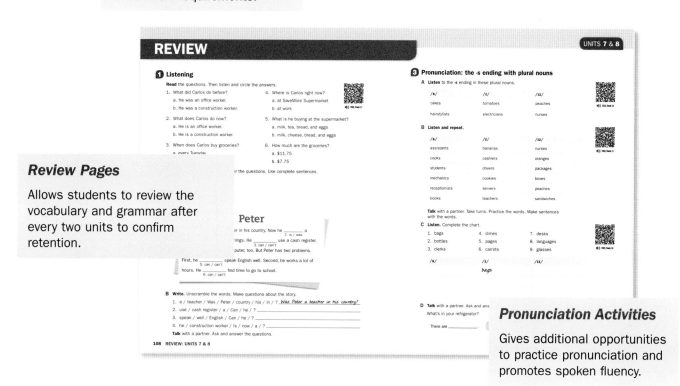

Pronunciation Activities

Gives additional opportunities to practice pronunciation and promotes spoken fluency.

CORRELATIONS

UNIT	CASAS Competencies	Florida Adult ESOL Low Beginning	LAUSD ESL Beginning Low Competencies
Welcome Unit Pages 2–5			
Unit 1 **Personal information** Pages 6–17	0.1.2, 0.1.3, 0.1.4, 0.1.5, 0.1.6, 0.2.1, 0.2.2, 2.1.1, 2.1.8, 2.4.1, 2.5.5, 2.7.2, 4.8.1, 6.0.1, 7.2.4, 7.4.3, 7.5.6	2.01.01, 2.01.02, 2.01.03, 2.01.04, 2.03.12, 2.03.16	I. 1, 2, 4, 5, 7 II. 9, 11 III. 16, 26 V. 40 VIII. 58a, 58b, 58c
Unit 2 **At school** Pages 18–29	0.1.2, 0.1.4, 0.1.5, 2.5.5, 4.5.3, 4.6.2, 4.6.5, 4.7.2, 4.7.4, 4.8.1, 6.0.1, 6.0.2, 6.1.1, 7.1.4, 7.4.5	2.01.02, 2.01.04, 2.03.12, 2.03.16, 2.04.01	I. 1 II. 9 III. 15
Unit 3 **Friends and family** Pages 32–43	0.1.2, 0.1.4, 0.1.8, 0.2.1, 0.2.4, 1.4.1, 2.6.1, 2.7.1, 2.7.2, 6.0.1, 6.0.2, 7.1.4, 7.2.4, 7.4.7, 7.4.8, 7.5.6, 8.1.3, 8.2.1, 8.3.1	2.01.01, 2.01.02, 2.01.03, 2.01.04, 2.01.05, 2.01.06, 2.03.12, 2.03.16, 2.04.01, 2.05.01, 2.05.02	I. 3, 6, 7 II. 12, 13 III. 19 IV. 38
Unit 4 **Health** Pages 44–55	0.1.1, 0.1.2, 0.1.3, 0.1.4, 0.2.1, 0.2.3, 2.1.8, 2.3.2, 2.5.3, 2.5.5, 3.1.1, 3.1.2, 3.1.3, 3.2.1, 3.2.3, 3.3.1, 3.4.1, 3.4.3, 3.5.7, 4.6.1, 4.8.1, 6.0.1, 7.2.2, 7.2.4, 7.2.6, 7.3.2, 7.5.5, 7.5.6	2.01.02, 2.01.03, 2.01.04, 2.01.05, 2.01.09, 2.01.10, 2.02.02, 2.03.12, 2.03.16, 2.04.09, 2.06.03	IV. 43, 44 VI. 44 VII. 57
Unit 5 **Around town** Pages 58–69	0.1.1, 0.1.2, 0.1.3, 0.1.4, 0.2.1, 0.2.3, 1.1.3, 1.3.7, 1.4.1, 1.9.2, 1.9.4, 2.2.1, 2.2.3, 2.2.5, 2.5.4, 2.6.3, 4.8.1, 5.2.4, 6.0.1, 6.6.5, 7.1.2, 7.1.4, 7.2.2, 7.2.4, 7.2.7, 7.3.2, 7.3.4, 7.4.8, 7.5.6, 8.3.2	2.01.04, 2.01.10, 2.02.01, 2.02.02, 2.03.12, 2.03.16, 2.04.09, 2.06.02, 2.06.03	I. 2 II. 9, 11 III. 17, 23, 23 V. 42 VI. 49

For more details and correlations to other state standards, go to: www.cambridge.org/ventures/correlations

NRS Educational Functioning Level Descriptors	English Language Proficiency and College and Career Readiness Standards
Interpretive: (1, 6, 7, 8) • Identify key words in conversations and a reading about introductions. • Recognize the meaning of common words and phrases about introductions. • Recognize key words in a paragraph describing a student's personal information • Recognize key words in a registration form **Productive: (3, 4, 7, 9, 10)** • Use possessive adjectives, subject pronouns, simple present of be and contractions • Write sentences giving personal information **Interactive: meaning (2, 5)** • Participate in conversations about introductions • Gather and record information about popular names	ELP Standards 1-10 Reading Anchors 1, 2, 3, 4, 5, 7, 9, 10 Speaking & Listening Anchors 1, 2, 3, 4, 6
Interpretive: (1, 6, 7, 8) • Identify key words in conversations and a reading about the classroom • Recognize the meaning of common words and phrases about the classroom • Recognize key words in sentences describing a classroom • Recognize key words in an inventory list **Productive: (3, 4, 7, 9, 10)** • Use prepositions of location (in, on, under), Where is?, singular and plural nouns, Yes / No questions , This / that and these / those, contractions • Write sentences about the location of items in the classroom **Interactive: meaning (2, 5)** • Participate in conversations about the classroom • Gather and record information into a chart about school employees	ELP Standards 1-10 Reading Anchors 1, 2, 3, 4, 5, 7, 9, 10 Speaking & Listening Anchors 1, 2, 3, 4, 6
Interpretive: (1, 6, 7, 8) • Identify key words in conversations and a reading about friends and family • Recognize the meaning of common words and phrases about friends and family • Recognize key words in a paragraph describing a family birthday party • Recognize key words in an insurance application form **Productive: (3, 4, 7, 9, 10)** • Use present continuous, Wh- questions, Yes/No questions and object pronouns (him, her, it, them) • Write sentences about your own family **Interactive: meaning (2, 5)** • Participate in conversations about friends and family • Gather and record information about people's birthdays and send an electronic card	ELP Standards 1-10 Reading Anchors 1, 2, 4, 5, 7, 9, 10 Speaking & Listening Anchors 1, 2, 3, 4, 6
Interpretive: (1, 6, 7, 8) • Identify key words in conversations and a reading about health problems • Recognize the meaning of common words and phrases about health problems • Recognize key words in a paragraph describing a sick family's visit to the doctor's office • Recognize key words in an appointment card **Productive: (3, 4, 7, 9, 10)** • Use simple present of have, questions with have, have and need, and contractions • Write an absence note to a child's teacher **Interactive: meaning (2, 5)** • Participate in conversations about health problems • Gather and record information about your health and emergency information	ELP Standards 1-10 Reading Anchors 1, 2, 4, 5, 7, 9, 10 Speaking & Listening Anchors 1, 2, 3, 4, 6
Interpretive: (1, 6, 7, 8) • Identify key words in conversations and a reading about places and directions • Recognize the meaning of common words and phrases about places and directions • Recognize key words in an e-mail describing a neighborhood • Recognize key words in a map **Productive: (3, 4, 7, 9, 10)** • Use prepositions of location (on, next to, across from, between, on the corner of), Where questions and affirmative and negative imperatives • Write a description of your neighborhood **Interactive: meaning (2, 5)** • Participate in conversations about places and directions • Gather and record information to create a community directory	ELP Standards 1-10 Reading Anchors 1, 2, 4, 5, 7, 9, 10 Speaking & Listening Anchors 1, 2, 3, 4, 6

UNIT	CASAS Competencies	Florida Adult ESOL Low Beginning	LAUSD ESL Beginning Low Competencies
Unit 6 **Time** Pages 70–81	0.1.2, 0.1.4, 0.2.4, 2.3.1, 2.3.2, 2.5.5, 2.6.1, 2.6.3, 2.7.1, 4.1.6, 4.1.7, 4.2.1, 4.3.1, 6.0.1, 6.0.3, 7.1.2, 7.1.4, 7.2.4, 8.1.1, 8.1.2, 8.1.3	2.01.04, 2.01.05, 2.01.10, 2.02.09, 2.02.10, 2.03.12	II. 12, 13 III. 16, 22, 23, 25, 26 VII. 55
Unit 7 **Shopping** Pages 84–95	0.1.2, 0.2.4, 1.1.6, 1.1.7, 1.2.1, 1.2.2, 1.2.5, 1.3.1, 1.3.6, 1.3.8, 1.5.1, 1.5.3, 1.6.4, 1.8.1, 1.8.2, 2.6.4, 6.0.1, 6.0.2, 6.0.3, 6.0.4, 6.1.1, 6.1.2, 6.2.1, 6.2.2, 6.2.5, 6.5.1, 6.6.7, 6.9.2, 7.1.3, 7.1.4, 7.2.3, 7.5.6, 8.2.1	2.01.04, 2.03.12, 2.04.01, 2.04.02, 2.05.06	IV. 30, 31, 35, 36 VII. 50, 51, 52
Unit 8 **Work** Pages 96–107	0.1.2, 0.2.1, 0.2.2, 1.9.6, 4.1.1, 4.1.2, 4.1.5, 4.1.6, 4.1.8, 4.4.2, 4.4.4, 4.4.7, 4.5.1, 4.6.2, 7.1.1, 7.1.4, 7.2.3, 7.2.4, 7.5.1, 7.5.6, 8.2.1, 8.2.6	2.01.02, 2.01.03, 2.01.04, 2.03.01, 2.03.02, 2.03.04, 2.03.05, 2.03.12, 2.03.13, 2.03.14, 2.03.15, 2.03.16	I. 7 II. 14 IV. 31, 35 VII. 50, 51, 54
Unit 9 **Daily living** Pages 110–121	0.1.2, 0.2.4, 1.4.1, 1.7.4, 2.3.2, 4.6.3, 7.1.4, 7.2.2, 7.4.8, 7.5.1, 7.5.5, 8.1.1, 8.1.4, 8.2.1, 8.2.2, 8.2.3, 8.2.4, 8.2.5, 8.2.6, 8.3.1	2.01.03, 2.01.04, 2.03.10, 2.03.12, 2.05.05	II. 12, 13 IV. 31, 35, 38 VII. 55
Unit 10 **Free time** Pages 122–133	0.1.2, 0.1.4, 0.2.4, 2.3.2, 2.6.1, 2.6.2, 2.6.3, 5.2.4, 6.0.1, 6.0.3, 7.1.4, 7.5.1, 7.5.6	2.01.03, 2.01.04, 2.01.10, 2.02.02, 2.03.12, 2.03.16	II. 12, 13 III. 19, 22, 23 VII. 52, 54, 55

For more details and correlations to other state standards, go to: www.cambridge.org/ventures/correlations

NRS Educational Functioning Level Descriptors	English Language Proficiency and College and Career Readiness Standards
Interpretive: (1, 6, 7, 8) ■ Identify key words in conversations and a reading about daily activities and time ■ Recognize the meaning of common words and phrases about daily activities and time ■ Recognize key words in a paragraph describing a person's schedule ■ Recognize key words in a schedule **Productive: (3, 4, 7, 9, 10)** ■ Use simple present tense, Wh- questions, prepositions of time (at, in, on), start/end and open/close ■ Write description of your schedule **Interactive: meaning (2, 5)** ■ Participate in conversations about daily activities and time ■ Gather and record information about businesses in your town	ELP Standards 1-10 Reading Anchors 1, 2, 4, 5, 7, 9, 10 Speaking & Listening Anchors 1, 2, 3, 4, 6
Interpretive: (1, 6, 7, 8) ■ Identify key words in conversations and a reading about food and money ■ Recognize the meaning of common words and phrases about food and money ■ Recognize key words in a paragraph describing a shopping trip ■ Recognize key words in a supermarket ad and receipt **Productive: (3, 4, 7, 9, 10)** ■ Use count/non-count nouns, How many?/ How much?, There is/There are, quantifiers with non-count nouns and some/any ■ Write a note about a shopping list **Interactive: meaning (2, 5)** ■ Participate in conversations about food and money ■ Gather and record information using ads to create a grocery list	ELP Standards 1-10 Reading Anchors 1, 2, 4, 5, 7, 9, 10 Speaking & Listening Anchors 1, 2, 3, 4, 6
Interpretive: (1, 6, 7, 8) ■ Identify key words in conversations and a reading about jobs and skills ■ Recognize the meaning of common words and phrases about jobs and skills ■ Recognize key words in a letter describing a person's job and work history ■ Recognize key words in a job application **Productive: (3, 4, 7, 9, 10)** ■ Use simple past of be (statements and questions), can, contractions and be with and and but ■ Write a paragraph about your skills **Interactive: meaning (2, 5)** ■ Participate in conversations about jobs and skills ■ Gather and record information about a job search	ELP Standards 1-10 Reading Anchors 1, 2, 4, 5, 7, 9, 10 Speaking & Listening Anchors 1, 2, 3, 4, 6
Interpretive: (1, 6, 7, 8) ■ Identify key words in conversations and a reading about home responsibilities ■ Recognize the meaning of common words and phrases about home responsibilities ■ Recognize key words in a letter describing daily events ■ Recognize key words in a job-duties chart **Productive: (3, 4, 7, 9, 10)** ■ Use simple past tense of irregular and regular verbs and Or questions ■ Write a letter describing household chores **Interactive: meaning (2, 5)** ■ Participate in conversations about home responsibilities ■ Gather and record information about a time-management calendar	ELP Standards 1-10 Reading Anchors 1, 2, 4, 5, 7, 9, 10 Speaking & Listening Anchors 1, 2, 3, 4, 6
Interpretive: (1, 6, 7, 8) ■ Identify key words in conversations and a reading about free-time activities ■ Recognize the meaning of common words and phrases about free-time activities ■ Recognize key words in an email and a letter describing vacation ■ Recognize key words in a TV schedule **Productive: (3, 4, 7, 9, 10)** ■ Use simple past of irregular verbs, future with be going to and contrasting past, present and future ■ Write a letter describing a past and future vacation **Interactive: meaning (2, 5)** ■ Participate in conversations about free-time activities ■ Gather and record information using the internet about public parks in your area	ELP Standards 1-10 Reading Anchors 1, 2, 4, 5, 7, 9, 10 Speaking & Listening Anchors 1, 2, 3, 4, 6

(Top row) Dennis Johnson, K. Lynn Savage; (bottom row) Gretchen Bitterlin, Donna Price, and Sylvia G. Ramirez. Together, the *Ventures* author team has more than 200 years teaching ESL as well as other roles that support adult immigrants and refugees, from teacher's aide to dean.

Gretchen Bitterlin has taught Citizenship, ESL, and family literacy through the San Diego Community College District and served as coordinator of the non-credit Continuing Education ESL program. She was an item writer for CASAS tests and chaired the task force that developed the TESOL Adult Education Program Standards. She is recipient of The President's Distinguished Leadership Award from her district and co-author of *English for Adult Competency*. Gretchen holds an MA in TESOL from the University of Arizona.

Dennis Johnson had his first language-teaching experience as a Peace Corps volunteer in South Korea. Following that teaching experience, he became an in-country ESL trainer. After returning to the United States, he began teaching credit and non-credit ESL at City College of San Francisco. As ESL site coordinator, he has provided guidance to faculty in selecting textbooks. He is the author of *Get Up and Go* and co-author of *The Immigrant Experience*. Dennis is the demonstration teacher on the *Ventures Professional Development DVD*. Dennis holds an MA in music from Stanford University.

Donna Price began her ESL career teaching EFL in Madagascar. She is currently associate professor of ESL and vocational ESL / technology resource instructor for the Continuing Education Program, San Diego Community College District. She has served as an author and a trainer for CALPRO, the California Adult Literacy Professional Development Project, co-authoring training modules on contextualizing and integrating workforce skills into the ESL classroom. She is a recipient of the TESOL Newbury House Award for Excellence in Teaching, and she is author of *Skills for Success*. Donna holds an MA in linguistics from San Diego State University.

Sylvia G. Ramirez is a Professor Emeritus at MiraCosta College, a teacher educator, writer, consultant, and a recipient of the California Hayward award for excellence in education, honoring her teaching and professional activities. She is an online instructor for the TESOL Core Certificate. Her MA is in education / counseling from Point Loma University, and she has certificates in ESOL and in online teaching.

K. Lynn Savage first taught English in Japan. She began teaching ESL at City College of San Francisco in 1974, where she has taught all levels of non-credit ESL and has served as Vocational ESL Resource Teacher. She has trained teachers for adult education programs around the country as well as abroad. She chaired the committee that developed *ESL Model Standards for Adult Education Programs* (California, 1992) and is the author, co-author, and editor of many ESL materials including *Crossroads Café*, *Teacher Training through Video*, *Parenting for Academic Success*, *Building Life Skills*, *Picture Stories*, *May I Help You?*, and *English That Works*. Lynn holds an MA in TESOL from Teachers College, Columbia University.

TO THE STUDENT

Welcome to **Ventures**! The dictionary says that "venture" means a risky or daring journey. Its meaning is similar to the word "adventure." Learning English is certainly a journey and an adventure. We hope that this book helps you in your journey of learning English to fulfill your goals. We believe that this book will prepare you for academic and career courses and give you the English skills you need to get a job or promotion, go to college, or communicate better in your community. The audio, grammar presentations, workbooks, and free Internet practice on the Arcade will help you improve your English outside class. Setting your personal goals will also help. Take a few minutes and write your goals below.

Good luck in your studies!

The Author Team
Gretchen Bitterlin
Dennis Johnson
Donna Price
Sylvia Ramirez
K. Lynn Savage

My goals for studying English

1. My first goal for studying English:	Date: _____
2. My second goal for studying English:	Date: _____
3. My third goal for studying English:	Date: _____

WELCOME

1 Meet your classmates

Look at the picture. What do you see?

2 The alphabet

A Listen. Students are introducing themselves. Check (✓) the names you hear.

_____ Eduardo   _____ Paolo   _____ Ryoko

_____ Pierre   _____ Tariq   _____ Kankou

◀)) CD1, Track 2

B Listen and write the letters.

Aa _A a_   Bb ___   Cc ___   Dd ___   Ee ___   Ff ___

Gg ___   Hh ___   Ii ___   Jj ___   Kk ___   Ll ___

Mm ___   Nn ___   Oo ___   Pp ___   Qq ___   Rr ___   Ss ___

Tt ___   Uu ___   Vv ___   Ww ___   Xx ___   Yy ___   Zz ___

◀)) CD1, Track 3

Talk with your partner. Take turns. Say a letter. Your partner points to the letter.

C Listen and repeat.

A What's your name?

B Helena.

A How do you spell that?

B H-E-L-E-N-A.

◀)) CD1, Track 4

Talk to five classmates. Write the names.

Class list
Helena
1.
2.
3.
4.
5.

❸ Numbers

A Listen and repeat.

🔊 CD1, Track 5

0 zero	1 one	2 two	3 three	4 four	5 five
6 six	7 seven	8 eight	9 nine	10 ten	
11 eleven	12 twelve	13 thirteen	14 fourteen	15 fifteen	
16 sixteen	17 seventeen	18 eighteen	19 nineteen	20 twenty	

Talk with a partner. Take turns. Say a number. Your partner points to the number.

B Listen. Circle the number you hear.

🔊 CD1, Track 6

1. 0   (6)   16
2. 3   7   20
3. 1   10   11
4. 2   5   15
5. 1   9   17
6. 11   12   20
7. 8   9   10
8. 3   5   13
9. 14   15   16

C Listen. Write the number you hear.

🔊 CD1, Track 7

1. _3_   3. ____   5. ____   7. ____   9. ____
2. ____   4. ____   6. ____   8. ____   10. ____

D Write. Match the number and the word.

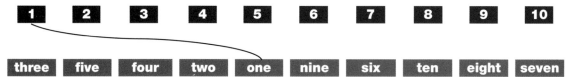

| 1 | 2 | 3 | 4 | 5 | 6 | 7 | 8 | 9 | 10 |

three   five   four   two   one   nine   six   ten   eight   seven

Talk with a partner. Take turns. Spell a number. Your partner says the number.

n-i-n-e
9

4 Days and months

A Listen and repeat.

CD1, Track 8

Sunday	Monday	Tuesday	Wednesday	Thursday	Friday	Saturday

Talk with a partner. Take turns. Say a day. Your partner points to the day.

B Write the full spelling.

1. Sun. _Sunday_
2. Mon. _____
3. Tues. _____
4. Wed. _____

5. Thurs. _____
6. Fri. _____
7. Sat. _____

C Listen and repeat.

CD1, Track 9

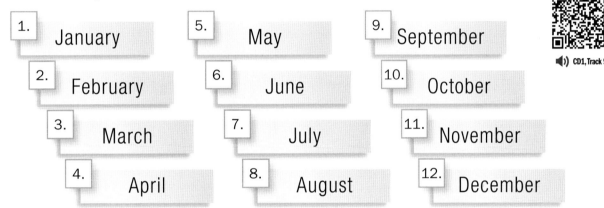

1. January
2. February
3. March
4. April

5. May
6. June
7. July
8. August

9. September
10. October
11. November
12. December

Talk with a partner. Say a number. Your partner says the month.

8   August

D Talk with a partner about your birthday. Take turns.

What month is your birthday?   June.

UNIT 1 PERSONAL INFORMATION

Lesson A Listening

1 Before you listen

A Look at the picture. What do you see?

B Point to: ■ first name ■ last name ■ city
■ zip code ■ area code ■ telephone number

REGISTRATION OFFICE

REGISTRATION HOURS
6 p.m. — 9 p.m.

LAST NAMES A-G

LAST NAMES H-P

LAST NAMES Q-Z

COURSE SCHEDULE

SUBJECT	TEACHER'S NAME	ROOM NUMBER

COURSE GUIDE

RICARDO

MR. CLARK

September

REGISTRATION FORM

Name	Svetlana Kulik
Phone	(707) 555-9073
Address	1041 Main Street Napa, California 94558

UNIT GOALS
Recognize names and vocabulary for personal identification
Make introductions   **Complete** a registration form

2 Listen

A **Listen.** Write the letter of the conversation.

1. ____

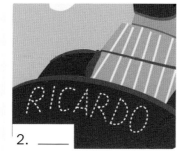

2. ____

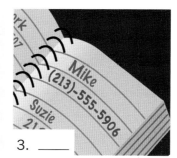

3. ____

◀)) CD1, Track 10

4. ____

5. ____

6. *a*

B **Listen again** to the conversations. Write the names and numbers you hear.

A. _____555-8907_____   D. _____

B. _____   E. _____

C. _____   F. _____

◀)) CD1, Track 10

Listen again. Check your answers.

3 After you listen

Write. Complete the sentences about yourself.

1. My first name is _____ .

2. My last name is _____ .

3. My area code is _____ .

4. My telephone number is _____ .

Talk with a partner. Talk about yourself.

My first name is Dahlia.   My first name is Yuri.

> **Saying telephone numbers**
> Stop at each number. Say *oh* for *zero*.
> 5   5   5 - 2   0   1   6
> *five - five - five   two - oh - one - six*

Lesson B What's your name?

1 Grammar focus: possessive adjectives

A possessive adjective before a noun shows ownership or relationship.

Her name is Mary.

QUESTIONS	What's = What is		ANSWERS	
What's	**your**	name?	**My**	name is Svetlana.
What's	**his**	name?	**His**	name is Steve.
What's	**her**	name?	**Her**	name is Mary.
What are	**their**	names?	**Their**	names are Ted and Rob.

 Watch

2 Practice

A Write. Complete the sentences. Use *his*, *her*, or *their*.

1. **A** What's _____*his*_____ first name?

   B _____ first name is Alfred.

2. **A** What's _____ first name?

   B _____ first name is Sue.

3. **A** What's _____ first name?

   B _____ first name is Tom.

4. **A** What's _____ last name?

   B _____ last name is Jones.

Listen and repeat. Then practice with a partner.

 CD1, Track 11

B Talk with a partner. Look at the student directory. Change the **bold** words and make conversations.

A What's **his** telephone number?

B **His** telephone number is **555-9314**.

STUDENT DIRECTORY

 1 555-9314

 2 555-9847

 3 555-2034

 4 555-5093

 5 555-6172

 6 555-8216

C **Listen.** Then listen again and repeat.

A What's your name?

B **Jennifer Kent**.

A Sorry. What's your first name?

B My first name is **Jennifer**.

A How do you spell that?

B **J-E-N-N-I-F-E-R**.

A OK. What's your last name?

B **Kent. K-E-N-T**.

◄)) CD1, Track 12

> **USEFUL LANGUAGE**
> *Please spell that.*
> *How do you spell* **Jennifer**?

Talk in a group. Ask questions and write the names.

First name	Last name
Jennifer	Kent

3 Communicate

A **Talk** with your classmates. Introduce a classmate.

> This is my classmate. Her first name is Jennifer. Her last name is Kent.

B **Talk** with a partner. Take turns and make new conversations.

A Good morning.

B Good morning.

A My name is Anna Gray. What's your name?

B Kate Harris.

A Nice to meet you.

B Nice to meet you, too.

A Hi. My name is Peter.

B Hi. My name is Alan.

A Nice to meet you, Alan.

B Nice to meet you, too, Peter.

> **CULTURE NOTE**
> Some people have two first names: *Mei-hwa.*
> Some people have two last names: *Baker-Price.*

📖 Use possessive adjectives (*my, your, his, her, their*) **UNIT 1** **9**

Lesson C Are you from Canada?

1 Grammar focus: subject pronouns; simple present of *be*

A subject pronoun can replace the name of a person.
Jennifer *is from Canada.* = ***She*** *is from Canada.*
Is, are, and *am* are *be* verbs.

QUESTIONS		ANSWERS			
Are you			I am.		I'm not. I'm
Is he	from Canada?	Yes,	he is.	No,	he isn't. He's
Is she			she is.		she isn't. She's
Are they			they are.		they aren't. They're

from the United States.

👁 Watch

I'm = I am	She's = She is	isn't = is not
He's = He is	They're = They are	aren't = are not

2 Practice

A Write. Complete the sentences.

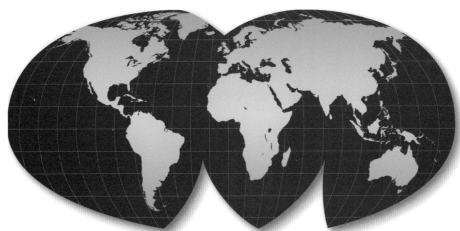

1. A _____Are_____ you from Canada?
   B No, I *'m not* _____ .

2. A _____ they from Somalia?
   B Yes, _____ .

3. A _____ she from Russia?
   B Yes, _____ .

4. A _____ he from Mexico?
   B Yes, _____ .

5. A _____ she from China?
   B No, _____ .

6. A _____ they from Brazil?
   B No, _____ .

7. A _____ he from Ecuador?
   B No, _____ .

8. A _____ you from South Korea?
   B Yes, _____ .

Listen and repeat. Then practice with a partner.

🔊 CD1, Track 13

B **Talk** with a partner. Change the **bold** words and make conversations.

INTERNATIONAL FESTIVAL

A **Is he** from **Mexico**?

B Yes, **he is**.

A **Are they** from **the United States**?

B No, **they aren't**.
   They're from **India**.

1. Japan?   2. the United States?   3. Mexico?   4. India?   5. Mexico?   6. Japan?

C **Listen and repeat.** Then practice with a partner.

A Where are you from, **Katia**?

B I'm from **Brazil**.

A **Brazil**? How do you spell that?

B **B-R-A-Z-I-L**.

> **USEFUL LANGUAGE**
> *Where are you from?*
> *Where do you come from?*
> *What country are you from?*

◀)) CD1, Track 14

❸ Communicate

Talk in a group. Where are your classmates from? Make guesses.

A This is Katia. Where is she from?

B Is she from Colombia?

A No, she isn't.

B Is she from Brazil?

A Yes, she is.

📖 Use subject pronouns (*I, you, he, she, they*); use *be* in the simple present **UNIT 1** 11

Lesson D Reading

1 Before you read

Talk. Svetlana starts school today. Look at the registration form. Answer the questions.

1. What's her last name?

2. What's her telephone number?

REGISTRATION FORM

Name	Svetlana Kulik
Phone	(707) 555-9073
Address	1041 Main Street Napa, California 94558

2 Read

Listen and read.

((•)) CD1, Track 15

A New Student

Svetlana Kulik is a new student. She is from Russia. Now she lives in Napa, California. Her address is 1041 Main Street. Her zip code is 94558. Her area code is 707. Her telephone number is 555-9073.

Address with 3 numbers
832 Main Street
eight thirty-two
Address with 4 numbers
1041 Main Street
ten forty-one

3 After you read

A **Read** the sentences. Are they correct? Circle *Yes* or *No*.

1. This reading is about a new teacher.   Yes   (No)

2. Her first name is Svetlana.   Yes   No

3. She is from Colombia.   Yes   No

4. Her address is 1014 Main Street.   Yes   No

5. Her zip code is 94558.   Yes   No

6. Her area code is 555-9073.   Yes   No

Write. Correct the sentences.

1. This reading is about a new student.

B **Write.** Answer the questions about Svetlana.

1. What is her last name? _____

2. Is she from Russia? _____

3. What is her address? _____

4. What is her telephone number? _____

4 Picture dictionary Personal information

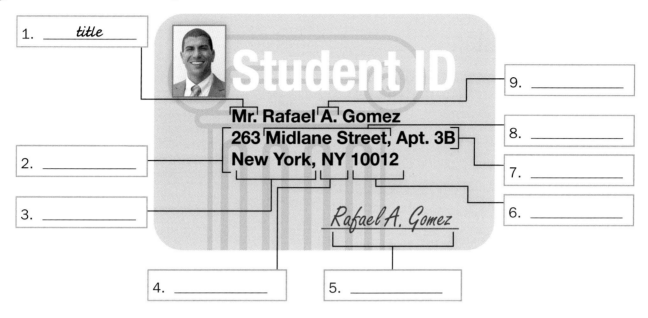

1. _____ *title* _____

9. _____

8. _____

7. _____

6. _____

2. _____

3. _____

4. _____

5. _____

Mr. Rafael A. Gomez
263 Midlane Street, Apt. 3B
New York, NY 10012

Rafael A. Gomez

A **Write** the words in the Picture dictionary. Then listen and repeat.

address	city	signature	street	zip code
apartment number	middle initial	state	title	

CD1, Track 16

B **Talk** with a partner. Use the words in 4A to ask questions. Complete the student ID with your partner's information.

What's your name?

My name is Rafael.

CULTURE NOTE

Use *Mr.* for a man.

Use *Ms.* for a woman.

Use *Mrs.* for a married woman.

Use *Miss* for an unmarried woman.

STUDENT ID

_____

_____

_____

_____

For college and career readiness practice, see pages 136–137.

Lesson E Writing

1 Before you write

A **Talk** with your classmates. Ask questions. Write the answers.

A What's your name?

B My name is **Liliana Lopez**.

A What's your telephone number?

B My telephone number is **555-2904**.

A Where are you from?

B I'm from **Mexico**.

 Begin names of people, streets, cities, states, and countries with capital letters. These are capital letters: *A B C D E . . . .* These are lowercase letters: *a b c d e . . . .*

Name	Telephone (phone) number	Country
Liliana Lopez	555–2904	Mexico

B **Write.** Complete the sentences. Use the words in the box.

> address   last name   zip code
> area code   telephone number

Svetlana is a new student.

1. Her _____ last name _____ is Kulik. She is from Russia.

2. Her _____ is 1041 Main Street.

3. Her _____ is 94558.

4. Her _____ is 555-9073.

5. Her _____ is 707.

C **Write.** Add capital letters.

P
~~p~~edro is a new student. He is single. He is from colombia. His last name is ramirez. His address is 285 pacheco street, houston, texas. His zip code is 77057. His telephone number is 555-7878. His area code is 713.

D **Read** about Pedro again. Complete the chart. Use capital letters.

First name	Last name	City	State
Pedro			

2 Write

Read the questions and write about yourself.

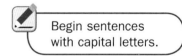

Begin sentences with capital letters.

1. What's your first name? _My first name is_ _____.

2. What's your last name? _____.

3. What's your address? _____.

4. What's your zip code? _____.

5. What's your phone number? _____.

6. Where are you from? _____.

3 After you write

A **Read** your sentences to a partner.

B **Check** your partner's sentences.

■ What is your partner's name?
■ Are the capital letters correct?

Lesson F Another view

1 Life-skills reading

REGISTRATION

Please print:

☐ Mr. ☐ Ms. ☐ Mrs.

(1) NAME: _____

                        Last   First   Middle

(2) ADDRESS: _____

                    Number   Street   Apt.

(3) _____

               City   State   Zip code

(4) TELEPHONE: check one: ☐ home ☐ cell _____

                                 Area code   Number

(5) COUNTRY OF ORIGIN: _____

(6) _____

                             Signature

A Read the questions. Look at the registration form. Fill in the answer.

1. Where do you print your country of origin?
   - Ⓐ line 1
   - Ⓑ line 2
   - ⬤ line 5
   - Ⓓ line 6

2. Where do you print your name?
   - Ⓐ line 1
   - Ⓑ line 3
   - Ⓒ line 5
   - Ⓓ line 6

3. Where do you sign your name?
   - Ⓐ line 1
   - Ⓑ line 3
   - Ⓒ line 5
   - Ⓓ line 6

4. What is *country of origin*?
   - Ⓐ your city
   - Ⓑ your home country
   - Ⓒ your country now
   - Ⓓ your state

B Write. Complete the form with your own information.

C Solve the problem. Which solution is best? Circle your opinion.

Anna is filling out a registration form. She is new in her city. She doesn't know her zip code. What should she do?

1. Write "X" on line 3.

2. Ask her friend.

3. Come back tomorrow.

4. Other: _____

2 **Grammar connections:** possessive adjectives and subject pronouns

> Possessive adjectives come before a noun or adjective.
> Subject pronouns come before a verb.

POSSESSIVE ADJECTIVES	SUBJECT PRONOUNS
My name is Isabel.	**I'm** from Guatemala.
Your name is Leo.	**You're** from Peru.
His name is Dusit.	**He's** from Thailand.
Her name is Amira.	**She's** from Iraq.
Their last name is Kim.	**They're** from South Korea.

Contractions
I'm = I am
you're = you are
he's = he is
she's = she is
they're = they are

 Watch

A **Talk** with a partner. Look at the picture. Take turns.

    A *His* name is Victor.

    B *He's* from Poland.

B **Work** in a group. Play the name game. Take turns.

My name is Isabel. I'm from Guatemala.

Your name is Isabel. You're from Guatemala. My name is Dusit. I'm from Thailand.

Your name is Dusit. You're from Thailand. Your name is Isabel. You're from Guatemala. My name is Amira. I'm from Iraq.

UNIT 2 AT SCHOOL

Lesson A Listening

1 Before you listen

A Look at the picture. What do you see?

B Point to: ■ a book ■ a desk ■ a map ■ a pencil
■ a clock ■ an eraser ■ a pen ■ a table

LESSON
Review: name, address, phone number
New: school vocabulary
Book: Ventures, pages 18–29

UNIT GOALS
Identify classroom objects   **Identify** location of classroom objects
Interpret information on a classroom inventory list

2 Listen

A Listen. Write the letter of the conversation.

 CD1, Track 17

1. ____

2. ____

3. ____

4. _a_

5. ____

6. ____

B Listen again to the conversations. Circle the location you hear.

 CD1, Track 17

A. on the desk	(in the drawer)	in the box
B. in the desk	in the drawer	in the box
C. on the floor	on the chair	on the table
D. in the desk	in the drawer	on the floor
E. in the desk	in the box	under the desk
F. under your chair	on your chair	under your desk

Listen again. Check your answers.

3 After you listen

Write. What's on the desk? What's in the drawer? What's under the chair?

book   clock   paper   pencil   rulers   stapler

on the desk	in the drawer	under the chair

1. ____stapler____   3. _____   5. _____

2. _____   4. _____   6. _____

Lesson B Where is the pen?

❶ Grammar focus: prepositions *in*, *on*, and *under*; *Where is?*

The prepositions *in*, *on*, and *under* tell the location of things. They answer the question *Where?*

QUESTIONS	Where's the pen?	Where's the pencil?	Where's the ruler?
ANSWERS	It's **in** the drawer.	It's **on** the book.	It's **under** the notebook.

Watch

Where's = Where is

❷ Practice

A Write. Complete the sentences. Use *in*, *on*, or *under*.

1. **A** Where's the book?
   B It's __on__ the shelf.

2. **A** Where's the pencil sharpener?
   B It's _____ the wall.

3. **A** Where's the dictionary?
   B It's _____ the table.

4. **A** Where's the calendar?
   B It's _____ the box.

5. **A** Where's the eraser?
   B It's _____ the drawer.

6. **A** Where's the calculator?
   B It's _____ the cabinet.

7. **A** Where's the stapler?
   B It's _____ the drawer.

8. **A** Where's the pencil?
   B It's _____ the table.

9. **A** Where's the ruler?
   B It's _____ the book.

Listen and repeat. Then practice with a partner.

🔊 CD1, Track 18

B **Listen.** Circle the items you hear.

CD1, Track 19

Talk with a partner. Look at the picture again. Change the **bold** words and make conversations.

A Excuse me. Where's the **calculator**?

B It's **in the cabinet.**

A Oh, thanks.

B You're welcome.

> **USEFUL LANGUAGE**
> Say *excuse me* to get someone's attention.

3 Communicate

Talk with a partner about your classroom.

Where's the computer?   It's on the table.

Lesson C Where are the pencils?

1 Grammar focus: singular and plural nouns

A singular noun names one thing. A plural noun names more than one thing.
Use an *s* at the end of most singular nouns to make plural.

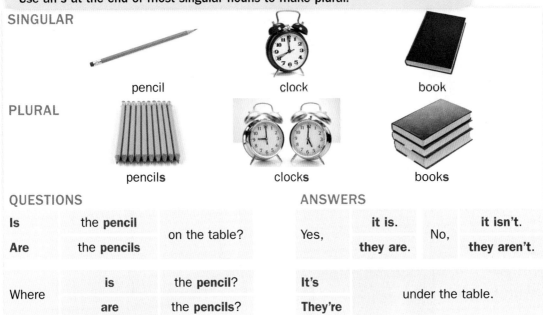

SINGULAR

pencil   clock   book

PLURAL

pencils   clocks   books

Watch

QUESTIONS			ANSWERS			
Is	the **pencil**	on the table?	Yes,	it is.	No,	it isn't.
Are	the **pencils**			they are.		they aren't.
Where	is	the **pencil**?	It's	under the table.		
	are	the **pencils**?	They're			

2 Practice

A Write. Look at the picture. Complete the conversations.

1. **A** Are the _____books_____ in the cabinet?
         (book / books)
   B Yes, _____they are_____ .

2. **A** Is the _____ under the clock?
         (calendar / calendars)
   B Yes, _____ .

3. **A** Are the _____ on the table?
         (ruler / rulers)
   B No, _____ .

4. **A** Are the _____ on the table?
         (pencil / pencils)
   B No, _____ .

5. **A** Are the _____ on the table?
         (calculator / calculators)
   B Yes, _____ .

Listen and repeat. Then practice with a partner.

CD1, Track 20

B Write. Complete the sentences. Use *is* or *are*.

1. Where ___*is*___ the laptop computer?
2. Where _____ the notebooks?
3. Where _____ the calendar?
4. Where _____ the dictionary?

5. Where _____ the maps?
6. Where _____ the pencil?
7. Where _____ the calculator?
8. Where _____ the books?

C Write. Look at the picture. Read the answers. Write the questions.

1. A *Where are the notebooks?*
   B They're in the filing cabinet.
2. A _____?
   B They're on the filing cabinet.
3. A _____?
   B It's on the wall.
4. A _____?
   B They're on the desk.

5. A _____?
   B It's on the small table.
6. A _____?
   B It's under the dictionary.
7. A _____?
   B They're in the box.
8. A _____?
   B They're under the small table.

Listen and repeat. Then practice with a partner.

◀)) CD1, Track 21

3 Communicate

Talk with a partner about things in your classroom.

A Is the map on the desk?
B Yes, it is.
A Are the books on the table?
B No, they aren't.
A Where are they?
B They're in the cabinet.

📖 Use singular and plural nouns; ask and answer *yes / no* and *where* questions   UNIT 2   **23**

Lesson D Reading

1 Before you read

Talk. It's the first day of class. Look at the picture. Answer the questions.

1. What do you see in the classroom?
2. Where are the things?

2 Read

Listen and read.

🔊 CD1, Track 22

Attention, new students!
Items in your new classroom.

- The laptop is on the small table.
- The pencils are in the basket on the desk.
- The erasers are in the basket.
- The books are in the bookcase.
- The calculators are in a box under the table.
- The markers are in the desk drawer.

Look at pictures before you read. They help you understand new words. *Basket* is a new word. Find the basket in the picture.

3 After you read

A **Read** the sentences. Are they correct? Circle **Yes** or **No.**

1. The laptop is on the desk.	Yes	(No)
2. The pencils are under the table.	Yes	No
3. The erasers are in the bookcase.	Yes	No
4. The calculators are under the table.	Yes	No
5. The markers are in the desk drawer.	Yes	No
6. The reading is about items in the classroom.	Yes	No

Write. Correct the sentences.

1. The laptop is on the <u>small table</u>.

B **Write.** Answer the questions about the classroom.

1. Where is the box? _____

2. Where is the basket? _____

4 Picture dictionary Classroom objects

1. <u>hole puncher</u>

2. _____

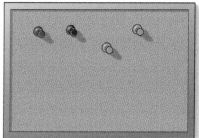

3. _____

4. _____

5. _____

6. _____

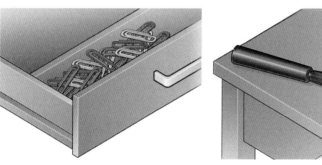

7. _____

8. _____

9. _____

A Write the words in the Picture dictionary. Then listen and repeat.

bulletin board	hole puncher	marker	paper clips	whiteboard
globe	index cards	notepads	scissors	

 CD1, Track 23

B Talk with a partner. Look at the pictures and make conversations.

  A Where's the **whiteboard**?

  B It's **on the wall**.

  A Where are the **paper clips**?

  B They're **in the drawer**.

For college and career readiness practice, see pages 138–139.

Lesson E Writing

1 Before you write

A Draw. Choose six objects. Draw two on the desk. Draw one on the wall. Draw two in the cabinet.
Draw one under the table. Write the words under the picture.

calculator	dictionary	map	pen	ruler
calendar	hole puncher	notebook	pencil	scissors
clock	laptop	notepad	pencil sharpener	whiteboard

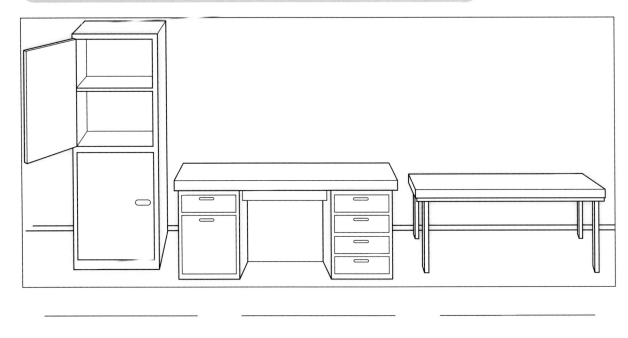

_____   _____   _____

_____   _____   _____

Talk with a partner. Tell about your picture. Draw your partner's objects here.

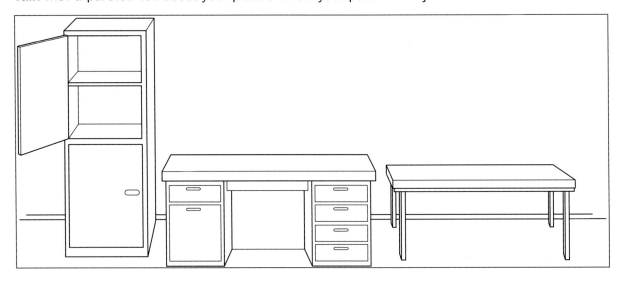

B **Write.** Look at the picture. Complete the sentences. Use *is* or *are* with *on*, *in*, or *under*.

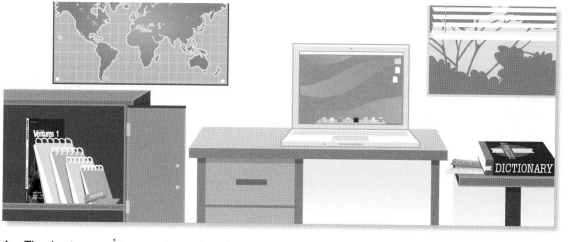

1. The laptop __is__ __on__ the desk.
2. The notepads _____ _____ the cabinet.
3. The book _____ _____ the cabinet.
4. The cabinet _____ _____ the map.
5. The map _____ _____ the wall.
6. The rulers _____ _____ the dictionary.

2 Write

A **Write.** Look at your classroom. What do you see? Complete the chart.

Singular	Plural
pen	*pencils*

B **Write** one sentence about each object.

1. *The pen is on the desk.*
2. *The pencils are in the drawer.*
3. _____
4. _____
5. _____
6. _____

 Start sentences with a capital letter (A, B, C). End sentences with a period (**.**).

3 After you write

A **Read** your sentences to a partner.

B **Check** your partner's sentences.

- What are four things in the classroom? Where are they?
- Are the capital letters and periods correct?

Lesson F Another view

1 Life-skills reading

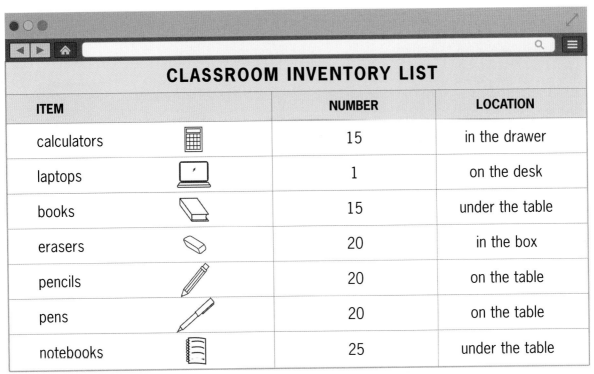

CLASSROOM INVENTORY LIST

ITEM		NUMBER	LOCATION
calculators		15	in the drawer
laptops		1	on the desk
books		15	under the table
erasers		20	in the box
pencils		20	on the table
pens		20	on the table
notebooks		25	under the table

A **Read** the questions. Look at the inventory list. Fill in the answer.

1. How many pencils are on the table?
   - A 5
   - B 15
   - C 20
   - D 25

2. What is another word for *item*?
   - A thing
   - B number
   - C location
   - D person

3. Where are the calculators?
   - A in the cabinet
   - B in the drawer
   - C on the desk
   - D under the table

4. What's on the table?
   - A laptops and calculators
   - B books and notebooks
   - C pencils and pens
   - D laptops and notebooks

B **Solve** the problem. Which solution is best? Circle your opinion.

Mr. Liang asks Ava for the notebooks. Where are the notebooks? Ava doesn't know. What should she do?

1. Ask another student.
2. Look at the classroom inventory list.
3. Ask the teacher.
4. Other: _____

2 Grammar connections: *this / that* and *these / those*

Use *this* and *these* to talk about things that are near you. Use *that* and *those* to talk about things that are far away from you.

This is a book.

That's a book.   that's = that is

These are books.

Those are books

Those are books.

Watch

A Work in a group. Put one or more objects in a bag. (Other classmates close their eyes.) Then take turns. Take an object from the bag. Ask questions.

No, those aren't my keys.

Hector, are these your keys?

Fen, are these your keys?

Yes, those are my keys.

B Talk with your group. Say what your object is. Get your object.

A That's my pencil.

B Here you are.

REVIEW

1 Listening

Read the questions. Then listen and circle the answers.

🔊 CD1, Track 24

1. What is Juan's last name?
   a. Perez *(circled)*
   b. Cruz

2. Where is he from?
   a. Mexico
   b. El Salvador

3. What is his apartment number?
   a. 1324
   b. 10

4. What is his zip code?
   a. 94548
   b. 94321

5. What is his area code?
   a. 213
   b. 555

6. What is his telephone number?
   a. 555-6301
   b. 555-0133

Talk with a partner. Ask and answer the questions. Use complete sentences.

2 Grammar

A Write. Complete the story.

A NEW STUDENT

Layla ___is___ a new student. _____ last name
    1. is / are   2. My / Her
is Azari. She _____ from Iran. She _____ a good
              3. is / are   4. is / are
student. Her pencils and a notebook _____ on her
                                     5. is / are
desk. A dictionary is _____ her bag. Her classmates
                      6. in / at
_____ in the classroom now.
7. isn't / aren't

B Write. Unscramble the words. Make questions about the story.

1. from / Where / Layla / is / ? _Where is Layla from?_

2. her / What's / name / last / ? _____

3. good / she / a / student / Is / ? _____

4. in / bag / What / is / her / ? _____

Talk with a partner. Ask and answer the questions.

30   REVIEW: UNITS 1 & 2

3 Pronunciation: syllables

A **Listen** to the syllables in these words.

CD1, Track 25

•   • •   • • •
name   address   apartment

B **Listen and repeat.** Say the word and clap one time for each syllable.

CD1, Track 26

•	• •	• • •
map	classroom	telephone
books	middle	initial
box	partner	signature
clock	whiteboard	computer
pens	ruler	sharpener
chair	notebook	calendar
desk	pencil	eraser

Talk with a partner. Take turns. Say a word. Your partner claps for each syllable.

C **Listen** to the words. Write the number of syllables you hear.

a. ___1___   b. _____   c. _____   d. _____

e. _____   f. _____   g. _____   h. _____

CD1, Track 27

Listen again and repeat. Clap one time for each syllable.

D **Write.** Find ten other words in your book. Make a list.

1.	6.
2.	7.
3.	8.
4.	9.
5.	10.

Talk with a partner. Say the words. Your partner says the number of syllables.

UNIT 3 FRIENDS AND FAMILY

Lesson A Listening

1 Before you listen

A Look at the picture. What do you see?

B Point to: ■ the mother ■ the father ■ the daughter
■ the son ■ the grandmother ■ the grandfather

UNIT GOALS
Identify family members **Identify** family activities
Complete a census form

2 Listen

A Listen. Write the letter of the conversation.

CD1, Track 28

1. _c_

2. _b_

3. _e_

4. _a_

5. _d_

6. _f_

B Listen again to the conversations. Who is calling? Circle the name you hear.

CD1, Track 28

A.	Mr. Brown	(Mrs. Brown)	Luisa
B.	(Mr. Cho)	Mrs. Cho	Carlos
C.	Mrs. Ramos	Carlos	(Mr. Ramos)
D.	Carlos	mother	(Angela)
E.	(Mary)	Carlos	sister
F.	Dr. Jones's office	(Dr. Smith's office)	Dr. Pham's office

Listen again. Check your answers.

3 After you listen

Who lives with you? Check (✓) your answers.

☐ my husband   ☐ my son   ☐ my mother   ☐ my sister

☐ my wife   ☐ my daughter   ☐ my father   ☐ my brother

Talk about your family. Work with a partner.

My husband and my son live with me. My mother and father live in Ecuador.

Lesson B What are you doing?

1 Grammar focus: present continuous; *What* questions

Use the present continuous for actions happening now.

QUESTIONS		ANSWERS	
What **are** you		I'm	
What's he	doing?	He's	reading.
What's she		She's	
What **are** they		They're	

The present continuous = *be* + verb + *-ing*:
read → I am reading.
talk → He is talking.
listen → They are listening.

 Watch

2 Practice

A Write. Complete the conversations.

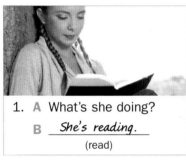

1. A What's she doing?
   B _She's reading._
      (read)

2. A What's he doing?
   B _he's sleeping_.
      (sleep)

3. A What are they doing?
   B _They're eating_.
      (eat)

4. A What's he doing?
   B _he's watching_ TV.
      (watch)

5. A What's she doing?
   B _She's talking_ on phone
      (talk)

6. A What are you doing?
   B _I'm studying_ .
      (study)

7. A What's she doing?
   B _she's talking a_ picture
      (take a picture)

8. A What are you doing?
   B _I'm drinking coffee_
      (drink coffee)

9. A What are they doing?
   B _They're playing_ basketball
      (play basketball)

Listen and repeat. Then practice with a partner.

◀)) CD1, Track 29

B **Talk** with a partner. Point to the picture. Change the **bold** words and make conversations.

A What's **she** doing?

B **She's listening to music.**

A What are **they** doing?

B **They're eating popcorn.**

C **Write.** Answer the question.

What are you doing?

I'm _____ .

3 Communicate

Talk. Practice with a partner.

A Hello?

B Hi, Ann. This is Paul.

A Oh, hi, Paul.

B What are you doing?

A I'm cooking dinner.

B Oh, sorry. I'll call back later.

Make new conversations.

Lesson C Are you working now?

1 Grammar focus: present continuous; Yes / No questions

Watch

Use the present continuous to ask about actions happening now.

QUESTIONS		ANSWERS				
Are you				I **am.**		I'm **not.**
Is he	**working?**	Yes,	he **is.**		No,	he **isn't.**
Is she			she **is.**			she **isn't.**
Are they			they **are.**			they **aren't.**

Spelling change
drive → driving
take → taking
smile → smiling

2 Practice

A Write. Complete the conversations.

1. A ___Is___ she ___working___ now?
   (work)
   B Yes, she is. She's very busy.

2. A ___is___ he ___driving___ to work?
   (drive)
   B Yes, he is. He's late.

3. A ___are___ they ___eating___ lunch now?
   (eat)
   B Yes, they are. They're hungry.

4. A ___is___ he ___helping___ his grandmother?
   (help)
   B Yes, he is. He's really helpful.

5. A ___is___ she ___takeing___ a break?
   (take)
   B Yes, she is. She's tired.

6. A ___are___ they ___buying___ water?
   (buy)
   B Yes, they are. They're thirsty.

7. A ___is___ she ___crying___ ?
   (cry)
   B Yes, she is. She's sad.

8. A ___are___ you ___smiling___ ?
   (smile)
   B Yes, I am. I'm happy.

Listen and repeat. Then practice with a partner.

CD1, Track 30

B **Look** at the picture. Check (✓) Yes or No.

	Yes	No
1. Is Joe driving to work?	☐	☑
2. Is Mike helping his father?	☑	☐
3. Is Lisa talking to her brother?	☑	☐
4. Is Karla eating lunch?	☑	☐
5. Is Jennifer working now?	☐	☑
6. Are Peter and Paul buying soda?	☐	☑

Talk with a partner. Ask and answer questions.

Is Joe driving to work?

No, he isn't. He's cooking lunch.

3 Communicate

Talk with a partner. Take turns. Act out and guess a word from the box.

busy	hungry	thirsty
happy	sad	tired

driving	studying
eating	working

Are you tired?

Yes, I am.

Are you working?

No, I'm not.

Lesson D Reading

1 Before you read

Talk. Juan is celebrating his birthday.
Look at the picture. Answer the questions.

1. What are the people doing?

2. Do you celebrate birthdays? How?

Photo Album

CD1, Track 31

2 Read

Listen and read.

The Birthday Party

My name is Juan. In this picture, it's my birthday. I am 70 years old. Look at me! I don't look 70 years old. My wife, my daughter, and my grandson are eating cake. My grandson is always hungry. My granddaughter is drinking soda. She's always thirsty. My son-in-law is playing the guitar and singing. Everyone is happy!

> Think about the title before you read. This helps you understand the story.

3 After you read

A Read the sentences. Are they correct? Circle **Yes** or **No**.

1. Juan's story is about his grandson's birthday party.   Yes   (No)
2. Juan is celebrating his birthday with his friends.   Yes   (No)
3. His wife, daughter, and grandson are eating cake.   (Yes)   No
4. His granddaughter is drinking soda.   (Yes)   No
5. His grandson is playing the guitar and singing.   (Yes)   (No)
6. Everyone is tired.   Yes   (No)

Write. Correct the sentences.

1. Juan's story is about <u>his</u> birthday party.

B Write. Answer the questions about Juan's party.

1. How old is Juan? _____

2. What is the family eating? _____

3. What is Juan's granddaughter doing? _____

4. What is his son-in-law doing? _____

④ **Picture dictionary** Family members

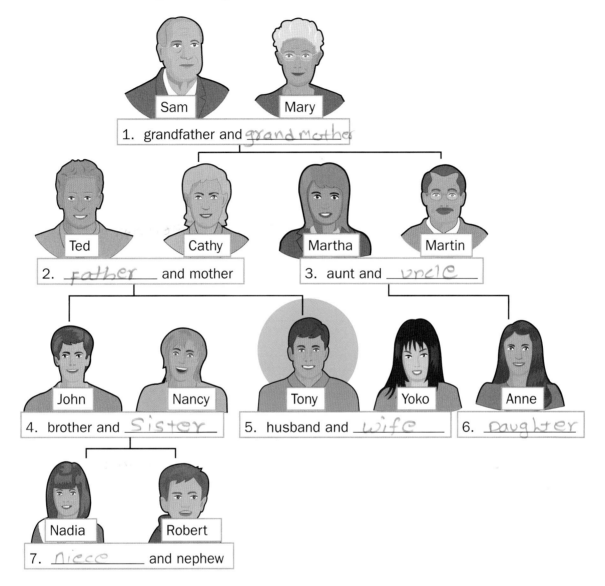

1. grandfather and *grand mother*

2. *father* and mother

3. aunt and *uncle*

4. brother and *Sister*

5. husband and *wife*

6. *Daughter*

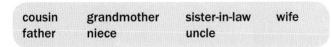

7. *niece* and nephew

A **Write.** Look at Tony. Complete his family tree. Then listen and repeat.

cousin	grandmother	sister-in-law	wife
father	niece	uncle	

🔊 CD1, Track 32

B **Talk** with a partner. Take turns. Ask and answer questions about Tony's family.

Who is Yoko?   She's Tony's wife.

USEFUL LANGUAGE
Dad = father
Mom = mother
Grandpa = grandfather
Grandma = grandmother
Tony's wife = wife of Tony

For college and career readiness practice, see pages 140–141.

Lesson E Writing

1 Before you write

A **Talk** with a partner. Ask and answer the questions. Write your partner's answers.

United States Census Bureau

What's your name?	My name is DJMerisan
Are you married or single?	
Do you have children?	
How many daughters?	
How many sons?	
How many sisters do you have?	
How many brothers do you have?	

B **Read.** Then write the words on the picture.

My name is David. I am single.

I live with my sister and her husband.

I have two nieces and one nephew.

In this picture, my nieces are <u>cooking</u>.

My nephew is <u>watching</u> TV.

My sister is <u>studying</u>. She's very smart.

Her husband is <u>reading</u> the newspaper.

2. *watching*

3. *Studying*

4. *reading*

1. *cooking*

❷ Write

A **Draw** your family. What are they doing?

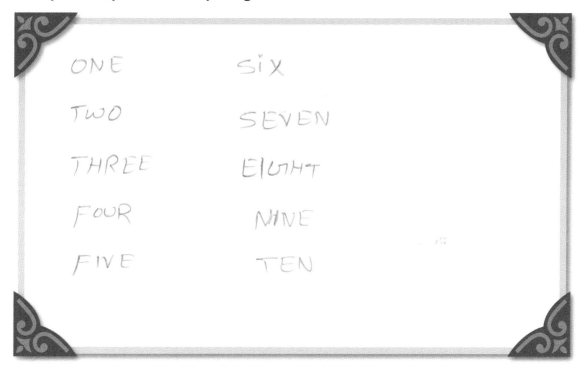

ONE   SIX

TWO   SEVEN

THREE   EIGHT

FOUR   NINE

FIVE   TEN

B **Write.** Answer the questions.

> 🖉 **Spell** numbers from one to ten:
> *I have one brother.*
> Write all other numbers: *I have **11** nieces.*

1. What's your name?
   My name is _____Silpa_____.

2. Are you married or single?
   I'm ___Married___.

3. How many children do you have?
   I ___have 2 children___.

4. Who do you live with?
   I live with ___My husband and kids___.

5. In the picture, what are they doing?
   _____
   _____
   _____

❸ After you write

A **Read** your sentences to a partner.

B **Check** your partner's sentences.

- How many people are in the family?
- Did your partner spell the numbers from one to ten?

Lesson F Another view

1 Life-skills reading

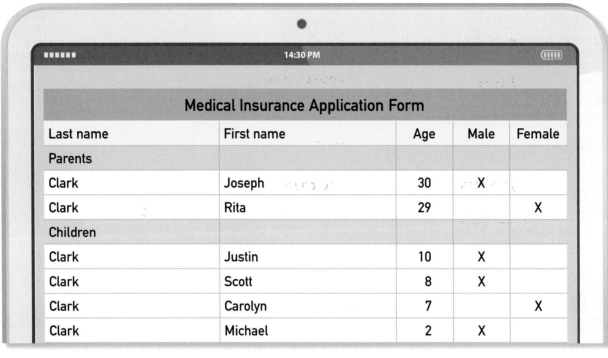

Medical Insurance Application Form

Last name	First name	Age	Male	Female
Parents				
Clark	Joseph	30	X	
Clark	Rita	29		X
Children				
Clark	Justin	10	X	
Clark	Scott	8	X	
Clark	Carolyn	7		X
Clark	Michael	2	X	

A **Read** the questions. Look at the form. Fill in the answer.

1. How many children do Mr. and Mrs. Clark have?
   - A 1
   - B 2
   - C 3
   - D (4)

2. On this form, what does the word *Parents* mean?
   - A brother and sister
   - B father and mother
   - C daughter and son
   - D aunt and uncle

3. How many sons do Mr. and Mrs. Clark have?
   - A 1
   - B 2
   - C (3)
   - D 4

4. Who is eight years old?
   - A Carolyn
   - B Justin
   - C Michael
   - D Scott

B **Solve** the problem. Which solution is best? Circle your opinion.

Mr. Clark gets health insurance for his family from his job now, but the pay is low. He can get a new job with more pay, but no health insurance. What should he do?

1. Keep the job with health insurance.
2. Take the new job with no insurance.
3. Look for a different job with health insurance.
4. Other: _____

❷ Grammar connections: object pronouns

Pronouns take the place of nouns. [Johnny Depp = him] When pronouns follow verbs, they are called *object pronouns*. The object pronouns are *me, you, him, her, it, us,* and *them*.

OBJECT PRONOUNS

Watch

I like <u>Johnny Depp.</u>	I like **him**.
I don't like <u>Beyonce.</u>	I don't like **her**.
Katia likes <u>chocolate.</u>	She likes **it**.
Peter likes <u>cats.</u>	He likes **them**.

A **Talk** with your classmates. Complete the chart.

A Do you like chocolate, Peter?

B No, I don't. I don't like *it*.

A Do you like chocolate, Katia?

C Yes, I do. I like *it*.

Find someone who likes . . .	Name
chocolate	*Katia*
Johnny Depp	
dogs	
milk	
Beyonce	
Prince William and Princess Kate	
TV	
birthdays	
Lionel Messi (soccer player)	
guitars	

B **Share** your group's information with the class.

Katia likes chocolate. Peter doesn't like it.

UNIT 4 HEALTH

Lesson A Listening

1 Before you listen

A Look at the picture. What do you see?

B Point to a person with: ■ a backache ■ a cough
■ a headache ■ a broken leg ■ an earache ■ a sore throat

UNIT GOALS
Identify common health problems   **Write** an email to excuse an absence
Identify remedies for common health problems

2 Listen

A   Listen. Write the letter of the conversation.

1. ____

2. _a_

3. ____

CD1, Track 33

4. ____

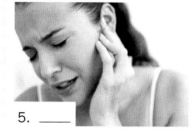

5. ____

6. ____

B   Listen again to the conversations. Circle the words you hear.

A.	I'm sorry to hear it.	I'm sorry to hear that.	I'm sorry about that.
B.	I hope it gets better soon.	I hope you get better soon.	I hope you get well soon.
C.	I hope it gets better soon.	I hope you get better soon.	I hope you get well soon.
D.	That's too bad.	That's terrible.	I'm sorry.
E.	That's too bad.	Oh, I'm sorry.	That's terrible.
F.	That's too bad.	Oh, that's terrible.	I'm sorry.

CD1, Track 33

Listen again. Check your answers.

3 After you listen

Talk with a partner. Take turns. Act out and guess the problem.

Sore throat?

Yes.

USEFUL LANGUAGE
Yes.
That's right.
No. Guess again.

Lesson B I have a headache.

1 Grammar focus: simple present of *have*

Use *have* with health problems.

STATEMENTS		
I	**have**	
You	**have**	a cold.
He	**has**	
She	**has**	

> **USEFUL LANGUAGE**
> *I have a **terrible** cold.*
> *I have a **bad** headache.*

Watch

2 Practice

A Write. Complete the sentences. Use *has* or *have*.

1. He __has__ a terrible cold.

2. I _____ a headache.

3. He _____ a backache.

4. You _____ a fever.

5 I _____ a broken arm.

6. He _____ a stomachache.

7. She _____ a bad cough.

8. You _____ a sore throat.

9. She _____ a cut.

Listen and repeat.

🔊 CD1, Track 34

B Talk with a partner. Change the **bold** words and make conversations.

A How **is she**?

B Not so good.

A What's wrong?

B **She has a cold.**

A I have **tissues**.

B Really? Thanks.

> **USEFUL LANGUAGE**
> *What's wrong?*
> *What's the matter?*

1. she / a cold / tissues

2. he / a headache / aspirin

3. you / a cough / cough medicine

4. she / a cut / a bandage

5. you / a sprained ankle / an ice pack

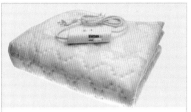

6. he / a backache / a heating pad

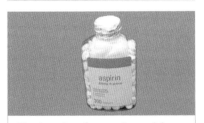

7. he / a fever / aspirin

8. you / earache / ear drops

9. she / sore throat / cough drops

3 Communicate

Talk with a partner. Ask and answer questions.

A What's the matter?

B I have a cold.

A Use tissues.

A What's the matter?

B I have a cough.

A Take cough medicine.

> **USEFUL LANGUAGE**
> *Use: tissues, a bandage, a heating pad, an ice pack*
> *Take: medicine, aspirin, vitamin C, cough drops*

Lesson C Do you have a cold?

1 Grammar focus: *Yes / No* questions with *have*

Ask *Yes / No* questions to get information. Use *do* or *does* with the verb *have*. Answers are usually short.

QUESTIONS			ANSWERS					
Do	I			you	**do.**		you	**don't.**
Do	you			I	**do.**		I	**don't.**
Does	he	**have** a fever?	Yes,	he	**does.**	No,	he	**doesn't.**
Does	she			she	**does.**		she	**doesn't.**
Do	we			you	**do.**		you	**don't.**
Do	they			they	**do.**		they	**don't.**

Watch

don't = do not
doesn't = does not

2 Practice

A Look at the picture. Complete the sentences. Use *do*, *does*, *don't*, or *doesn't*.

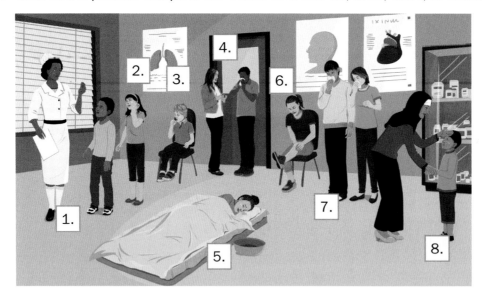

1. __Do__ I have a fever?
   _No, you don't._____

2. _____ she have a sore throat?
   _____

3. _____ he have a cough?
   _____

4. _____ you have a cold?
   _____

5. _____ she have the flu?
   _____

6. _____ she have a sprained ankle?
   _____

7. _____ they have colds?
   _____

8. _____ he have a fever?
   _____

Listen and repeat. Then practice with a partner.

CD1, Track 35

B **Talk** with a partner. Change the **bold** words and make conversations.

A **Mr. Jones** isn't at work today.

B Why not? Does **he** have the flu?

A No, not the flu. A **backache**.

1. Mr. Jones

a backache

2. Diana

a cold

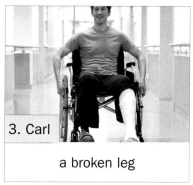

3. Carl

a broken leg

4. Mrs. Leeds

a stomachache

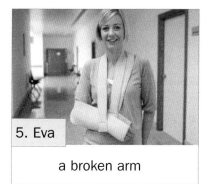

5. Eva

a broken arm

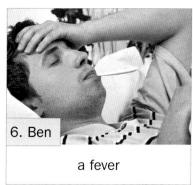

6. Ben

a fever

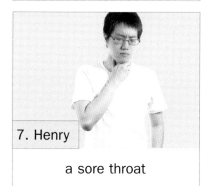

7. Henry

a sore throat

8. John and Jose

sprained ankles

9. Dick and Jane

earaches

3 Communicate

Talk with a partner. Take turns and make conversations.

A I don't feel well.

B Do you have a cold?

A No, I don't. I have a sore throat.

B That's too bad. I hope you feel better.

Ask and answer *Yes / No* questions with *have* **UNIT 4** **49**

Lesson D Reading

1 Before you read

Talk. Maria is in the doctor's office. Look at the picture. Answer the questions.

1. Who is with Maria?
2. What's wrong?

2 Read

Listen and read.

 CD1, Track 36

The Doctor's Office

Poor Maria! Everyone is sick! Maria and her children are in the doctor's office. Her son, Luis, has a sore throat. Her daughter, Rosa, has a stomachache. Her baby, Gabriel, has an earache. Maria doesn't have a sore throat. She doesn't have a stomachache. And she doesn't have an earache. But Maria has a very bad headache!

> Look at the exclamation points (!) in the reading. An exclamation point shows strong feeling.

3 After you read

A **Read** the sentences. Are they correct? Circle *Yes* or *No*.

1. Luis has a backache.	Yes	(No)
2. Rosa has a headache.	Yes	No
3. Gabriel has an earache.	Yes	No
4. Maria has a bad headache.	Yes	No
5. Everyone is happy today.	Yes	No
6. This story is about Maria and her children at the doctor's office.	Yes	No

Write. Correct the sentences.

1. Luis has a <u>sore throat</u>.

B **Write.** Answer the questions.

1. Does Maria have a cold? _____
2. Do Luis and Rosa have headaches? _____
3. What's the matter with Maria's children? _____

④ Picture dictionary Parts of the body

8. _____

1. _____ *nose* _____

2. _____

3. _____

7. _____

4. _____

6. _____

15. _____

16. _____

9. _____

17. _____

14. _____

13. _____

12. _____

11. _____

5. _____

10. _____

A **Write** the words in the Picture dictionary. Then listen and repeat.

| back | ear | finger | hand | knee | mouth | nose | stomach | toe |
| chin | eye | foot | head | leg | neck | shoulder | teeth | |

◀)) CD1, Track 37

B **Talk** with a partner. Change the **bold** word and make conversations.

A What's wrong?

B My **tooth** hurts.

A That's too bad.

one **tooth**

two **teeth**

For college and career readiness practice, see pages 142–143.

Lesson E Writing

1 Before you write

A Talk with your classmates.

1. Do you write emails?

2. Who do you write to?

B Read. Luis is sick today. Read the email from his mother to his teacher.

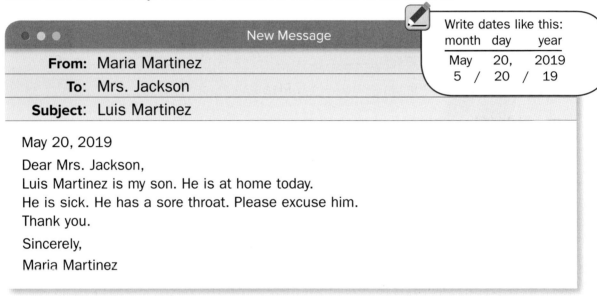

New Message

From: Maria Martinez

To: Mrs. Jackson

Subject: Luis Martinez

May 20, 2019

Dear Mrs. Jackson,
Luis Martinez is my son. He is at home today.
He is sick. He has a sore throat. Please excuse him.
Thank you.
Sincerely,
Maria Martinez

Write dates like this:

month	day	year
May	20,	2019
5 /	20 /	19

Read the email again. Circle the information.

1. the date

2. the teacher's name

3. the name of the sick child

4. what's wrong

5. the sender's name

Write. Answer the questions.

1. What is the date? _____

2. What is the teacher's name? _____

3. Who is sick? _____

4. What's the matter? _____

5. Who is the email from? _____

C **Write** about Rosa. She is sick, too. Complete the email.

| daughter   Dear   home   May 20, 2019   stomachache |

New Message

From: Maria Martinez

To: Mr. O'Hara

Subject: Rosa Martinez

May 20, 2019

_____ Mr. O'Hara,

Rosa Martinez is my _____. She is at _____ today.

She is sick. She has a _____. Please excuse her.

Thank you.
Sincerely,
Maria Martinez

2 Write

Write. Imagine your son or daughter is sick today. Complete the email to the teacher.

New Message

From:

To:

Subject:

_____

_____,

_____ is my _____. _____ is at

home today. _____ has a fever. Please excuse _____.

Thank you.
Sincerely,

_____

3 After you write

A **Read** your email to a partner.

B **Check** your partner's email.
- Who is sick? What's the matter?
- Is the date correct?

Lesson F Another view

1 Life-skills reading

Appointment Confirmation
Here is your appointment information.

Patient: __J. D. Avona__

Medical record number: __9999999__

Date: __Monday, October 23__

Time: __9:10 a.m.__

Doctor: __William Goldman, MD__

Address: __Eye Care Clinic__
__2025 Morse Avenue__

Cancellation Information

To cancel only: (973) 555-5645   7 days / 24 hours

To cancel and reschedule: (973) 555-5210   Mon-Fri 8:30 a.m. to 5:00 p.m.

A **Read** the questions. Look at the appointment confirmation card.
Fill in the answer.

1. What is the doctor's last name?
   - A Avona
   - B Goldman
   - C Morse
   - D William

2. What is the appointment for?
   - A ears
   - B eyes
   - C nose
   - D throat

3. What does *cancel* mean?
   - A change the appointment time
   - B change the appointment place
   - C stop the appointment
   - D keep the appointment

4. What do you do to reschedule?
   - A Call J. D. Avona.
   - B Call (973) 555-5645.
   - C Call (973) 555-5210.
   - D Go to the Eye Care Clinic.

B **Solve** the problem. Which solution is best? Circle your opinion.

Your English class is at the same time as your doctor's appointment. What should you do?

1. Not go to the class.

2. Cancel the appointment.

3. Talk to the teacher.

4. Other: _____

2 Grammar connections: *have* and *need*

Use *have* with health problems. Use *need* with medicine and objects.

have + problem	*need* + medicine / object
Do you **have** a headache?	Yes, I do. I **need** aspirin.
I **have** a headache.	You **need** aspirin.

Watch

A **Talk** with a partner. Look at the picture. Say what you need.
Your partner guesses what health problem you have. Take turns.

A I *need* a heating pad.

B Do you *have* a sprained ankle?

A No, I don't.

B Do you *have* a backache?

A Yes, I do!

B **Tell** the class about your partner's problems from 2A.

Julia has a backache. She needs a heating pad.

REVIEW

1 Listening

Read the questions. Then listen and circle the answers.

1. What's wrong with Connie?

   a. She has a backache.

   b. She has a headache.

2. What's wrong with Robert?

   a. He has an earache.

   b. He has a headache.

3. What's Robert doing?

   a. He's talking to the doctor.

   b. He's talking to the children.

4. What's Connie's daughter doing?

   a. She's sleeping.

   b. She's watching TV.

5. What's Connie's son doing?

   a. He's eating.

   b. He's watching TV.

6. What's wrong with Eddie?

   a. He has an earache.

   b. He has a stomachache.

Talk with a partner. Ask and answer the questions. Use complete sentences.

2 Grammar

A Write. Complete the story.

At the Hospital

This week, everyone in Anthony's family is sick. Anthony ____*has*____ a wife,
                                                         1. have / has

a son, and a daughter. Right now, they _____ sitting in a hospital room.
                                        2. is / are

Anthony's wife _____ a backache. The nurse _____ giving her
                3. have / has   4. is / are

medicine. The doctor _____ talking to Anthony. He _____ asking
                      5. is / are   6. is / are

questions about his children. They _____ the flu.
                                    7. have / has

B Write. Unscramble the words. Make questions about the story.

1. Is / home / family / at / Anthony's / ? _*Is Anthony's family at home?*_

2. is / doing / the nurse / What / ? _____

3. wrong / the children / with / What's / ? _____

Talk with a partner. Ask and answer the questions.

❸ Pronunciation: strong syllables

A **Listen** to the syllables in these words.

•
happy

•
fever

◀)) CD1, Track 39

B **Listen and repeat.** Clap for each syllable. Clap loudly for the strong syllable.

◀)) CD1, Track 40

•	• •	• • •	• • •
son	cooking	yesterday	tomorrow
wife	homework	grandmother	computer
head	toothache	grandfather	
ear	headache	newspaper	
foot	husband	studying	
leg	daughter	stomachache	

Talk with a partner. Take turns. Say a word. Your partner claps for each syllable.

C **Listen** for the strong syllable in each word. Put a dot (•) over the strong syllable.

•
1. father
2. earache
3. tired
4. birthday

5. thirsty
6. celebrate
7. finger
8. Brazil

9. repeat
10. elbow
11. reschedule
12. shoulder

◀)) CD1, Track 41

D **Write** eight words from Units 3 and 4. Put a dot over the strong syllable in each word.

1.	5.
2.	6.
3.	7.
4.	8.

Talk with a partner. Read the words.

UNIT 5 AROUND TOWN

Lesson A Listening

1 **Before you listen**

A Look at the picture. What do you see?

B Point to: ■ a grocery store ■ a library ■ a restaurant
■ a hospital ■ a house ■ a street

UNIT GOALS
Identify places around town   **Identify** locations of places
Write directions to a place

2 Listen

A **Listen.** Write the letter of the conversation.

1. ____

2. ____

3. _a_

◀)) CD1, Track 42

4. ____

5. ____

6. ____

B **Listen again** to the conversations. Circle the street you hear.

◀)) CD1, Track 42

A. 15th Avenue	(5th Avenue)	50th Avenue
B. C Street	G Street	Z Street
C. 7th Street	16th Street	70th Street
D. C Street	G Street	Z Street
E. Fir Avenue	First Avenue	Third Avenue
F. Thirteenth Avenue	Thirtieth Avenue	Third Avenue

Listen again. Check your answers.

3 After you listen

Write. How many places are in your neighborhood?

museums ___0___	libraries _____	schools _____
pharmacies _____	restaurants _____	post offices _____
bus stops _____	parks _____	hospitals _____

Work with a partner. Ask and answer questions

How many museums are in your neighborhood?   None.

> **USEFUL LANGUAGE**
> When *0* means *zero*,
> say *none*.

Lesson B It's on the corner.

1 Grammar focus: prepositions *on*, *next to*, *across from*, *between*, *on the corner of*; *Where is?*

On, next to, across from, and *between* are prepositions. They tell the location of things. They answer the question *Where?*

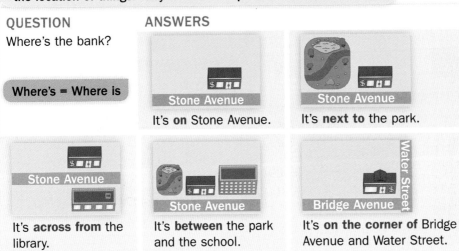

QUESTION
Where's the bank?

Where's = Where is

ANSWERS

It's **on** Stone Avenue.

It's **next to** the park.

It's **across from** the library.

It's **between** the park and the school.

It's **on the corner of** Bridge Avenue and Water Street.

👁 Watch

2 Practice

A Write. Look at the map. Complete the sentences.

1. A Where's the park?
   B It's _____*next to*_____ the bank.

2. A Where's the library?
   B It's _____ the bank.

3. A Where's the school?
   B It's _____ First Street and Grant Avenue.

4. A Where's the hospital?
   B It's _____ Grant Avenue.

5. A Where's the bank?
   B It's _____ the school and the park.

6. A Where's the post office?
   B It's _____ the library.

7. A Where's the museum?
   B It's _____ the park.

8. A Where's the car?
   B It's _____ Grant Avenue.

Listen and repeat. Then practice with a partner.

🔊 CD1, Track 43

B Listen and repeat.

A Excuse me. **Where's Kim's Coffee Shop?**

B It's **on Kent Street.**

A Sorry. Could you repeat that, please?

B It's **on Kent Street.**

A Oh, OK. Thanks.

> **USEFUL LANGUAGE**
> *Could you repeat that, please?*
> *Sorry, I didn't get that.*

CD1, Track 44

Talk with a partner. Change the **bold** words and make conversations.

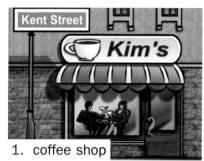

1. coffee shop

2. pharmacy

3. grocery store

Now practice this conversation with the map on page 60.

3 Communicate

A Talk with a partner. Look at the map on page 60. Take turns. Give directions. Guess the place.

A It's on the corner of First Street and Grant Avenue. It's across from the hospital.

B The school?

A That's right.

B Draw these places on the map. Talk with a partner. Ask and answer questions about your maps.

bank
bus stop
coffee shop
grocery store
hospital
house
museum
post office

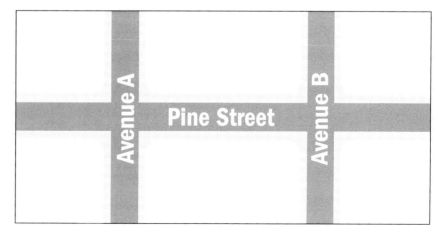

Lesson C Go two blocks.

1 Grammar focus: imperatives

Imperative sentences give commands. Use the base form of
the verb to start the sentence, not a subject:
~~You~~ Go straight ahead.

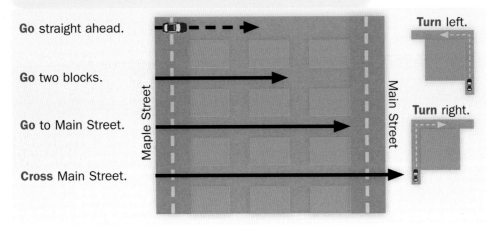

Go straight ahead.

Go two blocks.

Go to Main Street.

Cross Main Street.

Turn **left**.

Turn **right**.

👁 Watch

2 Practice

A Write. Match the pictures and the directions.

Cross Union Street.	Go three blocks.	Go to Union Street.	Turn left.
Go straight ahead.	Go to Main Street.	Go two blocks.	Turn right.

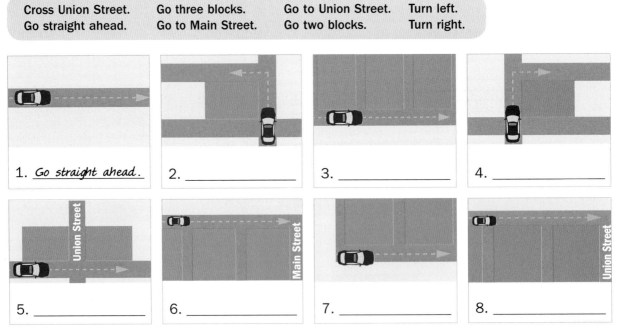

1. *Go straight ahead.*

2. _____

3. _____

4. _____

5. _____

6. _____

7. _____

8. _____

Listen and repeat.

🔊 CD1, Track 45

B Read the directions. Look at the map. Write the places.

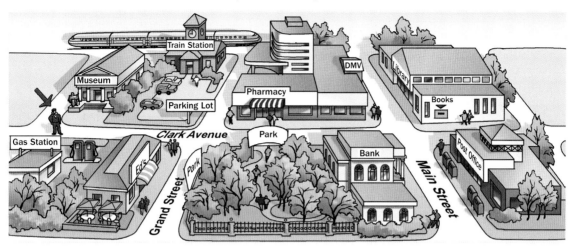

1. Go two blocks. Turn left. It's across from the library.

    the DMV

2. Go straight. Cross Grand Street. Turn right on Main Street. It's across from the post office.

    _____

3. Go to Grand Street. Turn left. It's next to the parking lot on Grand.

    _____

4. Go one block. Turn right on Grand Street. It's across from Ed's Restaurant.

    _____

Listen and repeat.

CD1, Track 46

C Talk with a partner. Look at the map in 2B. Change the **bold** words and make conversations.

A Excuse me. How do I get to the **DMV**?

B **Go two blocks. Turn left. It's on Main Street.**

A OK. **Go two blocks. Turn left. It's on Main Street.**

B Right.

A Thank you.

CULTURE NOTE
The DMV is the Department of Motor Vehicles. You can get a driver's license there.

1. DMV
2. parking lot
3. pharmacy
4. library
5. hospital
6. post office

3 Communicate

Talk with a partner. Give directions to a building on the map in 2B. Your partner names the building.

Go two blocks. Turn left. It's on Main Street.   The DMV.

Lesson D Reading

1 Before you read

Talk. Look at these pictures of Sandra's new neighborhood. Answer the questions.

1. What are the places in her neighborhood?

2. What can you do in these places?

2 Read

Listen and read.

◀) CD1, Track 47

New Message

Send

Hi Angela,

I love my new house. My neighborhood is great! Here are some pictures.
There is a school on my street. My children go to the school. They like it a lot.
There is a community center across from the school. My husband works at the
community center. He walks to work. There is a grocery store next to my house.
It's a small store, but we can buy a lot of things. There is a good Mexican
restaurant on Second Street. It's right across from my house.

I like it here, but I miss you.
Please write.

Your friend,
Sandra

When you see pronouns (*he*, *it*, *they*), ask
Who is the writer talking about? Look at the
sentences before a pronoun to find the answer.

3 After you read

A Read the sentences. Are they correct? Circle *Yes* or *No*.

1. Sandra lives on Summit Street.   Yes   (No)

2. There is a school on Sandra's street.   Yes   No

3. There is a community center next to the school.   Yes   No

4. Sandra's husband works at the community center.   Yes   No

5. Sandra's letter is about her new school.   Yes   No

Write. Correct the sentences.

1. Sandra lives on <u>Second</u> Street.

B Write. Answer the questions about Sandra's neighborhood.

1. Where is the school? _____

2. Where is the grocery store? _____

3. Does Sandra like the restaurant? _____

4 Picture dictionary Places around town

1. _a shopping mall_

2. _____

3. _____

4. _____

5. _____

6. _____

7. _____

8. _____

9. _____

A **Write** the words in the Picture dictionary. Then listen and repeat.

an apartment building	a hardware store	a police station
a courthouse	a high school	a senior center
a day-care center	a playground	a shopping mall

◀)) CD1, Track 48

B **Talk** with a partner about your neighborhood.

> There's a playground in my neighborhood.

Where is it?

> It's across from the bank.

CULTURE NOTE

Most elementary school students are 5 to 10 years old.

Most middle school students are 11 to 13 years old.

Most high school students are 14 to 18 years old.

For college and career readiness practice, see pages 144–145.

Lesson E Writing

1 Before you write

A Listen. Draw the way from the train station to the school.

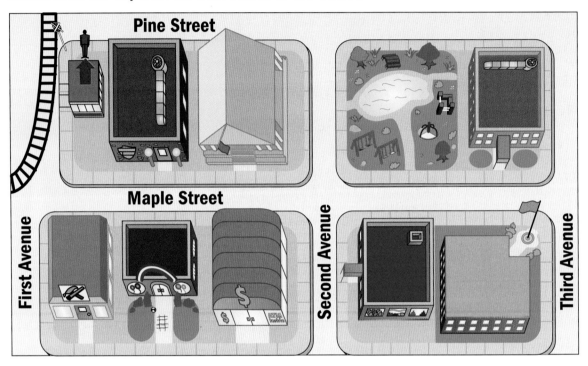

Write. Look at the map. Complete the directions from the train station to the school.

across from	go straight	on the corner of	turn right
cross	one block	straight ahead	

START

1. **From the train station, turn right.**

2. _____Go straight_____ **on Pine Street.**

3. _____ **on Second Avenue.**

4. **Go** _____ .

5. _____ **Maple Street. Then turn left on Maple Street.**

6. **Walk** _____ **to the corner.**

7. **The school is** _____ **Maple Street and Third Avenue.**

FINISH 8. **It's** _____ **the apartment building.**

Talk with a partner. Give different directions to get from the train station to the school.

B **Write.** Add capital letters.

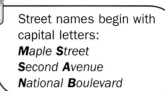

Street names begin with capital letters:
*M*aple *S*treet
*S*econd *A*venue
*N*ational *B*oulevard

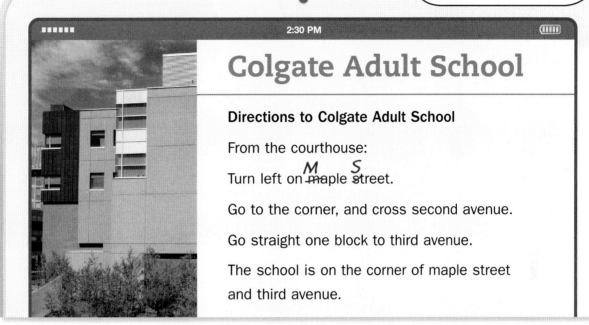

2:30 PM

Colgate Adult School

Directions to Colgate Adult School

From the courthouse:

Turn left on ~~maple~~ *M* street. *S*

Go to the corner, and cross second avenue.

Go straight one block to third avenue.

The school is on the corner of maple street and third avenue.

C **Write.** Work with a partner. Complete the chart. Write four streets near your school. Write four places near your school.

Streets	Places

2 Write

Draw a map first. Show directions to your school. Start from a bus stop, a train station, a subway stop, a restaurant, or your home.

Write the directions to your school.

3 After you write

A **Read** your directions to a partner.

B **Check** your partner's directions.

■ What are the street names?
■ Do all the street names have capital letters?

Lesson F Another view

1 Life-skills reading

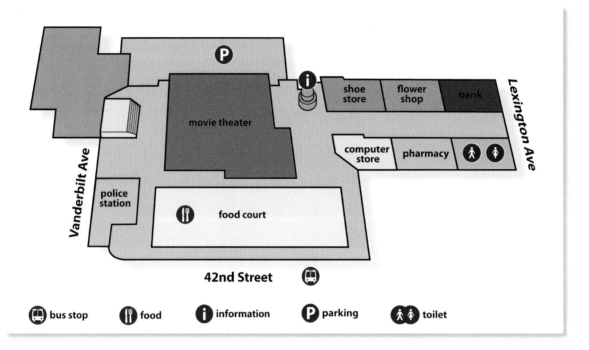

A **Read** the questions. Look at the map. Fill in the answer.

1. Where is the pharmacy?

   A It's between the shoe store and the bank.

   B It's on Lexington Avenue.

   C It's next to the computer store.

   D It's across from the shoe store.

2. What does *toilet* mean?

   A restroom

   B bathroom

   C ladies' and men's room

   D all of the above

3. Where is the police station?

   A It's on Vanderbilt Avenue.

   B It's next to the shoe store.

   C It's on Lexington Avenue.

   D It's on the corner of Lexington Avenue and 42nd Street.

4. Where is the flower shop?

   A It's next to the police station.

   B It's across from the computer store.

   C It's between the shoe store and the bank.

   D It's on Vanderbilt Avenue.

B **Solve** the problem. Which solution is best? Circle your opinion.

Sandra parked her car in one of the parking lots at the mall. She can't find her car. What should she do?

1. Call her husband.

2. Go to the parking lots and look.

3. Call the police.

4. Other: _____

2 Grammar connections: negative imperatives

Use *Don't* before the base form of the verb for negative imperatives.

AFFIRMATIVE	NEGATIVE
Turn right on Elm Street.	**Don't turn** left on Elm Street.
Use cell phones outside.	**Don't use** cell phones in the library.

Don't = Do not

Watch

A **Work** with a partner. Match the signs and the words.

1. _e_   2. ____   3. ____

4. ____   5. ____   6. ____

    a. Don't park here.
    b. Don't litter.
    c. Don't ride bicycles.
    d. Don't use cell phones.
    e. Don't turn left.
    f. Don't fish.

B **Work** with your partner. Where do the signs go? Write the numbers from 2A on the map.

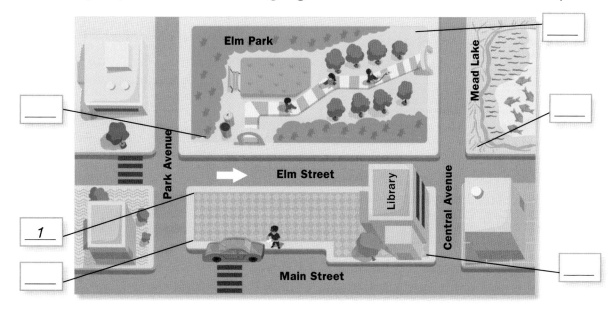

A Don't turn left on Elm Street. That's number one. That goes here.

B Don't use cell phones in . . .

Lesson A Listening

1 Before you listen

A Look at the picture. What do you see?

B Point to a person: ■ eating ■ talking ■ taking a nap
■ drinking coffee ■ reading a schedule ■ buying a snack

UNIT GOALS
Get information from a weekly planner   **Describe** own daily schedule
Interpret information on a course schedule

2 Listen

A **Listen.** Write the letter of the conversation.

1. ____    2. ____    3. ____

 CD2, Track 2

4. ____    5. ____    6. _a_

B **Listen again** to the conversations. Circle the time you hear.

A.	(10:30)	11:30	2:30	D.	10:15	10:45	10:40
B.	5:30	5:40	6:30	E.	10:45	12:45	2:45
C.	11:00	12:00	1:00	F.	11:30	7:30	12:30

 CD2, Track 2

Listen again. Check your answers.

3 After you listen

Talk with a partner. Take turns. Ask and tell the time.

What time is it?   It's ten o'clock.

1. ten o'clock   2. ten-thirty   3. six-fifteen   4. five-twenty

5. twelve-fifty   6. two-forty-five   7. seven-thirty   8. nine-oh-five

Lesson B What do you do in the evening?

1 Grammar focus: simple present; *What* questions

Use the simple present tense for a repeated or regular action.

QUESTIONS			ANSWERS	
What	**do** you **do**	in the evening? every evening?	I	read.
	does he **do**		He	reads.
	does she **do**		She	reads.
	do they **do**		They	read.

With *he* and *she*:
do → does
exercise → exercises
go → goes
study → studies
watch → watches

 Watch

2 Practice

A Write. Complete the sentences. Use *do* or *does* and the correct form of the verb.

1. **A** What ____*do*____ they do in the evening?
   B They ____*watch*____ TV.
   (watch / watches)

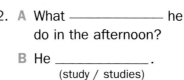

2. **A** What _____ he do in the afternoon?
   B He _____ .
   (study / studies)

3. **A** What _____ she do in the morning?
   B She _____ .
   (exercise / exercises)

4. **A** What _____ they do on Sunday?
   B They _____ to the park.
   (go / goes)

5. **A** What _____ she do every evening?
   B She _____ .
   (read / reads)

6. **A** What _____ he do in the afternoon?
   B He _____ a nap.
   (take / takes)

Listen and repeat. Then practice with a partner.

🔊 CD2, Track 3

B **Listen** to the Wilder family's schedule. Then listen and repeat.

)) CD2, Track 4

SATURDAY MORNING	SATURDAY AFTERNOON	SATURDAY EVENING

Jill

Jill watches TV.

She plays soccer.

She listens to music.

Mr. and Mrs. Wilder

Mr. and Mrs. Wilder go shopping.

They work in the garden.

They pay bills.

Harry

Harry does his homework.

He plays football.

He goes to a movie.

Listen. Then talk with a partner. Change the **bold** words and make conversations.

)) CD2, Track 5

A What **does Jill** do on **Saturday morning**?

B **She** usually **watches TV**.

1. Jill / Saturday morning
2. Mr. and Mrs. Wilder / Saturday evening
3. Mr. and Mrs. Wilder / Saturday morning
4. Harry / Saturday afternoon
5. Mr. and Mrs. Wilder / Saturday afternoon
6. Jill / Saturday evening
7. Harry / Saturday evening
8. Jill / Saturday afternoon
9. Harry / Saturday morning

3 Communicate

Talk with your classmates. Ask questions about the weekend.

What do you do on Saturday morning?   I usually go to the grocery store.

USEFUL LANGUAGE
Usually means
most of the time.
Always means
all of the time.

Use simple present; ask and answer *what* questions   UNIT 6   **73**

Lesson C I go to work at 8:00.

1 Grammar focus: *at*, *in*, *on*, and *from . . . to* with time; *When* questions

Use *when* to ask about the time something happens. Use the propositions *at*, *in*, *on* and *from . . . to* to talk about time.

Use *at* for a definite time.
Use *in* for months and parts of the day.
Use *on* for days and dates.
Use *from . . . to* for a period of time.

Watch

PREPOSITIONS OF TIME

at	1:30	in	the morning	on	Saturday	from	2:00 p.m.	to	3:00 p.m
	night		January		the weekend		Tuesday		Friday

QUESTIONS

When **do** you **go** to work?

When **does** he **have** class?

ANSWERS

I **go** to work **at** 8 o'clock.

He **has** class **on** Monday.

With *he* and *she*:
have → has

2 Practice

PTA meetings:
First Tuesday of the month

CULTURE NOTE
The PTA is the Parent-Teacher Association at a school. Parents and teachers meet in a group to talk about school.

A Write. Complete the sentences. Use *at*, *in*, *on* or *from . . . to*.

1. I have English class __on__ Tuesday and Thursday.

2. My sister usually has class _____ Saturday.

3. I do homework _____ night.

4. My father goes to work _____ the morning.

5. He always catches the bus _____ 8:45.

6. My mom goes to PTA meetings _____ the evening.

7. I usually go on vacation _____ July.

8. She has class _____ 9:00 a.m _____ 11:00 a.m.

B Write. Read the answers. Complete the questions.

1. A When ___do___ you ___go___ on vacation?

   B I usually go on vacation _____ July.

2. A When _____ your sister _____ class?

   B She usually has class _____ Saturday.

3. A When _____ your father _____ the bus?

   B He always catches the bus _____ 8:45.

4. A When _____ you _____ homework?

   B I always do homework _____ night.

5. A When _____ your brother _____ his homework?

   B He usualy does his homework _____ the evening.

6. A When _____ your mother _____?

   B She usually exercises _____ the morning.

Listen and repeat. Then practice with a partner.

CD2, Track 6

C **Listen.** Then talk with a partner. Change the **bold** words and make conversations.

CD2, Track 7

Mrs. Wilder's Schedule

SUNDAY	MONDAY	TUESDAY	WEDNESDAY	THURSDAY	FRIDAY	SATURDAY
2:00–4:00 p.m. rest	11:00 a.m. volunteer at the high school	6:00–7:00 a.m. exercise class 7:30 p.m. cooking class	2:30 p.m. driving lessons	4:00 p.m. Spanish class	6:30 p.m. PTA meeting	9:00 a.m. go shopping 3:00 p.m. visit mother

A When does Mrs. Wilder **rest**?

B She **rests on Sunday**.

A What time?

B **From 2:00 to 4:00 p.m.**

1. rest
2. volunteer at the high school
3. take driving lessons
4. visit her mother
5. have cooking class
6. have Spanish class
7. go shopping
8. go to the PTA meeting
9. have exercise class

CULTURE NOTE
Many people in the U.S. do volunteer work in their free time. Volunteers do not receive money for their work.

USEFUL LANGUAGE
She *has* cooking class on Tuesday.
She *goes to* cooking class on Tuesday.

3 Communicate

Write. What are five things you do every week? Make a list.

1. call my mother
2. go to English class
3. work
4. visit friends
5. go to the grocery store

Talk with a partner. Ask questions about your partner's list.

When do you call your mother?　I usually call my mother on Sunday at nine o'clock at night.

Lesson D Reading

1 Before you read

Talk. Bob has a new job. Look at the picture. Answer the questions.

1. What is Bob wearing?
2. What is his new job?

2 Read

Listen and read.

 CD2, Track 8

Meet Our New Employee: Bob Green

Please welcome Bob. He is a new security guard. He works the night shift at the East End Factory. Bob starts work at 11:00 at night. He leaves work at 7:00 in the morning.

Bob likes these hours because he can spend time with his family. Bob says, "I eat breakfast with my wife, Arlene, and my son, Brett, at 7:30 every morning. I help Brett with his homework in the afternoon. I eat dinner with my family at 6:30. Then we watch TV. At 10:30, I go to work."

Congratulations to Bob on his new job!

> To help you remember, ask questions as you read:
> **Who** is this reading about?
> **What** is this reading about?
> **When** does Bob work?

3 After you read

A Read the sentences. Are they correct? Circle **Yes** or **No**.

1. This story is about a new boss.   Yes   (No)
2. He starts work at 7:00 at night.   Yes   No
3. He likes to spend time with his family.   Yes   No
4. Bob helps Brett with his homework.   Yes   No

Write. Correct the sentences.

1. *This story is about a new <u>employee</u>.*

B Write. Answer the questions about Bob's schedule.

1. Where does Bob work? _____

2. Who is Arlene? _____

3. What does Bob do at 7:30 every morning? _____

4. When does the Green family watch TV? _____

❹ **Picture dictionary** *Daily activities*

1. _____*get up*_____

2. _____

3. _____

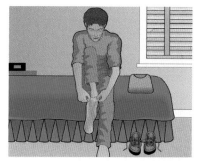

4. _____

5. _____

6. _____

7. _____

8. _____

9. _____

A **Write** the words in the Picture dictionary. Then listen and repeat.

eat breakfast	get dressed	take a shower
eat dinner	get up	take the children to school
eat lunch	go to bed	walk the dog

🔊)) CD2, Track 9

B **Talk** with a partner. Ask and answer questions about your daily activities.

When do you eat breakfast?   I usually eat breakfast at 6:45.

For college and career readiness practice, see pages 146–147.

Lesson E Writing

1 Before you write

A **Write.** What do you do in the morning, afternoon, and evening?

Complete the chart.

Morning	Afternoon	Evening
get up		
get dressed		

Talk with a partner about your daily schedule.

What do you do in the morning?

I get up. I get dressed . . .

Write sentences.

Morning

I get up.

I get dressed.

_____

_____

Afternoon

_____

_____

_____

_____

Evening

_____

_____

_____

_____

UNIT 6

B **Write.** Complete the paragraph. Use *in*, *on*, and *at*.

Hamid
August 10

My Daily Schedule

Leave space at the beginning of a paragraph. This space is an *indent*.

 Let me tell you about my daily schedule. _On_ Monday, I usually get up ____ 6:30 ____ the morning. I eat breakfast and get dressed. ____ 8:00, I go to work. I work at a department store. I eat lunch ____ 12:30. ____ the afternoon, I take a break ____ 3:30. I finish work ____ 5:00. I go to a fast-food restaurant or a coffee shop for dinner. I get home ____ 6:45 or 7:00. I read ____ the evening. I go to bed ____ 10:00.

2 Write

Write a paragraph about your daily schedule.

3 After you write

A **Read** your paragraph to a partner.

B **Check** your partner's paragraph.

■ What does your partner do in the evening?
■ Is there an indent at the beginning of the paragraph?

Write a paragraph about a daily schedule **UNIT 6** **79**

Lesson F Another view

1 Life-skills reading

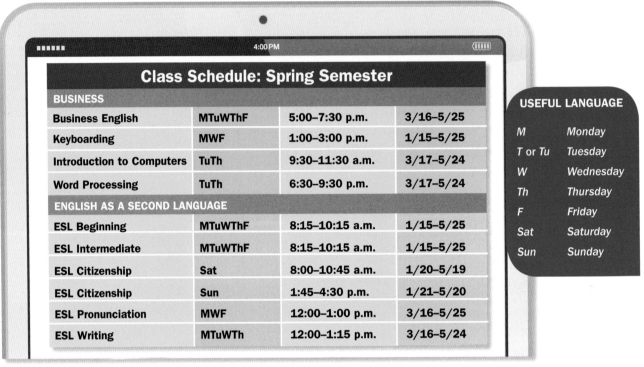

Class Schedule: Spring Semester

BUSINESS

Business English	MTuWThF	5:00–7:30 p.m.	3/16–5/25
Keyboarding	MWF	1:00–3:00 p.m.	1/15–5/25
Introduction to Computers	TuTh	9:30–11:30 a.m.	3/17–5/24
Word Processing	TuTh	6:30–9:30 p.m.	3/17–5/24

ENGLISH AS A SECOND LANGUAGE

ESL Beginning	MTuWThF	8:15–10:15 a.m.	1/15–5/25
ESL Intermediate	MTuWThF	8:15–10:15 a.m.	1/15–5/25
ESL Citizenship	Sat	8:00–10:45 a.m.	1/20–5/19
ESL Citizenship	Sun	1:45–4:30 p.m.	1/21–5/20
ESL Pronunciation	MWF	12:00–1:00 p.m.	3/16–5/25
ESL Writing	MTuWTh	12:00–1:15 p.m.	3/16–5/24

USEFUL LANGUAGE

M	Monday
T or Tu	Tuesday
W	Wednesday
Th	Thursday
F	Friday
Sat	Saturday
Sun	Sunday

A **Read** the questions. Look at the schedule. Fill in the answer.

1. Which classes meet on Monday, Wednesday, and Friday?

   A ESL Beginning and ESL Intermediate

   B Keyboarding and ESL Writing

   C Keyboarding and ESL Citizenship

   D Keyboarding and ESL Pronunciation

2. When does the Introduction to Computers class start?

   A on January 15

   B on March 16

   C on March 17

   D on March 19

3. When is the Word Processing class?

   A on Monday, Wednesday, and Friday

   B on Tuesday and Thursday

   C on Monday, Tuesday, and Thursday

   D on Monday, Tuesday, and Wednesday

4. When does the spring semester end?

   A in January

   B in February

   C in March

   D in May

B **Solve** the problem. Which solution is best? Circle your opinion.

You want to take the Citizenship Class on Saturday morning. You can't attend Saturday classes in January. What should you do?

1. Not take the class.

2. Take the Sunday class.

3. Talk to the teacher.

4. Other: _____

❷ Grammar connections: *start / end* and *open / close*

Use *start* and *end* for events. Use *open* and *close* for places.

What time does the meeting **start**?   What time does the store **open**?

What time does it **end**?   What time does it **close**?

👁 **Watch**

A Talk with a partner. Ask and answer questions about the notices. Take turns.

A What time does the computer club meeting start?

B At 5:00 p.m. What time does the library close?

A At 8:00 p.m.

Computer Club Meeting
Every Tuesday
5:00 p.m. – 7:30 p.m.
At the Lincoln Library
Library hours:
8:00 a.m. – 8:00 p.m.

The History of Rock Music

See a great show about rock music!

Show: 7:00 p.m. – 9:15 p.m., Wednesday

Ticket office hours: 6:00 p.m. – 11:00 p.m.

Cooking Class with Yolanda

Learn to cook with Yolanda Gomez at Yoli's Café.

9:00 a.m. – 11:00 a.m. on Saturdays

Restaurant hours: 12:00 p.m. – 10:00 p.m.

Basketball Game

Rockets vs. Leopards

Game time: 7:30 p.m.– 10:00 p.m., Friday

Gym hours: 4:30 p.m. – 10:30 p.m.

B Talk with your partner. Write times for the signs. Then share your information with the class.

A What time does the park open?

B How about 9:00 a.m.?

A No. That's too late. How about 7:00 a.m.?

B OK. And it closes at . . .

City Park Hours
_____ to _____ every day
Free Music
_____ to _____ on Sundays

Free Beginner English Class
_____ to _____ on Fridays in Room 28
at Central Community Center
Center Hours: _____ to _____
Monday – Friday

REVIEW

1 Listening

Read. the questions. Then listen and circle the answers.

CD2, Track 10

1. Where is the DMV?

   a. on Broadway

   b. on Fifth Avenue

2. What is the address number?

   a. 550

   b. 515

3. Is the DMV between the coffee shop and the grocery store?

   a. Yes, it is.

   b. No, it isn't.

4. Is the DMV between the bank and the coffee shop?

   a. Yes, it is.

   b. No, it isn't.

5. Is the DMV across from the hospital?

   a. Yes, it is.

   b. No, it isn't.

Talk with a partner. Ask and answer the questions. Use complete sentences.

2 Grammar

A Write. Complete the story.

Kate's Day

Kate is very busy. She's a wife, a mother, and a volunteer at the library. ___*In*___
                                                             1. In / On

the morning, she _____ breakfast with her husband. _____ 8:30, she
                   2. has / have   3. At / In

_____ the children to school. Her house is _____
       4. take/takes   5. on / on the corner of

Tenth and Pine. The school is _____ the post office. Kate volunteers
                               6. across from / between

_____ the library _____ 12 _____ 2. At 3:30, She _____ her
7. on / at   8. to / from   9. to / from   10. get / gets

children from school. The family _____ dinner at 6:00. _____
                        11. eat / eats   12. On / In

the evening, they _____ TV.
        13. watch / watches

B Write. Unscramble the words. Make questions about the story.

1. morning / Kate / do / What / does / the / in / ? *What does Kate do in the morning?*

2. school / Where / the / is / ? _____

3. get / When / children / does / her / Kate / ? _____

4. What time / the family / eat / dinner / does / ? _____

Talk with a partner. Ask and answer the questions.

3 Pronunciation: intonation in questions

A **Listen** to the intonation in these questions.

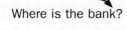 Where is the bank?

Is the bank on Broadway?

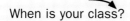 When is your class?

Is your class in the morning?

 ◀)) CD2, Track 11

B **Listen and repeat.**

 ◀)) CD2, Track 12

Wh- questions

1. **A** Where is the post office?
   B It's on First Street.

2. **A** What time do they eat dinner?
   B They eat dinner at 6:30.

Yes/No questions

3. **A** Are you from Mexico?
   B Yes, I am.

4. **A** Does he start work at 7:00?
   B No, he doesn't.

C **Talk** with a partner. Ask and answer the questions.

1. What time do you go to bed?
2. When is your birthday?
3. Where is your supermarket?
4. What time is your English class?
5. Do you visit your friends on the weekend?
6. Do you work in the evening?
7. Do you volunteer?
8. Do you watch TV in the afternoon?

D **Write** five questions.

   What's your name?

1. _____

2. _____

3. _____

4. _____

5. _____

Talk with a partner. Ask and answer the questions. Use correct intonation.

What's your name?   My name is Teresa.

Lesson A Listening

1 Before you listen

A Look at the picture. What do you see?

B Point to: ■ apples ■ bananas ■ bread ■ cheese ■ cookies
■ milk ■ a cashier ■ a shopping cart ■ a stock clerk

Shirley

Dan

UNIT GOALS
Identify food items **Make** a shopping list
Interpret information in a supermarket ad

2 Listen

A Listen. Write the letter of the conversation.

◄)) CD2, Track 13

1. ____

2. ____

3. _a_

4. ____

5. ____

6. ____

B Listen again to the conversations. Write the price that you hear.

A. $ ___2.69___   C. $ _____ / lb.   E. _____ ¢ / lb.

B. _____ ¢ each   D. $ _____ / lb.   F. $ _____

◄)) CD2, Track 13

Listen again. Check your answers.

3 After you listen

Add the prices of all the items. What is the total?

Sales Receipt		
bananas	3 lb	$1.98
apples	2 lb	$2.98
bread	2	$7.58
cheese	1/2 lb	$3.50
potatoes	3 lb	$2.97
milk	2	$5.38
Total		_____

USEFUL LANGUAGE
69¢ / lb. =
sixty-nine cents a pound

$1.98 = *one ninety-eight*
OR
one dollar and ninety-eight cents

Listen for and identify food items and prices **UNIT 7 85**

Lesson B How many? How much?

1 Grammar focus: count / non-count nouns; *How many?* / *How much?*

Some things we count: one apple, two apples, three apples . . .
Some things we don't count: ~~one sugar, two sugars, three sugars~~ . . .
Use *How many?* to ask questions about count nouns.
Use *How much?* to ask questions about non-count nouns.

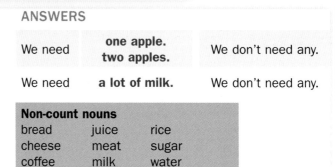

QUESTIONS		ANSWERS		
How many apples	do we need?	We need	**one apple.** **two apples.**	We don't need any.
How much milk	do we need?	We need	**a lot of milk.**	We don't need any.

Count nouns			Non-count nouns		
an apple	a cookie	an orange	bread	juice	rice
a banana	an egg	a peach	cheese	meat	sugar
a carrot	an onion	a pie	coffee	milk	water

Watch

2 Practice

A Look at the pictures. Circle only the count nouns.

1.
2.
3.
4.
5.
6.
7.
8.
9.
10.
11.
12.

Listen and repeat.

CD2, Track 14

B Write. Look at the pictures on page 86. Complete the chart. Write the food words.

1. *carrots*   5.   9.

2. *water*   6.   10.

3.   7.   11.

4.   8.   12.

C Write. Complete the questions. Use *many* or *much*.

1. How ___many___ eggs do we need?
2. How ___much___ juice do we need?
3. How _____ milk do we need?
4. How _____ pies do we need?
5. How _____ bread do we need?
6. How _____ potatoes do we need?
7. How _____ rice do we need?
8. How _____ meat do we need?

Listen and repeat.

CD2, Track 15

D Talk with a partner. Change the **bold** words and make conversations.

A We need some **apples**.
B How **many apples** do we need?
A **Two.**

A We need some **milk**.
B How **much milk** do we need?
A **Not much.**

1. apples / two
2. milk / not much
3. bananas / five
4. bread / a lot
5. oranges / six
6. cheese / not much
7. eggs / a dozen
8. onions / not many

> **USEFUL LANGUAGE**
> *How many do we need?*
> You can answer *A few, Not many,* or *A lot.*
> *How much do we need?*
> You can answer *A little, Not much,* or *A lot.*

❸ Communicate

Talk with a partner. Pretend you are making a fruit salad for four friends. Check (✓) six items. Then make conversations.

How many apples do we need? We need three.

☐ apples   ☐ cherries   ☐ pineapples
☐ bananas   ☐ orange juice   ☐ strawberries
☐ blueberries   ☐ oranges   ☐ sugar

Lesson C Are there any bananas?

1 Grammar focus: *There is / There are*

Use *There is* with non-count nouns and singular count nouns.
Use *There are* with plural count nouns.

STATEMENTS

There is	a banana	
There are	two bananas	on the table.
There is	bread	

👁 Watch

QUESTIONS

Is there	a banana	
Are there	any bananas	on the table?
Is there	any bread	

ANSWERS

	is.			**isn't.**
Yes, **there**	**are.**	No, **there**		**aren't.**
	is.			**isn't.**

2 Practice

A Write. Complete the sentences. Use *there is* or *there are*.

1. _There_ _is_ sugar on the table.
2. _____ _____ 6 eggs in the refrigerator.
3. _____ _____ one apple on the table.
4. _____ _____ many peaches in the box.
5. _____ _____ bread on the shelf.
6. _____ _____ an orange on the table.
7. _____ _____ onions in the drawer.
8. _____ _____ meat in the refrigerator.

Listen and repeat. Then practice with a partner.

🔊 CD2, Track 16

B Write. Complete the sentences. Use *Is there, Are there, there is, there isn't, there are,* or *there aren't.*

1. A _Is_ _there_ any meat in the refrigerator?
   B Yes, _there_ _is_ .
2. A _____ _____ any oranges?
   B Yes, _____ _____.
3. A _____ _____ any cheese?
   B No, _____ _____.
4. A _____ _____ any sugar?
   B No, _____ _____.
5. A _____ _____ any milk in the refrigerator?
   B Yes, _____ _____.
6. A _____ _____ any coffee?
   B Yes, _____ _____.
7. A _____ _____ any apples?
   B No, _____ _____.
8. A _____ _____ any cherries?
   B Yes, _____ _____.

Listen and repeat. Then practice with a partner.

🔊 CD2, Track 17

C Write. Complete the sentences. Use *There is* or *There are*.

1. ____There____ ____is____ one loaf of bread.

2. _____ _____ two cartons of apple juice.

3. _____ _____ three boxes of tea.

4. _____ _____ four bottles of water.

5. _____ _____ one package of ground meat.

6. _____ _____ six cans of soda.

7. _____ _____ one bag of flour.

8. _____ _____ two packages of cheese.

Listen and repeat.

D Talk with a partner. Look at the picture. Make conversations.

CD2, Track 18

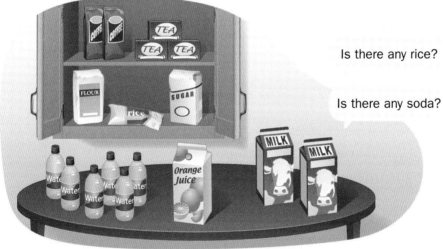

Is there any rice?

Yes, there is a bag of rice on the shelf.

Is there any soda?

No, there isn't.

1. rice	3. milk	5. tea	7. sugar	9. flour
2. soda	4. coffee	6. cheese	8. water	10. meat

3 Communicate

Talk with a partner. Ask and answer these questions.

1. What's in your refrigerator?

2. What's on your kitchen shelves?

Lesson D Reading

1 Before you read

Talk. Shirley and Dan are shopping.
Look at the picture. Answer the questions.

1. Where are they?

2. What are they doing?

2 Read

Listen and read.

🔊) CD2, Track 19

Regular Customers

Shirley and Dan are regular customers at SaveMore Supermarket. They go to SaveMore three or four times a week. The cashiers and stock clerks at SaveMore know them and like them. There are fruit and vegetables, meat and fish, and cookies and cakes in the supermarket. But today, Shirley and Dan are buying apples, bananas, bread, and cheese. There is one problem. The total is $16.75. They only have a ten-dollar bill, five one-dollar bills, and three quarters!

 When you don't understand a word, look for clues.
Do you understand *regular customer*?
Clue: They go to SaveMore *three or four times a week.*

3 After you read

A Read the sentences. Are they correct? Circle *Yes* or *No*.

1. This story is about regular customers at a restaurant.   Yes   (No)

2. Shirley and Dan go to SaveMore three or four times a day.   Yes   No

3. The cashiers and stock clerks know them.   Yes   No

4. Shirley and Dan are buying meat and fish.   Yes   No

5. Shirley and Dan have $16.00.   Yes   No

B Write. Correct the sentences.

1. This reading is about regular customers at a <u>supermarket</u>.

C Write. Answer the questions about Shirley and Dan.

1. How much money do Shirley and Dan have? _____

2. How many quarters do they have? _____

3. How much more money do they need? _____

4 Picture dictionary Money

1. __a penny__
2. _____
3. _____
4. _____

5. _____
6. _____
7. _____
8. _____

9. _____
10. _____
11. _____
12. _____

A Write the words in the Picture dictionary. Then listen and repeat.

a check	a dime	a nickel	a quarter
a credit card	a five-dollar bill	a one-dollar bill	a ten-dollar bill
a debit card	a half-dollar	a penny	a twenty-dollar bill

 CD2, Track 20

B Talk with a partner. Look at the pictures.
Change the **bold** words and make conversations.

A Do you have change for a **dollar**?

B Sure. What do you need?

A I need **four quarters**.

B Here you are.

USEFUL LANGUAGE
You can say:
a one-dollar bill OR a dollar
a five-dollar bill OR five dollars
a ten-dollar bill OR ten dollars

1.

2.

3.

4.

For college and career readiness practice, see pages 148–149.

Lesson E Writing

1 Before you write

A Talk with a partner. Ask and answer questions.

1. When do you go shopping?

2. What are the names of some supermarkets in your neighborhood?

3. What do you usually buy at the supermarket?

B Read the text. Make a shopping list.

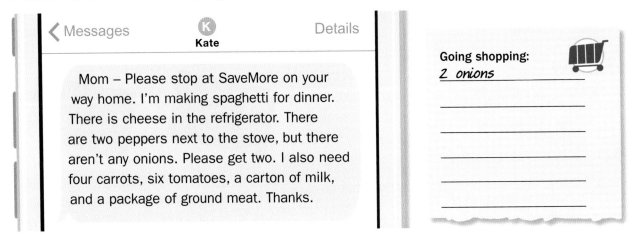

Messages   Ｋ   Details
Kate

Mom – Please stop at SaveMore on your way home. I'm making spaghetti for dinner. There is cheese in the refrigerator. There are two peppers next to the stove, but there aren't any onions. Please get two. I also need four carrots, six tomatoes, a carton of milk, and a package of ground meat. Thanks.

Going shopping:
2 onions
_____
_____
_____
_____
_____

C Write. Look at the picture. What is she buying? Write the words.

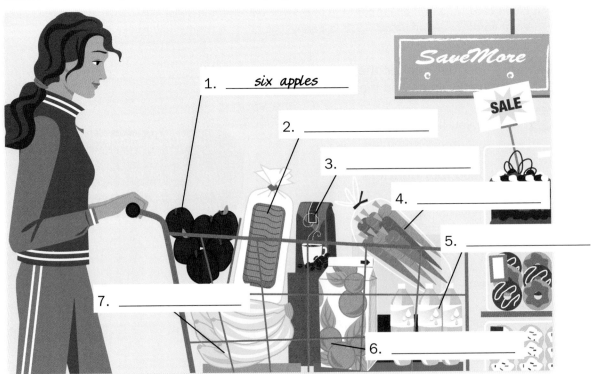

1. ___six apples___
2. _____
3. _____
4. _____
5. _____
6. _____
7. _____

D **Write.** Correct the text. Add commas.

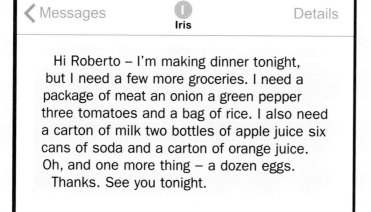

Messages   Iris   Details

> Hi Roberto – I'm making dinner tonight, but I need a few more groceries. I need a package of meat an onion a green pepper three tomatoes and a bag of rice. I also need a carton of milk two bottles of apple juice six cans of soda and a carton of orange juice. Oh, and one more thing – a dozen eggs.
> Thanks. See you tonight.

> Put a comma (,) after each item when there is a list of three or more items.
> *Please buy five oranges, two apples, and a peach.*

2 Write

Write a text asking someone to go shopping for you.

3 After you write

A **Read** your text to a partner.

B **Check** your partner's text.

- What food does your partner need?
- Are the commas correct?

Lesson F Another view

1 Life-skills reading

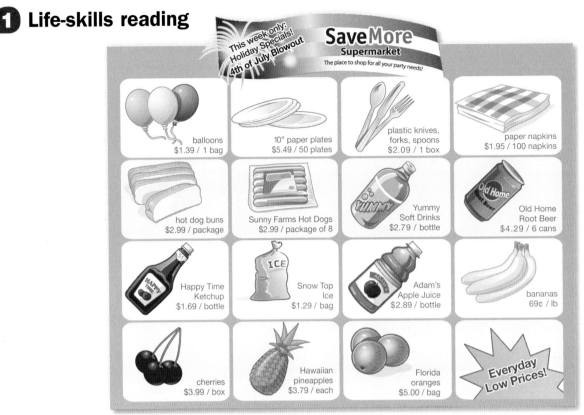

A **Read** the questions. Look at the ad. Fill in the answer.

1. What's the name of the store?
   - (A) SaveMore Supermarket
   - (B) Everyday Low Prices
   - (C) This week only
   - (D) 4th of July Blowout

2. How much are 50 paper plates?
   - (A) 10¢
   - (B) $2.09
   - (C) $5.49
   - (D) $5.94

3. How much are three bags of oranges?
   - (A) $1.00
   - (B) $5.00
   - (C) $10.00
   - (D) $15.00

4. How much are six cans of root beer and a bag of ice?
   - (A) $1.29
   - (B) $5.58
   - (C) $4.29
   - (D) $8.48

B **Solve** the problem. Which solution is best? Circle your opinion.

Mary buys oranges, cherries, and bananas at SaveMore Supermarket. The total is $9.75. She gives the clerk a twenty-dollar bill. At home, Mary looks in her wallet. There is only a five-dollar bill and a quarter. What should she do?

1. Nothing.

2. Go back to the store.

3. Count her money again.

4. Other: _____

2 Grammar connections: *some* and *any*

Use *some* with positive statements. Use *any* with negative statements.
(not → any)

👁 **Watch**

some	any
We need **some** bread.	We don't need **any** bread.
We want **some** apples.	We don't want **any** apples.

A **Talk** with a partner. Look at the list and the picture. Ask and answer. Take turns.

A Do we need bread?

B Yes, we do. We don't have *any* bread.

A Do we need apples?

B No, we don't. We have *some* apples.

Shopping List:

bread	coffee
~~apples~~	juice
bananas	sugar
tomatoes	rice
onions	cookies

B **Work** in a group. Plan a party for 15 people. Use the ad on page 94. You have $35.

A Do we need balloons?

B Yes! We want some balloons. How about 2 bags?

C OK. That's $2.78. What about soft drinks?

D No. Let's not have any soft drinks. How about some apple juice?

Item	Number	Cost
Balloons	2 bags	$2.78
Total:		

Lesson A Listening

1 Before you listen

A Look at the picture. What do you see?

B Point to: ■ a server ■ a busperson ■ a cashier ■ a cook
■ an electrician ■ a nurse ■ a nursing assistant ■ a construction worker

Red Oak Cafe

Specials
half sandwich,
soup, drink
$6.95

Mai Linh

UNIT GOALS
Identify common jobs   Describe skills
Complete a job application

2 Listen

A Listen. Write the letter of the conversation.

1. ____

2. ____

CD2, Track 21

3. ____

4. _a_

5. ____

6. ____

B Listen again to the conversations. Write the years or dates you hear.

A. from __2012__ to __2016__

D. from _____ to _____

B. from _____ to _____

E. in _____

C. from _____ to _____

F. _____ years ago

CD2, Track 21

Listen again. Check your answers.

3 After you listen

Where do the people work? Write the words.

| busperson | cashier | doctor | nurse | receptionist | server |

1. ____doctor____

2. _____

3. _____ hospital

4. _____

5. _____

6. _____ restaurant

Lesson B I was a teacher.

1 Grammar focus: simple past of *be*

Use *was* with *I, he, she,* and *it*. Use *were* with *you, we,* and *they*.

QUESTIONS			ANSWERS		
Were	you	a student?		I **was**.	I **wasn't**. I **was** a teacher.
Was	he	a student?		he **was**.	he **wasn't**. He **was** a teacher.
Was	she	a student?	Yes,	she **was**.	No, she **wasn't**. She **was** a teacher.
Were	you	students?		we **were**.	we **weren't**. We **were** teachers.
Were	they	students?		they **were**.	they **weren't**. They **were** teachers.

wasn't = was not | weren't = were not

👁 Watch

2 Practice

A Write. Look at the pictures. Complete the sentences. Use *is, are, was,* or *were*.

JOB HISTORY FOR *Amy Cho*

2010 – present	*Nurse*
2005 – 2010	*Teacher*

1. She _____was_____ a teacher before. Now she _____is_____ a nurse.

JOB APPLICATION

Jane's experience

2015 – present	Manager
2010 – 2015	Cashier

2. She _____ a manager now. She _____ a cashier before.

EMPLOYMENT HISTORY

John and Jack's work history
2016 – present	Electricians
2010 – 2016	Students

3. They _____ students before. Now they _____ electricians.

JOB APPLICATION FOR
Ben Liao
JOB HISTORY:

2009 – present
Construction Worker
2005 – 2009
Server

4. He _____ a server before. Now _____ _____ a construction worker.

Employment history

Adam Hill

2017 – present	Nursing Assistant
2010 – 2017	Server

5. He _____ a server before. Now _____ _____ a nursing assistant.

Work experience for

SARA AND RAUL LOPEZ

2015 – present	Managers
2010 – 2015	Cooks

6. Now they are _____. _____ _____ cooks before.

Listen and repeat.

B **Talk** with a partner. Look at the pictures. Change the **bold** words and make conversations.

1. **A** Was **she** a **teacher**?
   B Yes, **she** was.

2. **A** Were they **receptionists**?
   B No, they weren't. They were **nurses**.

1. a teacher?

2. receptionists?

3. a server?

4. doctors?

5. a cook?

6. a cashier?

3 Communicate

Talk with three classmates. Complete the chart.

A Sylvia, what do you do now?

B Now? I'm a homemaker.

A Oh, really? Were you a homemaker before?

B No, I wasn't. I was a receptionist in a bank.

> **USEFUL LANGUAGE**
> In conversation, *What do you do?* means *What's your job?* OR *What's your occupation?*

Name	Job now	Job before
Sylvia	a homemaker	a receptionist

Write two sentences about your classmates. Use information from the chart.

Sylvia is a homemaker now. She was a receptionist before.

Lesson C Can you cook?

1 Grammar focus: *can*

Use *can* + verb in base form to show the ability to do something.

STATEMENTS			QUESTIONS			ANSWERS						
I				you			I			I		
He	**can**	cook.	**Can**	he	cook?	Yes,	he	**can.**	No,	he	**can't.**
She				she			she			she		
They				they			they			they		

can't = cannot

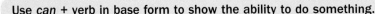 Watch

2 Practice

A Write. Complete the sentences. Use **yes**, **no**, **can**, or **can't**.

1. A ___Can___ she speak Spanish?
   B ___Yes___, she ___can___.

2. A ___Can___ he drive a truck?
   B ___No___, he ___can't___.

3. A _____ he fix a car?
   B _____, he _____.

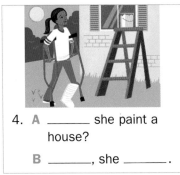

4. A _____ she paint a house?
   B _____, she _____.

5. A _____ they work with computers?
   B _____, they _____.

6. A _____ you cook?
   B _____, I _____.

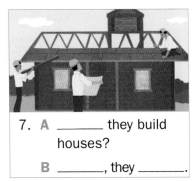

7. A _____ they build houses?
   B _____, they _____.

8. A _____ she read a book?
   B _____, she _____.

9. A _____ you operate on someone?
   B _____, I _____.

Listen and repeat. Then practice with a partner.

 CD2, Track 23

B **Write.** Look at the pictures. Complete the sentences.

build things   fix cars   paint   sell things   take care of children   take care of plants

1. A painter can

_____*paint*_____ .

2. A salesperson can

_____ .

3. A carpenter can

_____ .

4. A gardener can

_____ .

5. A child-care worker can

_____ .

6. An auto mechanic can

_____ .

Listen and repeat.

◀)) CD2, Track 24

C **Talk** with a partner. Look at the pictures in 2B. Change the **bold** words and make conversations.

A Hi. I'm looking for a job. Can you help me?

B What can you do?

A I'm a **painter**. I can **paint** very well.

③ Communicate

Talk with a partner. Ask and answer questions.

What can you do?   I can cook. I can work with computers.

Lesson D Reading

1 Before you read

Talk. Mai Linh is looking for a new job. Look at the picture. Answer the questions.

1. Who are the people in the picture?
2. Where are they?
3. What is Mai Linh's volunteer job now?

Harmon Hills Nursing Home

2 Read

A Listen and read.

CD2, Track 25

New Message

Send

Dear Ms. Carter:

I am writing to recommend my student Mai Linh Lam.

Mai Linh was a teacher in Vietnam. She is looking for a new job in the United States. She is a certified nursing assistant now. She volunteers in a nursing home Monday through Friday from 12:00 to 4:30. She takes care of senior citizens.

Mai Linh has many good skills. She can write reports. She can help elderly people move around and sit down. She can help them eat. She can also speak English and Vietnamese. These skills are useful in her job, and she is very good at her work.

Sincerely,

Elaine Maxwell

VALLEY ADULT SCHOOL

> Verb forms can tell you if something happened in the past or is happening now. *Mai Linh was a teacher in Vietnam. She is looking for a new job.*

3 After you read

A Read the sentences. Are they correct? Circle *Yes* or *No*.

1. Elaine's email is to apply for a job.   Yes   (No)
2. Mai Linh volunteers in a hospital.   Yes   No
3. She can write reports.   Yes   No
4. She finishes work at 8:30.   Yes   No
5. She is good at her job.   Yes   No

CULTURE NOTE
For some jobs, you need a certificate. You have to take a test to get the certificate.

I'm certified. means *I have a certificate.*

Write. Correct the sentences.

1. Elaine's email is to <u>recommend someone for a job</u>.

B Write. Answer the questions about Mai Linh.

1. What was Mai Linh's job before? _____

2. Is Mai Linh certified? _____

3. What are her work skills? _____

4 Picture dictionary Occupations

1. ___housekeeper___

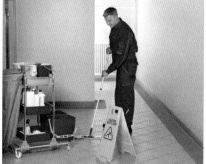

2. _____

3. _____

4. _____

5. _____

6. _____

A **Write** the words in the Picture dictionary. Then listen and repeat.

custodian	factory worker	housekeeper
dental assistant	hairstylist	pharmacist technician

◀)) CD2, Track 26

B **Work** with a partner. Match the words in the Picture dictionary with these places.

1. a beauty salon ____hairstylist____
2. a dental office _____
3. a factory _____

4. a hotel _____
5. an office building _____
6. a pharmacy _____

Talk with a partner. Point to a picture in the dictionary. Ask and answer questions about the occupations.

What's her occupation?

She's a housekeeper.

USEFUL LANGUAGE
occupation = job

Where does she work?

She works in a hotel.

For college and career readiness practice, see pages 150–151.

Lesson E Writing

1 Before you write

A **Write.** Check (✓) what you can do.

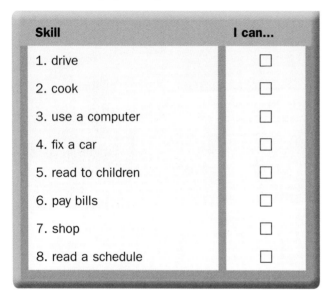

Skill	I can...
1. drive	☐
2. cook	☐
3. use a computer	☐
4. fix a car	☐
5. read to children	☐
6. pay bills	☐
7. shop	☐
8. read a schedule	☐

Talk with a partner.

A What about number 1? Can you drive?

B Yes, I can. What about you?

A I can drive, too. I just got my driver's license last month

B **Read.** Answer the questions.

> ● ● ●   New Message   (Send)
>
> My name is Carla. I am a homemaker. I work at home. I have many skills. I can do housework. I can drive a car, and I can fix a car, too. I can speak two languages. I can cook tasty meals for my family. I can help my children with their homework, and I can use a computer.

1. What are Carla's skills? _____

_____

2. What can Carla do that you can do, too? _____

_____

② Write

A **Write** about your occupation. Complete the sentences.

I am a _____.

I work at _____.

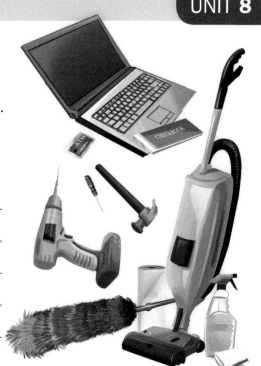

B **Write.** What are your skills? Make a list.

_____

_____

_____

_____

_____

C **Write** a paragraph about your skills.

③ After you write

A **Read** your paragraph to a partner.

B **Check** your partner's paragraph.

- What are your partner's skills?
- Is the spelling correct?

 Check your spelling. Use a dictionary if necessary. Correct spelling is important in writing.

Lesson F Another view

1 Life-skills reading

Application for Employment	
1. Name	2. Soc. Sec. No. 000-99-9103
3. Address	4. Phone
5. Are you 16 years or older? Yes No	6. Position desired

Employment History (List most recent job first.)

Dates	Employer Name and Address	Position
7.		
8.		
9.		

10. Important: Show your Social Security card at the time you present this application.

A Read the questions. Look at the job application. Fill in the answer.

1. Where do you write the job you want?

   - A line 5
   - B line 6
   - C line 8
   - D line 10

2. The form says *List most recent job first.* Which of the following dates is the most recent?

   - A 2012–2014
   - B 2015–2017
   - C 2015–present
   - D 2010–2016

3. What do you show with your application?

   - A a library card
   - B a photograph
   - C a driver's license
   - D a Social Security card

4. Where do you write your phone number?

   - A line 4
   - B line 5
   - C line 8
   - D line 9

B Solve the problem. Which solution is best? Circle your opinion.

Carla is filling out a job application. She had two jobs before, but she can't remember the dates. What should she do?

1. Leave it blank.

2. Take the application home.

3. Call her old employer.

4. Other: _____

2 Grammar connections: *be* with *and* and *but*

Use *and* to show things that are the same. Use *but* to show things that are different.

Sid **is** at work today, **and** he **was** at work yesterday.

Ana **isn't** at work today, **and** she **wasn't** at work yesterday.

Natt **is** at work today, **but** she **wasn't** at work yesterday.

Len and Eva **aren't** at work today, **but** they **were** at work yesterday.

Watch

A **Work** with a partner. Look at the pictures. Talk about the people. Take turns.

A John is at work today, and he was at work yesterday.

B Carmen is at work today, but she wasn't at work yesterday.

Today
John Sandra Maggie Pedro
Carmen Phil Mike Lisa

Yesterday
John Sandra Maggie Larry
Laura Bao Mike Lisa

B **Talk** in a group. Tell about your classmates. Take turns.

Mario: I'm here today, but I wasn't here yesterday.

Ina: Mario is here today, but he wasn't here yesterday. I'm here today, and I was here yesterday.

Bing: Mario is here today, but he wasn't here yesterday. Ina is here today, and she was here yesterday. I'm here . . .

REVIEW

1 Listening

Read the questions. Then listen and circle the answers.

🔊 CD2, Track 27

1. What did Carlos do before?

   a. He was an office worker.

   b. He was a construction worker.

2. What does Carlos do now?

   a. He is an office worker.

   b. He is a construction worker.

3. When does Carlos buy groceries?

   a. every Tuesday

   b. every Thursday

4. Where is Carlos right now?

   a. at SaveMore Supermarket

   b. at work

5. What is he buying at the supermarket?

   a. milk, tea, bread, and eggs

   b. milk, cheese, bread, and eggs

6. How much are the groceries?

   a. $11.75

   b. $7.75

Talk with a partner. Ask and answer the questions. Use complete sentences.

2 Grammar

A **Write.** Complete the story.

Peter

Peter ___was___ a server in his country. Now he _____ a
     1. is / was   2. is / was
cashier. He can do many things. He _____ use a cash register.
                                    3. can / can't
He _____ use a computer, too. But Peter has two problems.
    4. can / can't
First, he _____ speak English well. Second, he works a lot of
         5. can / can't
hours. He _____ find time to go to school.
          6. can / can't

B **Write.** Unscramble the words. Make questions about the story.

1. a / teacher / Was / Peter / country / his / in / ? _Was Peter a teacher in his country?_

2. use / cash register / a / Can / he / ? _____

3. speak / well / English / Can / he / ? _____

4. he / construction worker / Is / now / a / ? _____

Talk with a partner. Ask and answer the questions.

③ Pronunciation: the -s ending with plural nouns

A **Listen** to the *-s* ending in these plural nouns.

/s/	/z/	/ɪz/
cakes	tomatoes	peaches
hairstylists	electricians	nurses

◀)) CD2, Track 28

B **Listen and repeat.**

/s/	/z/	/ɪz/
assistants	bananas	nurses
cooks	cashiers	oranges
students	drivers	packages
mechanics	cookies	boxes
receptionists	servers	peaches
books	teachers	sandwiches

◀)) CD2, Track 29

Talk with a partner. Take turns. Practice the words. Make sentences with the words.

C **Listen.** Complete the chart.

1. bags
2. bottles
3. clerks
4. dimes
5. pages
6. carrots
7. desks
8. languages
9. glasses

◀)) CD2, Track 30

/s/	/z/	/ɪz/
	bags	

D **Talk** with a partner. Ask and answer the question. Use correct pronunciation.

What's in your refrigerator?

There are _____.   There is _____.

UNIT 9 DAILY LIVING

Lesson A Listening

1 Before you listen

A Look at the picture. What do you see?

B Point to a person: ■ cleaning the bathroom ■ emptying the trash ■ mopping the floor ■ vacuuming the rug ■ ironing clothes

UNIT GOALS
Identify household chores and objects   **Interpret** a job duties chart
Write an email about chores

2 Listen

A   Listen. Write the letter of the conversation.

CD2, Track 31

1. ____

2. ____

3. __a__

4. ____

5. ____

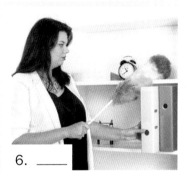
6. ____

B   Listen again to the conversations. Circle the time expression you hear.

CD2, Track 31

A. (last night)	last week	last weekend
B. the day before yesterday	yesterday	yesterday morning
C. last night	yesterday	the day before yesterday
D. yesterday morning	every day last week	yesterday
E. yesterday	yesterday morning	the day before yesterday
F. last night	last weekend	last week

Listen again. Check your answers.

3 After you listen

Work with a partner. Put the words from the box in the correct category.

a bill	the floor	a shirt	the trash
a dress	the rug	a ticket	the wastebasket

iron	empty	vacuum	pay
a dress			

Lesson B I cleaned the living room.

1 Grammar focus: simple past with regular verbs

For regular verbs, add *–ed* to the base form to make statements about the past. Use *did* with the base form to make questions about the past.

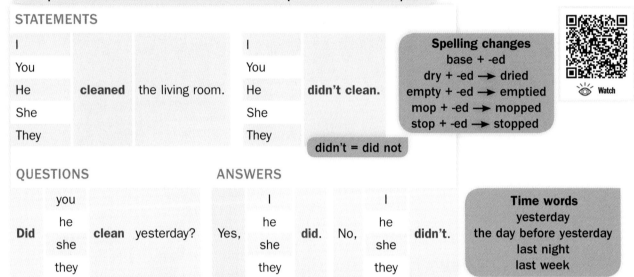

STATEMENTS

| I You He She They | **cleaned** | the living room. |

| I You He She They | **didn't clean.** |

didn't = did not

Spelling changes
base + -ed
dry + -ed → dried
empty + -ed → emptied
mop + -ed → mopped
stop + -ed → stopped

👁 Watch

QUESTIONS

| **Did** | you he she they | **clean** yesterday? |

ANSWERS

| Yes, | I he she they | **did.** | No, | I he she they | **didn't.** |

Time words
yesterday
the day before yesterday
last night
last week

2 Practice

A Write. Look at the picture. What did Yousef do? What didn't Yousef do? Complete the sentences.

1. Yousef ___cooked___ dinner.
   (cook)

2. He ___didn't clean___ the kitchen.
   (clean)

3. He _____ the shelves.
   (dust)

4. He _____ the floor.
   (mop)

5. He _____ the dishes.
   (wash)

6. He _____ the shirts.
   (iron)

7. He _____ the trash.
   (empty)

8. He _____ the dishes.
   (dry)

Listen and repeat.

🔊 CD2, Track 32

B Write. Look at the picture. Answer the questions.

1. A Did Mr. Ramirez mop the floor?
   B *Yes, he did.*

2. A Did Mrs. Ramirez empty the trash?
   B _____

3. A Did Monica mop the floor?
   B _____

4. A Did Mr. and Mrs. Ramirez wash the dishes?
   B _____

5. A Did Roberto dry the dishes?
   B _____

6. A Did Luis vacuum the rug?
   B _____

7. A Did Monica vacuum the rug?
   B _____

8. A A Did Luis wash the dishes?
   B _____

Listen and repeat. Then practice with a partner.

◀)) CD2, Track 33

3 Communicate

Talk with your classmates. Write their names on the chart.

Anna, did you cook dinner last night?   Yes, I did.

Find a classmate who:	Classmate's name
cooked dinner last night	
emptied the trash yesterday	
washed the dishes every night last week	
dried the dishes the day before yesterday	
vacuumed last weekend	
ironed clothes last week	

📖 Use the simple past with regular verbs **UNIT 9** **113**

Lesson C I paid the bills.

1 Grammar focus: simple past with irregular verbs

Irregular verbs in the simple past do not use *-ed*. They form the past in other ways. See the list of some irregular verbs.

STATEMENTS

| I He She they | **paid** | the bills. | I He She they | **didn't pay** | the bills. |

QUESTIONS

| Who | **bought** | groceries last week? |
| What | **did** | she **buy**? |

ANSWERS

| I You He She they | **did.** |
| | **bought** groceries. |

Irregular verbs

buy ➡ bought
get ➡ got
do ➡ did
make ➡ made
pay ➡ paid
sweep ➡ swept

👁 Watch

2 Practice

A Write. Look at the pictures. Complete the sentences.

Last night, Linda had to pay the bills. But first, she ___*bought*___ groceries
                                                    1. buy

after work. She _____ $15. She _____ home, and she _____ dinner.
                2. pay   3. get   4. make

She _____ soup and salad. She washed and _____ the dishes. After dinner,
     5. make   6. dry

she was very tired. She _____ the kitchen floor, but she _____ the bills!
                     7. sweep   8. not pay

Listen and check your answers.

🔊 CD2, Track 34

B **Write.** Look at the notes. Answer the questions.

Mom,
Thanks for buying the groceries.
I vacuumed the rug in the living room.
I dusted the shelves, too.
Love,
Erica

Dad,
I got the mail and made the beds.
Can I have my allowance now?
Sasha

Sasha,
I cut the grass, but I didn't do the laundry.
Can you do the laundry, please?
Dad

Sasha,
I did the laundry.
Your allowance is on the table. Have fun at the movie theater.
Mom

1. **A** Who bought the groceries?
   B *Mom did.*

2. **A** What else did mom do?
   B *She did the laundry.*

3. **A** Who got the mail?
   B _____

4. **A** What else did Sasha do?
   B _____

5. **A** Who vacuumed the rug?
   B _____

6. **A** What else did Erica do?
   B _____

7. **A** What did Dad do?
   B _____

8. **A** Where is the allowance for Sasha?
   B _____

Listen and repeat. Then practice with a partner.

CD2, Track 35

3 Communicate

Talk with a partner. What chores did you do yesterday? Check (✓) the boxes.

☐ paid the bills   ☐ did the laundry   ☐ swept the floor   ☐ washed the dishes
☐ bought the groceries   ☐ made the bed   ☐ got the mail   ☐ vacuumed the rug

Work in a group. Ask and answer questions.

Who paid the bills yesterday?   I did.   I didn't.

Lesson D Reading

1 Before you read

Talk. Lucas is writing a note. Look at the picture.
Answer the questions.

1. Where is he?

2. What do you think Lucas is writing about?

2 Read

Listen and read.

Dear Karen,

    Welcome home! We were very busy today.
Jeff ironed the clothes. Chris emptied the trash.
Sharon mopped the floor. Ben vacuumed the rug
and dusted the furniture. The house is clean for
you!

    I cooked dinner. There is food on the stove.

                       Your tired husband,
                            Lucas

Good readers ask
themselves questions
before they start
reading, such as
Who wrote the letter?

) CD2, Track 36

3 After you read

A Read the sentences. Are they correct? Circle **Yes** or **No**.

1. Jeff washed the clothes.	Yes	(No)
2. Sharon swept the floor.	Yes	No
3. Ben vacuumed the rug.	Yes	No
4. Karen cooked dinner.	Yes	No
5. This note is about family chores.	Yes	No

Write. Correct the sentences.

1. Jeff ironed the clothes.

B Write. Answer the questions about the note.

1. Who dusted the furniture? _____

2. Did Sharon empty the trash? _____

3. Who is Karen? _____

4 Picture dictionary *Household objects*

1. _____*a sponge*_____

2. _____

3. _____

4. _____

5. _____

6. _____

7. _____

8. _____

9. _____

A Write the words in the Picture dictionary. Then listen and repeat.

a broom	a dustpan	a lawn mower	a sponge	a vacuum cleaner
a bucket	an iron	a mop	a stove	

CD2, Track 37

B Write. Match the objects with the actions.

1. an iron __*d*__   a. vacuum
2. a sponge _____   b. sweep
3. a stove _____   c. mop
4. a lawn mower _____   d. iron
5. a mop _____   e. cook
6. a vacuum cleaner _____   f. wash
7. a broom _____   g. cut grass

For college and career readiness practice, see pages 152–153.

Lesson E Writing

1 Before you write

A **Talk** with a partner. Ask and answer the questions.

1. Who does the chores in your home? What chores?

2. Are there special times to do those chores?

3. What is your favorite chore?

B **Talk.** Interview three classmates. Write two chores each person did last week and one chore they didn't do.

Name	Chores you did	Chores you didn't do
Katia	bought the groceries walked the dog	didn't vacuum the rugs

C **Write.** Complete the email. Use the simple past form of the verbs.

New Message

Send

Dear Mom,

I ___bought___ milk from the supermarket. It's in the refrigerator. I also
1. buy

_____ the shelves and _____ the floor, but I didn't _____
2. dust   3. sweep   4. wash

the dishes. Did you _____ a new sponge? Did you _____ the rug
5. buy   6. vacuum

yesterday? I also _____ my bed.
7. make

See you later,

Irina

D Write. Complete the email. Use the correct simple past form.

buy   cook   dry   mop   pay   sweep   walk   wash

● ● ● New Message

(Send)

Hi Tom,

I ____*cooked*____ dinner for you. It's on the stove. I _____ the dishes,

but I didn't _____ them. Sorry, I didn't have time. I _____ a new broom

at the store. I _____ the kitchen floor with it. I _____ the

floor, too, with the new mop. I didn't _____ the dog.

Did you _____ the bills? It's the end of the month. Please remember.

I'll see you tonight.

Love,

Mary

---

2 Write

Write an email to a family member. Write the chores you did and didn't do.

● ● ● New Message

(Send)

---

3 After you write

A Read your email to a partner.

B Check your partner's email.

■ What are two chores your partner wrote about?
■ Are the past verb forms correct?

Lesson F Another view

1 Life-skills reading

SaveMore Supermarket	JOB DUTIES	Monday (day)	January 23 (date)	
Duties	**Employee**	**Initials**	**Time Completed**	
Sweep the floor.	Joshua Liu	JL	9:15 p.m.	
Mop the floor.	Kim Casey	KC	9:30 p.m.	
Mop the floor.	Roger Brown	RB	9:30 p.m.	
Clean the bathroom.	Ann Hamilton	AH	8:30 p.m.	
Empty the trash cans.	Steve Johnson	SJ	8:45 p.m.	
Turn off the lights.	Victor Morales	VM	10:00 p.m.	
Lock the doors.	Victor Morales	VM	10:00 p.m.	

Problems? Contact Job Duties Supervisor at x298.

A **Read** the questions. Look at the chart. Fill in the answer.

1. Who swept the floor?
   - A Ann
   - B Victor
   - C Kim and Roger
   - D Joshua

2. When did Steve empty the trash cans?
   - A at 8:30 p.m.
   - B at 8:45 p.m.
   - C at 9:15 p.m.
   - D at 10:00 p.m.

3. Who turned off the lights and locked the doors?
   - A Joshua
   - B Kim
   - C Victor
   - D Roger

4. What is *Time Completed*?
   - A time started
   - B time stopped
   - C time off
   - D time worked

B **Solve** the problem. Which solution is best? Circle your opinion.

Today is Tuesday. Victor forgot to write his initials on the Job Duties chart and write the time completed. He doesn't work Wednesday. What should he do?

1. Call Joshua and ask him to do it.

2. Call the supervisor.

3. Do nothing. Talk to the supervisor on Thursday.

4. Other: _____

2 Grammar connections: *or* questions

Use *or* when there are two choices in a question.

Did Juan wash **or** sweep the floor?
He swept the floor.

Watch

A **Work** with a partner. Talk about the pictures. Ask and answer. Take turns.

A Did Feng wash or dry the dishes?

B He washed the dishes.

A Did Mei wash or dry the dishes?

B She dried the dishes.

1. Feng / Mei

2. Santiago / Monica

3. Donna / Tina

4. Paco / Ivan

5. Angie / Tommy

6. Donald / Teresa

B **Talk** with your partner. Ask and answer. Use simple past. Take turns.

Did you wash the dishes or use a dishwasher yesterday?

I used a dishwasher.

1. wash the dishes yesterday / use a dishwasher yesterday

2. eat lunch at home last Monday / have lunch at work last Monday

3. stay home last weekend / go out last weekend

4. wash your clothes at home last week / go to the laundromat last week

5. mop the floors yesterday / vacuum the rugs yesterday

UNIT 10 FREE TIME

Lesson A Listening

1 Before you listen

A Look at the picture. What do you see?

B Point to these activities: ■ camping ■ fishing ■ hiking
■ canoeing ■ swimming ■ having a picnic

Marco

Mr. Lopez

Mrs. Lopez

NATURAL HARDWOOD LUMP CHARCOAL

UNIT GOALS
Write a letter about a vacation   **Interpret** information on a TV schedule
Talk about past and future free-time activities

2 Listen

A Listen. Write the letter of the conversation.

1. ____

2. ____

3. ____

CD2, Track 38

4. _a_

5. ____

6. ____

B Listen again to the conversations. Write the time word you hear.

A. I went hiking _____*yesterday*_____ .

B. We went camping _____ .

C. I was on vacation all _____ .

D. Where were you _____?

E. I'm going to go swimming _____ .

F. I went fishing _____ .

Listen again. Check your answers.

3 After you listen

CD2, Track 38

What do you do on your vacation? Check (✓) the boxes.

☐ go camping
☐ go fishing
☐ go hiking
☐ go swimming
☐ (other) _____

☐ have a picnic
☐ relax / rest
☐ spend time with my family
☐ volunteer
☐ (other) _____

Talk with a partner. Ask and answer questions.

What do you do on your vacation?

> I go hiking, swimming, and spend time with my family.

Lesson B What did you do yesterday?

1 Grammar focus: simple past with irregular verbs

Irregular verbs in the simple past do not use *-ed*. They form the past in other ways. See the list of some irregular verbs.

Watch

QUESTIONS				ANSWERS	
	did you **do**			I	
	did he **do**			He	
What	**did** she **do**	yesterday?		She	**went to the zoo.**
	did you **do**			We	
	did they **do**			We	

Irregular verbs

drive	→ drove		ride	→ rode
eat	→ ate		see	→ saw
go	→ went		sleep	→ slept
have	→ had		take	→ took
read	→ read		write	→ wrote

2 Practice

A Write. Answer the questions.

1. **A** What did Carl and Gina do last weekend?

   B <u>*They went to the zoo.*</u>
   (go to the zoo)

2. **A** What did Paul do yesterday?

   B _____
   (take a driving test)

3. **A** What did Diane do last night?

   B _____
   (write a letter)

4. **A** What did Mrs. Nelson do last weekend?

   B _____
   (see the fireworks)

5. **A** What did Mr. Brown do last weekend?

   B _____
   (go fishing)

6. **A** What did Mr. and Mrs. Velez do last Saturday?

   B _____
   (go dancing)

7. **A** A What did John do yesterday afternoon?

   B _____
   (ride his bicycle)

8. **A** What did Ana do last night?

   B _____
   (eat some pizza)

9. **A** What did Sophia and Alex do last weekend?

   B _____
   (drive to the mountains)

Listen and repeat. Then practice with a partner.

CD2, Track 39

B **Write.** Complete the sentences. Use the correct simple past form.

| eat | go | have | ride | write |

1. We ____*went*____ swimming in the pool last weekend.

2. I _____ my bike yesterday.

3. Silvia _____ emails to all her friends last week.

4. They _____ dinner very late last night.

5. We _____ a picnic last Sunday.

C **Talk** with a partner. Look at the schedule. Change the **bold** words and make conversations.

Jeff Yu's Vacation Schedule

SUNDAY	MONDAY	TUESDAY	WEDNESDAY	THURSDAY	FRIDAY	SATURDAY
go to the museum	drive to the lake	ride my motorcycle	take swimming lessons	go hiking	go on a picnic in the park	see a movie

A What did Jeff do on **Sunday**?

B He **went to the museum**.

3 Communicate

Talk with three classmates. Complete the chart.

Sara, what did you do last night?

I read a book.

What did you do . . .	Name	Name	Name
last night?			
yesterday morning?			
yesterday afternoon?			
the day before yesterday?			
last weekend?			

Lesson C What are you going to do?

1 Grammar focus: future with *be going to*

Watch

Use *be going to* + verb in base form for actions you plan to do in the future.

QUESTIONS				ANSWERS		
What	**are** you	**going to**	do tomorrow?	I'm	**going to**	take a trip.
	is he			He's		
	is she			She's		
	are they			They're		

Time words
today
tomorrow
tonight
next week
next month

2 Practice

A Write. Read the schedule. Answer the questions.

1. **A** What's Marta going to do next Monday?
   B *She's going to take a test* .

2. **A** What's Dad going to do next Monday?
   B _____.

3. **A** What are Mom and Dad going to do next Thursday?
   B _____.

4. **A** What's Paco going to do next Tuesday?
   B _____.

5. **A** What's Alfredo going to do next Wednesday?
   B _____.

6. **A** What's Mom going to do next Saturday?
   B _____.

7. **A** What are Alfredo and Marta going to do next Friday?
   B _____.

8. **A** What's Paco going to do next Saturday?
   B _____.

9. **A** What are Mom and Dad going to do next Sunday?
   B _____.

10. **A** What's Alfredo going to do next Thursday?
    B _____.

Listen and repeat. Then practice with a partner.

Next Week's Schedule Santiago Family

Mon	Marta – take a test Dad – pay the rent
Tues	Paco – play soccer Marta – volunteer at school
Wed	Alfredo – ride his bike
Thurs	Dad and Mom – go dancing Alfredo – take a guitar class
Fri	Alfredo and Marta – go to a party
Sat	Mom – do the laundry Paco – wash the car
Sun	Mom and Dad – go on a picnic

CD2, Track 40

B **Talk** with a partner. Change the **bold** words and make conversations.

 A What's **Brian** going to do today?

B **He's going to go to the beach.**

A That sounds like fun.

> **USEFUL LANGUAGE**
> You can say:
> *He's going to go to the beach.*
> or *He's going to the beach.*

1. Brian / go to the beach
2. Ali / go shopping
3. Lisa / play soccer
4. Hiro and Lee / go fishing
5. Andrea / take a trip
6. Ray / go to a birthday party
7. Paula and Sylvia / go hiking

3 Communicate

Talk to your classmates. Write their names and activities on the chart.

Yuri, what are you going to do next weekend?   I'm going to fix my car.

Name	Next weekend
Yuri	fix the car

Lesson D Reading

1 Before you read

Talk. Mrs. Lopez sent a picture of her family to a friend. Look at the picture. Answer the questions.

1. Who are the people in the picture?

2. What did they do?

3. What are they going to do next?

2 Read

Listen and read.

CD2, Track 41

New Message

Send

Dear Ming,

Last weekend, we went camping in the mountains. I went hiking. My husband and our sons went fishing. They also went swimming in the lake. We all had a great time!

Tonight we're going to eat fish for dinner. After dinner, we're going to watch a movie. Later tonight, we're going to be very busy. We are going to do the laundry. With three boys, we have a lot of dirty clothes!

See you soon,

Maria

> Look for words that show past or future time to help you understand.
> *Last weekend*
> *Tonight*

---

3 After you read

A Read the sentences. Are they correct? Circle **Yes** or **No**.

1. Last weekend, the Lopez family went shopping. Yes (No)

2. Maria's email is about her family's activities last weekend and next weekend. Yes No

3. Mr. Lopez and his sons went fishing last weekend. Yes No

4. The Lopez family is going to eat pizza for dinner. Yes No

5. After dinner, they are going to watch a movie. Yes No

6. They have a lot of clean clothes. Yes No

Write. Correct the sentences.

1. Last weekend, the Lopez family went <u>camping</u>.

B Write. Answer the questions about the Lopez family.

1. Who went swimming in the lake? _____

2. What is the Lopez family going to do later tonight? _____

3. Is the Lopez family going to be busy tonight? _____

4 **Picture dictionary** Sports

1. ___football___

2. _____

3. _____

4. _____

5. _____

6. _____

7. _____

8. _____

9. _____

A **Write** the words in the Picture dictionary. Then listen and repeat.

Use *play* with these words:

| baseball | basketball | football | ice hockey | ping-pong | soccer |

Use *go* with these words:

| ice skating | skiing | surfing |

◀)) CD2, Track 42

B **Talk** with a partner. Look at the pictures and make conversations.

> What's he going to do?

> He's going to play football.

> **CULTURE NOTE**
> In the United States, football and soccer are different sports.

For college and career readiness practice, see pages 154–155.

Lesson E Writing

1 Before you write

A **Talk** with four classmates. Ask questions. Write the answers.

A Where did you go on your last vacation?

B I went to Arizona.

A Who did you go with?

B I went with my wife.

A What did you do?

B We visited the Grand Canyon.

Name	Where?	Who with?	Did what?
Omar	Arizona	wife	visited the Grand Canyon

B **Read** Maria's email. Answer the questions.

New Message

Send

Dear Colleen,

I had a nice vacation. I went to Oregon. I went camping with my family. I read a book and rested. I went hiking. My husband and sons went fishing. We ate fish for dinner every night. Next year, we are going to drive to New York. We are going to visit my mother and see the Statue of Liberty.

Did you have a nice vacation? What are you going to do on your next vacation?

See you soon,

Maria

---

1. Where did Maria go on vacation? _She went to Oregon._____

2. What did Maria do? _____

3. What did her husband and sons do? _____

4. Where is Maria's family going next year? _____

5. What are they going to do? _____

❷ Write

A Write. Answer the questions.

1. Where did you go on your last vacation?

   _____

   _____

a beach

2. Who did you go with?

   _____

   _____

3. What did you do?

   _____

   _____

4. Where are you going to go on your next vacation?

   _____

   _____

a zoo

5. Who are you going to go with?

   _____

   _____

6. What are you going to do?

   _____

   _____

B Write a letter about your vacations. Use the information from 2A.

❸ After you write

Begin a new paragraph when you change your ideas from the past to the future.

A Read your letter to a partner.

B Check your partner's letter.

- ■ What are the past activities?
- ■ What are the future activities?
- ■ Are there different paragraphs for past and future activities?

Lesson F Another view

1 Life-skills reading

Saturday TV Schedule

	6:00	7:00	8:00	9:00
CHANNEL 7	Local news	Soccer		Swimming competition
CHANNEL 9	Cooking show	Boating program	*Great Places to Hike*	*Strange Animals*
CHANNEL 14	National news	Movie: *Camp Sunshine*		*Kids' Favorite Vacations*
CHANNEL 18	World news	*Fantastic Fishing*	Dancing competition	
CHANNEL 23	*Outdoor Adventures*	Baseball		

A Read the questions. Look at the TV schedule. Fill in the answer.

1. When is *Outdoor Adventures* going to be on?

   - (A) at 6:00 p.m.
   - (B) at 7:00 p.m.
   - (C) at 8:00 p.m.
   - (D) at 9:00 p.m

2. What are they going to show at 9 p.m. on Channel 9?

   - (A) *Great Places to Hike*
   - (B) *Kids' Favorite Vacations*
   - (C) *Fantastic Fishing*
   - (D) *Strange Animals*

3. How many channels are going to show the news at 6 p.m.?

   - (A) one channel
   - (B) two channels
   - (C) three channels
   - (D) five channels

4. What does *Local news* mean?

   - (A) news about sports
   - (B) news about the world
   - (C) news about the city I live in
   - (D) news about the United States

B Solve the problem. Which solution is best? Circle your opinion.

Joseph and his wife, Ana, are watching TV. Joseph wants to watch the baseball game, but Ana wants to watch the dancing competition. What can they do?

1. Watch ½ of the baseball game and then watch the dancing competition.

2. Change the channels again and again to see both.

3. Joseph or Ana can go to a friend's house.

4. Other: _____

132 UNIT 10

2 Grammar connections: past, present, and future

Use the simple past to talk about last weekend. Use the simple present to talk about weekends in general. Use the future to talk about next weekend.

SIMPLE PAST	SIMPLE PRESENT	FUTURE WITH *BE GOING TO*
Boris **went** to the movies last weekend.	Boris usually **cleans** his apartment on the weekends.	Boris **is going to go** hiking next weekend.

Watch

A **Talk** in a group. Complete the chart.

   A What **did** you **do** last weekend, Boris?

   B I **went** to the movies.

   A What **do** you **do** every weekend?

   B I **usually clean** my apartment.

   A What are you **going to do** next weekend?

   B I'm **going to go** hiking.

Name	Last weekend	Every weekend	Next weekend
Boris	went to the movies	cleans his apartment	is going to go hiking

B **Share** your group's information with the class.

   A Boris went to the movies last weekend. He usually cleans his apartment every weekend. He's going to go hiking next weekend.

   B Ling visited her sister last weekend. She usually . . .

REVIEW

1 Listening

Read the questions. Then listen and circle the answers.

🔊 CD2, Track 43

1. When did Melissa's family go on a picnic?

   a. on Saturday

   b. on Sunday

2. What did they eat in the park?

   a. hot dogs

   b. hamburgers

3. When did Ivan's family do their chores?

   a. on Saturday

   b. on Sunday

4. Did Ivan wash the dishes?

   a. Yes, he did.

   b. No, he didn't.

5. What did Ivan's wife do?

   a. She washed the clothes.

   b. She vacuumed the rugs.

6. Who dusted the furniture?

   a. Tommy

   b. Lisa

Talk with a partner. Ask and answer the questions. Use complete sentences.

2 Grammar

A Write. Complete the story.

Two Weekends

Sam and Jenny ___*had*___ a big party last weekend. On Saturday
         1. have / had

morning, Jenny _____ the house and _____ dinner. Sam
      2. clean / cleaned   3. make / made

_____ the trash and _____ the patio.
4. empty / emptied   5. sweep / swept

    Next weekend, they're going to _____ to the mountains. Sam is
               6. drive / drove

going to _____ fishing. Jenny is going to _____ swimming
     7. go / went   8. go / went

in a lake.

B Write. Unscramble the words. Make questions about the story.

1. clean / When / Jenny / did / the house / ? _When did Jenny clean the house?_

2. dinner / Sam / make / Did / ? _____

3. Sam / do / did / What / ? _____

4. next / do / going to / they / What / are / weekend / ?

   _____

Talk with a partner. Ask and answer the questions.

③ Pronunciation: the *-ed* ending in the simple past

A **Listen** to the *-ed* ending in these simple past verbs.

◀)) CD2, Track 44

/d/	/t/	/I d/
cleaned	cooked	dusted
He cleaned his house.	They cooked dinner.	I dusted the living room.
dried	talked	folded
I dried all the dishes.	She talked on the phone.	He folded his clothes.
emptied	washed	painted
They emptied the trash.	She washed the car.	They painted the house.

B **Listen and repeat.**

◀)) CD2, Track 45

/d/	/t/	/I d/
exercised	camped	celebrated
played	fished	folded
turned	walked	visited

C **Listen** and check (✓) the correct column.

◀)) CD2, Track 46

	/d/	/t/	/I d/		/d/	/t/	/I d/
1. studied	✓			5. waited			
2. ironed				6. hiked			
3. mopped				7. vacuumed			
4. rested				8. worked			

Talk with a partner. Take turns. Make a sentence with each verb.

D **Talk** with a partner. Ask and answer the questions. Use correct pronunciation.

1. What did you do last weekend?   2. What did you do yesterday?

Last weekend, I . . .   Yesterday, I . . .

Reading Tip: Last names on a list go from A–Z. What last name is after <u>Abadi</u>?

Class Registration List

School: *Youngstown Adult School,*
         Downtown Site
Class: *English as a Second Language*
Level: *1*
Instructor: *Tony Brown*
Time: *10:15 a.m.*

Last Name	First Name	Male	Female	Phone Number	Date of Birth	Country of Origin
Abadi	Yana		✓	924-6848	10-19-1984	Syria
Cruz	Maria		✓	561-7927	1-16-1971	Mexico
Fedorin	Alex	✓		398-9505	3-9-1993	Russia
Fernandez	Mario	✓		none	5-30-1981	El Salvador
Hong	Kathy		✓	239-1844	9-4-1997	Korea
Hong	Katie		✓	239-1844	9-4-1997	Korea
Hua	Jun	✓		561-3027	8-22-1979	China

1 Check your understanding

1. What is this reading about?
   a. a class registration list
   b. a school address list
2. How many students are on this list?
   a. 7 students
   b. 8 students
3. What is the teacher's last name?
   a. Tony
   b. Brown
4. Circle your answer and complete the sentence.
   Kathy and Katie **are / are not** sisters because _____.

② Build your vocabulary

A Look at the pictures. Find the words in the class registration list. Then write the words below the pictures.

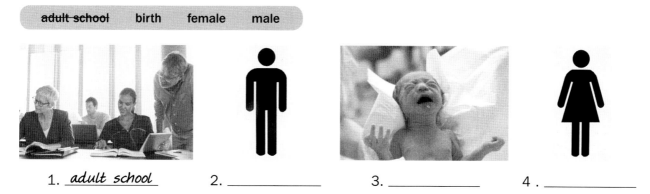

~~adult school~~   birth   female   male

1. _adult school_   2. _____   3. _____   4. _____

B Find the academic words in Column 1 in the class registration list and underline them. Then complete the chart.

Academic word	Phrase or sentence from registration list	Best definition	My sentence
1. instructor	*Instructor: Tony Brown*	ⓐ teacher b. student	*I like my English instructor.*
2. site		a. place b. number	

③ Talk with a partner

Answer each question with evidence from the class registration list. Use the phrase in the Useful Language box.

1. When is Alex Fedorin's birthday?
2. Where is Mario Fernandez from?
3. What is Jun's telephone number?

> **USEFUL LANGUAGE**
> According to the class
> registration list, . . .

④ Analyze the texts (**Objective:** Compare two texts on the same topic.)

Review the following texts to answer the questions below: (1) page 12, *A New Student* and (2) page 136, *Class Registration List*.

1. What is the topic of both readings?
   a. telephone numbers   b. personal information
2. What is one way they are similar?
   a. Both have lists of students.   b. Both have student information.
3. What is one way they are different?
   a. One is a list. One is not a list.   b. One is about a man. One is about a woman.

Reading Tip: Order forms have headings, like "Number", at the top. What are the headings on this form?

Order Form

Every month Jaime orders office supplies. He uses this form. The order form has four categories – office supplies, number, price per item and total price. The order form must be accurate. He must order the correct supplies.

Office Supplies	Number	Price	Total Price (Includes 6% tax)
Scissors	20	$ 3.99	$84.59
Boxes of pencils	15	$ 9.99	$158.84
Calculators	10	$14.99	$158.89
Boxes of markers	25	$ 7.99	$211.74
Notepads	50	$ 4.99	$264.47

1 Check your understanding

1. What is this reading about?
   a. Jaime's order form
   b. Jaime's coworkers
2. How much does one calculator cost?
   a. $10
   b. $14.99
3. How many boxes of pencils does Jaime order?
   a. 15
   b. 25
4. Circle your answer and complete the sentence.
   I think the office uses **notepads / calculators** more because _____.

Ventures 1
3rd Edition
STUDENT'S BOOK

2 Build your vocabulary

A Look at the pictures. Find the words in the reading. Then write the words below the pictures.

| boxes | form | price | ~~supplies~~ |

1. __*supplies*__   2. _____   3. _____   4. _____

B Find the academic words in Column 1 in the reading and underline them. Then complete the chart.

Academic word	Phrase or sentence from reading	Best definition	My sentence
1. accurate	*The order form must be accurate.*	ⓐ correct b. wrong	*My homework must be accurate.*
2. categories		a. whole b. groupings	

3 Talk with a partner

Answer each question with evidence from the reading. Use the phrase in the Useful Language box.

1. How many scissors does Jaime order?
2. What is the total price for the calculators?
3. Does the total price include the tax?

> **USEFUL LANGUAGE**
> According to the order form, . . .

4 Analyze the texts

> **Objective:** Compare two texts on the same topic.

Review the following texts to answer the questions below: (1) page 24, *Attention new students!* and (2) page 138, *Order Form.*

1. What is the topic of both readings?
   a. supplies   b. coworkers
2. How are they similar?
   a. Both list calculators, pencils and markers.   b. Both list calculators, pencils, and notebooks.
3. How are they different?
   a. One reading has five supplies. One reading has ten supplies.
   b. One reading is about school supplies. One reading is about work supplies.

Reading Tip: A paragraph is a group of sentences about one idea. How many sentences are in this paragraph?

The 60th Birthday in Chinese Culture

In Chinese culture, the 60th birthday is very important. The Chinese believe that a person begins a new life after the 60th birthday. The children and grandchildren have a big party for the 60-year-old. People at the party eat special foods such as noodles, peaches and eggs. The noodles symbolize a long life. The children and grandchildren give flowers, cakes and money in red envelopes. Chinese people only celebrate birthdays every 10 years after the 60th birthday.

1 Check your understanding

1. What is this reading about?
   a. an American birthday celebration
   b. a Chinese birthday celebration
2. What do noodles symbolize?
   a. a long life
   b. good luck
3. Who gives the party for the 60-year-old?
   a. the parents
   b. the children and grandchildren
4. Circle your answer and complete the sentence.
   I think the 60th birthday is / **is not** important in China because *begins a new life* .

2 Build your vocabulary

A Look at the pictures. Find the words in the paragraph. Then write the words below the pictures.

| flowers | ~~noodles~~ | peaches | red envelope |

   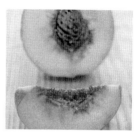

1. ___noodles___   2. _____   3. _____   4 . _____

B Find the academic words in Column 1 in the reading and underline them. Then complete the chart.

Academic word	Phrase or sentence from reading	Best definition	My sentence
1. culture	*In Chinese culture,.....*	a. people ⓑ way of life	*Family is important in my culture.*
2. symbolize		a. represent b. talk about	

3 Talk with a partner

Answer each question with evidence from the paragraph. Use the phrase in the Useful Language box.

1. What do people eat at a Chinese 60th birthday party?
2. What do the children and grandchildren give to the 60-year-old?
3. How often do the Chinese celebrate birthdays after the 60th birthday?

> **USEFUL LANGUAGE**
> According to the paragraph, . . .

4 Analyze the texts

> **Objective:** Compare two texts on the same topic.

Review the following texts to answer the questions below: (1) page 38, *The Birthday Party* and (2) page 140, *The 60th Birthday in Chinese Culture*.

1. What is the topic of the two readings?
   a. families
   b. birthday parties
2. How are they similar?
   a. Both are about birthday parties for older people.
   b. Both are about birthday parties for younger people.
3. How are they different?
   a. One is about birthday parties in China. One is about a birthday party in the United States.
   b. One is about a child's birthday party. One is about a birthday party for a sixty-year-old.

Reading Tip: A table has columns and rows. This table has two rows and three columns. What is the head of each column?

Don't Catch a Cold!

Colds spread from person to person. For example, your friend has a cold. You "catch" the cold from your friend. Look at the table below. Look at the symptoms, or signs, of a cold. How can your friend's cold transfer to you?

Illness	Symptoms	How it spreads
a cold	• runny nose • cough • sneeze	• hands touch a runny nose and then other objects • germs from coughs and sneezes fall on objects

Don't catch your friend's cold. Here is the best strategy: Wash your hands often. Use warm water and soap. Wash for 20 seconds.

1 Check your understanding

1. What is the reading about?
    a. how a cold spreads
    b. causes of a cold
2. What are the symptoms of a cold?
    a. hands touching objects
    b. runny noses, coughs and sneezes
3. How does a cold spread?
    a. from washing hands
    b. from germs
4. Circle your answer and complete the sentence.
    You **should / shouldn't** wash your hands often because _____.

2 Build your vocabulary

A Look at the pictures. Find the words in the reading. Write the words below the pictures.

> cough   germs   ~~runny nose~~   sneeze

   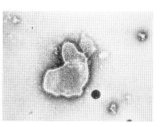

1. _runny nose_   2. _____   3. _____   4. _____

B Find the academic words in Column 1 in the article and underline them. Then complete the chart.

Academic word	Phrase or sentence from article	Best definition	My sentence
1. strategy	*Here is the best strategy*	a. a symptom (b.) a plan	*One strategy for learning English is to take a class.*
2. transfer		a. not move b. move	

3 Talk with a partner

Answer each question with evidence from the article. Use the phrase in the Useful Language box.

1. What is another word for symptom?
2. What is one symptom of a cold?
3. What happens when you sneeze?

> **USEFUL LANGUAGE**
> According to the article, . . .

4 Analyze the texts

> **Objective:** Compare two texts on the same topic.

Review the following texts to answer the questions below: (1) page 50, *The Doctor's Office* and (2) page 142, *Don't Catch a Cold!*

1. What is the topic of both readings?
   a. health   b. medicine
2. What is one way they are similar?
   a. Both talk about colds.   b. Both talk about a doctor's office.
3. What is one way they are different?
   a. One is about patients. One is about doctors.   b. One is about people. One is about symptoms.

Reading Tip: Arrows on a map mean something. What do the arrows mean in the directions below?

Directions to the Library

Sandra likes her new neighborhood. There's a school, playground and grocery store in the area. She wants to know the location of a library in her community. She uses her tablet to get directions from her house to the library.

directions.com

From: 4400 Jewell St., Duluth, MN 55803

To: 4275 Cass St., Duluth, MN 55803

5 min

1.1 mi

Start out going **south** on Jewell St toward Grand Ave.

1. Take the 1st **right** onto Grand Ave.
   Then go 0.11 miles
2. Take the 1st **right** onto Union St.
   Then go 0.13 miles
3. Turn **left** onto 2nd Ave.
   Then go 0.66 miles
4. Turn **left** onto Cass St.
   Then go 0.24 miles

4275 Cass St, Duluth, MN 55803 is on the **left**.

1 Check your understanding

1. What is this reading about?
   a. directions to the playground
   b. directions to the library
2. What does Sandra want to find?
   a. the library
   b. the school
3. How does Sandra find the location of the library?
   a. on her tablet
   b. on her phone
4. Circle your answer and complete the sentence.
   I think Sandra **can /can't** walk to the library because _____.

2 Build your vocabulary

A Look at the pictures. Find the words in the reading. Write the words below the pictures.

| neighborhood | playground | south | ~~toward~~ |

1. __toward__

2. _____

3. _____

4. _____

B Find the academic words in Column 1 in the reading and underline them. Then complete the chart.

Academic word	Phrase or sentence from reading	Best definition	My sentence
1. area	There's a school, playground, and grocery store in the area.	a. a place to borrow books (b.) part of a country, city, or town	My school is in a safe area.
2. community		a. a group of people b. a group of foods	

3 Talk with a partner

Answer each question with evidence from the reading. Use the phrase in the Useful Language box.

1. Why does Sandra like her new neighborhood?
2. What is the address of the library?
3. How long does it take to drive from Sandra's house to the library?

> **USEFUL LANGUAGE**
> According to the reading, . . .

4 Analyze the texts

Objective: Compare two texts on the same topic.

Review the following texts to answer the questions below: (1) page 64, the *Hi Angela* email and (2) page 144, *Directions to the Library*.

1. What is the topic of the two readings?
   a. places in the neighborhood   b. directions to the library
2. What is one way they are similar?
   a. Both are about downtown.   b. Both are about Sandra's neighborhood.
3. What is one way they are different?
   a. One has a school. One has a pharmacy.   b. One describes a neighborhood. One gives directions to a place.

Reading Tip: We use *a.m.* and *p.m.* with time. Before 12 o'clock noon is *a.m.* After 12 o'clock noon is *p.m.* 7:30 a.m. is in the morning. 7:30 p.m. is at night. Look at the schedule below. Who goes to work at night? Who goes to work in the morning?

Schedule of Tasks

Aaron and Kristin are married and have two children. They both work outside of the home. Aaron works from 11:00 p.m. to 7:00 a.m. Monday through Friday. Kristin works from 8:00 a.m. to 5:00 p.m. Monday through Friday. They create a schedule. It is a list of home tasks.

Aaron's Tasks		Kristin's Tasks	
7:30 a.m.	Make breakfast	7:30 a.m.	Leave for work
8:15 a.m.	Take children to school	5:30 p.m.	Make dinner
9:00 a.m.	Sleep	7:30 p.m.	Clean up kitchen
3:00 p.m.	Pick up children	8:00 p.m.	Make lunches
3:30 p.m.	Help children with homework	8:30 p.m.	Get children ready for bed
10:30 p.m.	Leave for work	10:30 p.m.	Sleep

1 Check your understanding

1. What is the reading about?
   a. Aaron's schedule
   b. Both Aaron and Kristin's schedules
2. What does Aaron do at 10:30 p.m.?
   a. sleeps
   b. leaves for work
3. What does Kristin do at 8:30 p.m.?
   a. leaves for work
   b. gets children ready for bed
4. Complete the sentence.
   Aaron and Kristin probably **like / don't like** to work different shifts because _____.

2 Build your vocabulary

A Look at the pictures. Find the words in the reading. Write the words below the pictures.

homework   leave   ~~list~~   pick up

1. ___*list*___   2. _____   3. _____   4. _____

B Find the academic words in Column 1 in the reading and underline them. Then complete the chart.

Academic word	Phrase or sentence from reading	Best definition	My sentence
1. create	*They create a schedule.*	(a.) make b. buy	*The teacher creates a class list.*
2. tasks		a. job to find b. work to do	

3 Talk with a partner

Answer each question with evidence from the reading. Use the phrase in the Useful Language box.

1. Who makes breakfast?
2. Who picks up the children?
3. When are Aaron and Kristin home at the same time?

> **USEFUL LANGUAGE**
> According to the schedule, . . .

4 Analyze the texts

> **Objective:** Compare two texts on the same topic.

Review the following texts to answer the questions below: (1) page 76, *Meet Our New Employee: Bob Green* and (2) page 146, *Schedule of Tasks*.

1. What is the topic of both readings?
   a. schedules   b. work tasks
2. How are they are similar?
   a. Both are about activities with family.   b. Both are about activities at work.
3. How are they different?
   a. One is about a married person. One is about a single person.
   b. One is about a night employee. One is about a night employee and a day employee.

Reading Tip: Receipts can have symbols and abbreviations. Look at the supermarket receipt. Find the symbols "@", "%" and "$." Find the abbreviations *reg, lb,* **and** *doz.* **What do they mean?**

SaveMore Supermarket #4

```
2200 Peach St., Pensacola FL 32506
555-463-2300
11/08/16                        12:41:46

Cashier:                        Kimberly

100% WHOLE GRAIN BREAD            $3.49
CHEESE 1 lb                       $4.99
  Reg price $5.99       $1.00 savings
BANANAS 2.33 lb @ $ .78/lb        $1.82
FUJI APPLES 3.5 lb @ $1.99/lb     $6.97
TOMATO SAUCE 3 @ $ .75            $2.25
LARGE EGGS 1 doz                  $3.79
BROWN SUGAR 2 lb                  $2.99
DOG FOOD 2 @ $14.99              $29.98
  Reg Price 1 @ $16.99  $4.00 savings

              Subtotal    $56.28
              7.5% tax     $4.22
              Total       $60.50
              Cash        $60.50
              8 items


        You saved $5.00.

    Thank you for your purchase.
```

1 Check your understanding

1. What is this reading about?
   a. a hardware store receipt   b. a grocery store receipt
2. How much is one pound of bananas?
   a. $2.33   b. $ .78
3. How much are 12 eggs?
   a. $3.79   b. $1.00
4. Circle your answer and complete the sentence.
   I think the customer **has / doesn't have** a dog because _____.

Ventures 1
3ʳᵈ Edition
STUDENT'S BOOK

2 Build your vocabulary

A Look at the pictures. Find the words in the reading. Write the words below the pictures.

cash   ~~cashier~~   subtotal   total

1. ___cashier___   2. _____   3. _____   4. _____

B Find the academic words in Column 1 on the receipt and underline them. Then complete the chart.

Academic word	Phrase or sentence from receipt	Best definition	My sentence
1. items	8 items	(a.) different things b. different people	The supermarket sells many items.
2. purchase		a. something you eat b. something you buy	

3 Talk with a partner

Answer each question with evidence from the receipt. Use the phrase in the Useful Language box.

1. What is the address of the supermarket?
2. How much is the tax?
3. What is the regular price of cheese?

> **USEFUL LANGUAGE**
> According to the receipt, . . .

4 Analyze the texts

> **Objective:** Compare two texts on the same topic.

Review the following texts to answer the questions below: (1) page 90, *Regular Customers* and (2) page 148, *SaveMore Supermarket #4.*

1. What is the topic of both readings?
   a. Supermarket shopping
   b. Supermarket receipts
2. How are they are similar?
   a. In both, customers pay with a debit card.
   b. In both, the customers are at SaveMore Supermarket.
3. How are they different?
   a. One has 4 items. One has 8 items.
   b. One is about food. One is about clothes.

Reading Tip: Each bulleted item (•) on a list is an important idea. Look at the Help Wanted job advertisement. How many important ideas are there?

Help Wanted
Gentle Palms Senior Daycare Center

Job openings: Care assistant
Work in a friendly environment.
Part-time and full-time positions are available.

Work activities include:
- Prepare snacks.
- Help seniors to eat and move around.
- Tell the medical staff when an individual has pain.

Go to our website for an employment application and to learn about other jobs at our center. www.adultseniorcare.com

1 Check your understanding

1. What is this reading about?
   a. children
   b. seniors
2. What job is available?
   a. care assistant
   b. child care worker
3. What are two work activities?
   a. help seniors and talk to medical staff
   b. prepare meals and make beds
4. Circle your answer and complete the sentence.
   I think this **is / isn't** a good job because _____.

2 Build your vocabulary

A Look at the pictures. Find the words in the reading. Write the words below the pictures.

care assistant   friendly   pain   ~~seniors~~

1. _seniors_   2. _____   3. _____   4. _____

B Find the academic words in Column 1 in the help wanted advertisement and underline them. Then complete the chart.

Academic word	Phrase or sentence from advertisement	Best definition	My sentence
1. available	*Part-time and full-time positions are available.*	(a.) open b. busy	*I am available to work part time.*
2. individual		a. animal b. person	

3 Talk with a partner

Answer each question with evidence from the help wanted advertisement. Use the phrase in the Useful Language box.

1. Where is the job opening?
2. How do you apply for this job?
3. Who do you tell about pain?

> **USEFUL LANGUAGE**
> According to the advertisement, . . .

4 Analyze the texts

> **Objective:** Compare two texts on the same topic.

Review the following texts to answer the questions below: (1) page 102, the recommendation letter and (2) page 150, *Help Wanted*.

1. What is the topic of the two readings?
   a. work
   b. volunteering
2. What is one way they are similar?
   a. Both are about seniors.
   b. Both are about nursing homes.
3. What is one way they are different?
   a. One is about seniors. One is about children.
   b. One is about a nursing home. One is about a daycare center.

Reading Tip: The chart has two headings – *Soup Kitchen Duties* and *Time*. The chart has five rows below the two headings. Read information in the rows from left to right. What information is in the first row?

Volunteer Duties

Anh volunteers at a soup kitchen on Tuesdays. She assists with five soup kitchen duties. Anh likes to volunteer. She likes to help others.

Soup Kitchen Duties	Time
1. Make soup	5:00 – 5:30 p.m.
2. Slice bread	5:30 – 6:00 p.m.
3. Serve soup	6:00 – 7:30 p.m.
4. Wash and dry dishes	7:30 – 8:30 p.m.
5. Mop floors	8:30 – 9:00 p.m.

1 Check your understanding

1. What is this reading about?
   a. Anh's work duties   b. Anh's volunteer duties
2. What does Anh do from 6:00 to 7:30?
   a. makes soup   b. serves soup
3. What does Anh do from 8:30 to 9:00 p.m.?
   a. mops floors   b. washes and dries dishes
4. Circle your answer and complete the sentence.
   I think Anh **likes / doesn't like** to volunteer because _____.

2 Build your vocabulary

A Look at the pictures. Find the words in the reading. Write the words below the pictures.

duties   serve   slice   ~~soup~~

1. _____soup_____   2. _____   3. _____   4. _____

B Find the academic words in Column 1 in the reading and underline them. Then complete the chart.

Academic word	Phrase or sentence from reading	Best definition	My sentence
1. assists	*She assists with five soup kitchen duties.*	a. stops b. helps ✓	*I assist my teacher before class.*
2. volunteers		a. works for free b. works for money	

3 Talk with a partner

Answer each question with evidence from the reading. Use the phrase in the Useful Language box.

1. When does Anh volunteer at the soup kitchen?
2. When does Anh serve soup?
3. When does Anh wash and dry the dishes?

> **USEFUL LANGUAGE**
> According to the reading . . .

4 Analyze the texts   **Objective:** Compare two texts on the same topic.

Review the following texts to answer the questions below: (1) page 116, *Letter to Karen* and (2) page 152, *Volunteer Duties*.

1. What is the topic of both readings?
   a. chores / duties with pay   b. chores / duties with no pay
2. How are they are similar?
   a. Both describe chores.   b. Both describe work for no pay.
3. How are they different?
   a. One is about household chores. One is about volunteer duties.
   b. One is about jobs at a restaurant. One is about duties at a soup kitchen.

Reading Tip: Read the headings (titles) first. They tell you the topics, or categories, of information. What are the four headings on this sign?

CAMPING RULES

Camping
- Camp and fish only in marked areas.
- Don't drink from glass containers.
- Only start fires in fire pits.
- Put all garbage and litter in appropriate containers.

Pets
- Keep your pet on a leash at all times.
- No pets in swimming areas.

Fireworks
- Fireworks are prohibited.

Noise
- Quiet hours are between 10:00 p.m. and 6:00 a.m.
- No loud music.

1 Check your understanding

1. What is this reading about?
   - a. camping activities
   - b. rules for camping
2. Where can you camp?
   - a. in marked areas
   - b. next to the fishing area
3. Where can't you take pets?
   - a. to the fishing area
   - b. to the swimming areas
4. Circle your answer and complete the sentence.

   You **can / can't** drink from glass containers because _____.

Ventures 1
3rd Edition
STUDENT'S BOOK

UNIT 10

College and Career Readiness

2 Build your vocabulary

A Look at the pictures. Find the words in the reading. Write the words below the pictures.

fire   fireworks   leash   litter

1. ___fire___   2. _____   3. _____   4. _____

B Find the academic words in Column 1 on the sign and underline them. Then complete the chart.

Academic word	Phrase or sentence from sign	Best definition	My sentence
1. appropriate	*Put all garbage and litter in appropriate containers.*	(a.) right b. not right	*I need to wear the appropriate clothes to a job interview.*
2. prohibited		a. allowed b. not allowed	

3 Talk with a partner

Answer each question with evidence from the sign. Use the phrase in the Useful Language box.

1. Where do you put your garbage?
2. When are quiet hours?
3. Where can you start a fire?

USEFUL LANGUAGE
According to the sign, . . .

4 Analyze the texts

Objective: Compare two texts on the same topic.

Review the following texts to answer the questions below: (1) page 128, *Email message to Ming* and (2) page 154, *Camping Rules*.

1. What is the topic of both readings?
   a. camping
   b. Sunday activities
2. How are they similar?
   a. Both talk about family chores.
   b. Both talk about swimming and fishing.
3. How are they different?
   a. One is rules for camping. One is an email about a camping trip.
   b. One talks about chores on a camping trip. One talks about chores at home.

Ventures STUDENT'S BOOK 3rd Edition   College and Career Readiness   UNIT 10   **155**

AUDIO SCRIPT

Welcome

Page 3, Exercise 2A
CD1, Track 2
Conversation A
A Hi, I'm Paolo. What's your name?
B I'm Ryoko.
A How do you spell that?
B R-Y-O-K-O.

Conversation B
A Hi, Kankou. How's it going?
This is my friend Eduardo.
B Nice to meet you, Eduardo.

Page 3, Exercise 2B
CD1, Track 3
A, B, C, D, E, F, G, H, I, J, K, L, M, N, O, P,
Q, R, S, T, U, V, W, X, Y, Z

Page 3, Exercise 2C
CD1, Track 4
A What's your name?
B Helena.
A How do you spell that?
B H-E-L-E-N-A.

Page 4, Exercise 3A
CD1, Track 5
zero, one, two, three, four, five, six,
seven, eight, nine, ten, eleven, twelve,
thirteen, fourteen, fifteen, sixteen,
seventeen, eighteen, nineteen, twenty

Page 4, Exercise 3B
CD1, Track 6
1. six   4. fifteen   7. eight
2. twenty   5. nine   8. five
3. one   6. twelve   9. sixteen

Page 4, Exercise 3C
CD1, Track 7
1. three   6. zero
2. eight   7. twenty
3. eighteen   8. four
4. twelve   9. fifteen
5. one   10. eleven

Page 5, Exercise 4A
CD1, Track 8
Sunday, Monday, Tuesday, Wednesday,
Thursday, Friday, Saturday

Page 5, Exercise 4C
CD1, Track 9
1. January
2. February
3. March
4. April
5. May
6. June
7. July
8. August
9. September
10. October
11. November
12. December

Unit 1: Personal information

Page 7, Exercises 2A and 2B
CD1, Track 10
Conversation A
A What's your telephone number?
B My telephone number is 555-8907.
A Was that 555-8807?
B No, it's 555-8907.

Conversation B
A What's your area code?
B My area code?
A Yes.
B It's 213.
A 213. OK, thanks.

Conversation C
A What's your last name?
B Clark. Mr. Clark.
A Clark? Please spell that.
B C-L-A-R-K.
A Thank you.

Conversation D
A What's your address?
B 1041 Main Street.
A 1014 Main Street?
B No, 1041.
A OK. Thank you.

Conversation E
A What's your first name?
B Ricardo.
A R-I-K-A . . .
B No, R-I-C-A-R-D-O.
A OK, R-I-C-A-R-D-O. Thanks.

Conversation F
A What's your zip code?
B 94558.
A Is that 94458?
B No, 94558.
A OK. Thanks.

Page 8, Exercise 2A
CD1, Track 11
1. **A** What's his first name?
   B His first name is Alfred.
2. **A** What's her first name?
   B Her first name is Sue.
3. **A** What's his first name?
   B His first name is Tom.
4. **A** What's their last name?
   B Their last name is Jones.

Page 9, Exercise 2C
CD1, Track 12
A What's your name?
B Jennifer Kent.
A Sorry. What's your first name?
B My first name is Jennifer.
A How do you spell that?
B J-E-N-N-I-F-E-R.
A OK. What's your last name?
B Kent. K-E-N-T.

Page 10, Exercise 2A
CD1, Track 13
1. **A** Are you from Canada?
   B No, I'm not.
2. **A** Are they from Somalia?
   B Yes, they are.
3. **A** Is she from Russia?
   B Yes, she is.
4. **A** Is he from Mexico?
   B Yes, he is.
5. **A** Is she from China?
   B No, she isn't.
6. **A** Are they from Brazil?
   B No, they aren't.
7. **A** Is he from Ecuador?
   B No, he isn't.
8. **A** Are you from South Korea?
   B Yes, I am.

Page 11, Exercise 2C
CD1, Track 14
A Where are you from, Katia?
B I'm from Brazil.
A Brazil? How do you spell that?
B B-R-A-Z-I-L.

Page 12, Exercise 2
CD1, Track 15
A New Student

Svetlana Kulik is a new student. She is from
Russia. Now she lives in Napa, California.
Her address is 1041 Main Street. Her
zip code is 94558. Her area code is 707.
Her telephone number is 555-9073.

Page 13, Exercise 4A
CD1, Track 16
1. title   6. zip code
2. address   7. apartment number
3. city   8. street
4. state   9. middle initial
5. signature

Unit 2: At school

Page 19, Exercises 2A and 2B
CD1, Track 17
Conversation A
A Where are the pens?
B The pins?
A No, the pens.
B Oh, they're in the drawer.
A Thanks.

Conversation B
A Where's the calculator?
B The what?
A The calculator.
B Oh. Look in the desk.
A Thank you.

Conversation C
A Where's the notebook?
B The notebook?
A Yes.
B I see it on the table.
A Oh, good.

Conversation D
A Erika, where's the stapler?
B The what?
A The stapler.
B It's in the drawer.
A Thanks, Erika.

Conversation E
A Where are the rulers?
B Excuse me?
A Where are the rulers?
B Are they in the box?
A Oh, yes. Now I see them.

Conversation F
B Where's my book?
A Your book?
B Yeah.
A It's on the floor under your chair.
B Oh, good. Thanks.

Page 20, Exercise 2A
CD1, Track 18
1. A Where's the book?
   B It's on the shelf.
2. A Where's the pencil sharpener?
   B It's on the wall.
3. A Where's the dictionary?
   B It's under the table.
4. A Where's the calendar?
   B It's under the box.
5. A Where's the eraser?
   B It's in the drawer
6. A Where's the calculator?
   B It's in the cabinet.
7. A Where's the stapler?
   B It's in the drawer.
8. A Where's the pencil?
   B It's under the table.
9. A Where's the ruler?
   B It's in the book.

Page 21, Exercise 2B
CD1, Track 19
1. A Excuse me. Where's the calculator?
   B It's in the cabinet.
   A Oh, thanks.
   B You're welcome.
2. A Excuse me. Where's the pen?
   B It's on the table.
   A Oh, thanks.
   B You're welcome.
3. A Excuse me. Where's the dictionary?
   B It's under the table.
   A Oh, thanks.
   B You're welcome
4. A Excuse me. Where's the pencil sharpener?
   B It's in the cabinet.
   A Oh, thanks.
   B You're welcome.
5. A Excuse me. Where's the ruler?
   B It's under the books on the table.
   A Oh, thanks.
   B You're welcome.
6. A Excuse me. Where's the eraser?
   B It's on the table.
   A Oh, thanks.
   B You're welcome.

Page 22, Exercise 2A
CD1, Track 20
1. A Are the books in the cabinet?
   B Yes, they are.
2. A Is the calendar under the clock?
   B Yes, it is.
3. A Are the rulers on the table?
   B No, they aren't.
4. A Are the pencils on the table?
   B No, they aren't.
5. A Are the calculators on the table?
   B Yes, they are.

Page 23, Exercise 2C
CD1, Track 21
1. A Where are the notebooks?
   B They're in the filing cabinet.
2. A Where is the calculators?
   B They're on the filing cabinet.
3. A Where is the calendar?
   B It's on the wall.
4. A Where are the maps?
   B They're on the desk.
5. A Where is the laptop computer?
   B It's on the small table.
6. A Where is the pencil?
   B It's under the dictionary.
7. A Where are the books?
   B They're in the box.
8. A Where are the rulers?
   B They're under the small table.

Page 24, Exercise 2
CD1, Track 22
Attention, new students!
Items in your new classroom.
· The laptop is on the small table.
· The pencils are in the basket on the desk.
· The erasers are in the basket.
· The books are in the bookcase.
· The calculators are in a box under the table.
· The markers are in the desk drawer.

Page 25, Exercise 4A
CD1, Track 23
1. hole puncher
2. notepads
3. bulletin board
4. whiteboard
5. index cards
6. scissors
7. paper clips
8. marker
9. globe

Review: Units 1 and 2

Page 30, Exercise 1
CD1, Track 24
A Good morning, class. We have a new student today. His name is Juan.
B Hello, Juan.
A Do you want to ask Juan some questions?
C What's your last name?
D My last name is Perez. P-E-R-E-Z.
E What's your middle name?
D Ricardo.
F Where are you from?
D I'm from El Salvador.
C Where do you live?

D My address is 350 Lincoln Avenue, Apartment 10. The zip code is 94321.
A Very good. Any other questions?
F What's your telephone number?
D 213-555-6301.
A Welcome, Juan.

Page 31, Exercise 3A
CD1, Track 25
name
address
apartment

Page 31, Exercise 3B
CD1, Track 26

map	ruler
books	notebook
box	pencil
clock	telephone
pens	initial
chair	signature
desk	computer
classroom	sharpener
middle	calendar
partner	eraser
whiteboard	

Page 31, Exercise 3C
CD1, Track 27

a. from	e. Colombia
b. China	f. Canada
c. student	g. talk
d. name	h. city

Unit 3: Friends and family

Page 33, Exercises 2A and 2B
CD1, Track 28
Conversation A
A Hello?
B Hi, Luisa. This is Mrs. Brown. Is your grandmother home?
A Yes, she is. She's watching TV.
B Can I talk to her?
A Sure, just a minute.

Conversation B
A Hello?
B Hi . . . Carlos? This is Mr. Cho. Is your father home?
A Yes, he is, but he's sleeping right now.
B Oh, I'm sorry. I can call again later.
A OK, thanks.

Conversation C
A Hello?
B Hi, Carlos. This is Mr. Ramos. Is your grandfather there?
A Yes, he is, but he's eating lunch right now.
B OK. I'll call him later.
A Thanks.

Conversation D
A Hello?
B Hi, this is Angela. Is your mother there?
A Yes, she is. But she's busy. She's cooking dinner.
B Oh, OK. I'll call back after dinner.
A OK, thanks.

Conversation E

A Hello?
B Hi, Carlos. This is Mary. Is your sister home?
A She's here, but she's studying.
B Oh, OK. Please ask her to call me later.
A Sure. No problem.

Conversation F

A Hello?
B Hello. Is this Mrs. Gonzalez?
A Yes, it is.
B This is Dr. Smith's office. Is your husband home?
A Yes, he is, but he's resting.
B Oh, OK. Please ask him to call our office.

Page 34, Exercise 2A
CD1, Track 29

1. A What's she doing?
   B She's reading.
2. A What's he doing?
   B He's sleeping.
3. A What are they doing?
   B They're eating.
4. A What's he doing?
   B He's watching TV.
5. A What's she doing?
   B She's talking.
6. A What are you doing?
   B I'm studying.
7. A What's she doing?
   B She's taking a picture.
8. A What are you doing?
   B I'm drinking coffee.
9. A What are they doing?
   B They're playing basketball.

Page 36, Exercise 2A
CD1, Track 30

1. A Is she working now?
   B Yes, she is. She's very busy.
2. A Is he driving to work?
   B Yes, he is. He's late.
3. A Are they eating lunch now?
   B Yes, they are. They're hungry.
4. A Is he helping his grandmother?
   B Yes, he is. He's really helpful.
5. A Is she taking a break?
   B Yes, she is. She's tired.
6. A Are they buying water?
   B Yes, they are. They're thirsty.
7. A Is she crying?
   B Yes, she is. She's sad.
8. A Are you smiling?
   B Yes, I am. I'm happy.

Page 38, Exercise 2
CD1, Track 31

The Birthday Party
My name is Juan. In this picture, it's my birthday. I am 70 years old. Look at me! I don't look 70 years old. My wife, my daughter, and my grandson are eating cake. My grandson is always hungry. My granddaughter is drinking soda. She's always thirsty. My son-in-law is playing the guitar and singing. Everyone is happy!

Page 39, Exercise 4A
CD1, Track 32

1. grandfather and grandmother
2. father and mother
3. aunt and uncle
4. brother and sister-in-law
5. husband and wife
6. cousin
7. niece and nephew

Unit 4: Health

Page 45, Exercises 2A and 2B
CD1, Track 33

Conversation A

A What's the matter? You aren't reading.
B No, I'm not.
A Why not?
B I have a headache.
A Oh, I'm sorry to hear that.

Conversation B

A Are you alright?
B No, not really. I have a fever.
A Get some rest. I hope you get well soon.
B Thank you. I'm sure I will.

Conversation C

A What's the matter?
B I have a sprained ankle.
A A sprained ankle? Try an ice pack.
B Thanks for the advice.
A I hope it gets better soon.
B Thanks. I'm sure it will.

Conversation D

A Are you OK?
B No, not really. I have a stomachache.
A A stomachache? That's too bad.
B Yes, a really bad stomachache.
A Well then, take it easy.
B Thanks. I will.

Conversation E

A You don't look well. What's wrong?
B I have a sore throat.
A Oh, I'm sorry. Get some rest.
B Thank you. I will.

Conversation F

A You don't look well. What's wrong?
B I have an earache.
A An earache, huh?
B Yeah.
A I'm sorry.

Page 46, Exercise 2A
CD1, Track 34

1. He has a terrible cold.
2. I have a headache.
3. He has a backache.
4. You have a fever.
5. I have a broken arm.
6. He has a stomachache.
7. She has a bad cough.
8. You have a sore throat.
9. She has a cut.

Page 48, Exercise 2A
CD1, Track 35

1. A Do I have a fever?
   B No, you don't.

2. A Does she have a sore throat?
   B No, she doesn't.
3. A Does he have a cough?
   B Yes, he does.
4. A Do you have a cold?
   B Yes, I do.
5. A Does she have the flu?
   B Yes, she does.
6. A Does she have a sprained ankle?
   B No, she doesn't.
7. A Do they have colds?
   B Yes, they do.
8. A Does he have a fever?
   B Yes he does.

Page 50, Exercise 2
CD1, Track 36

The Doctor's Office
Poor Maria! Everyone is sick! Maria and her children are in the doctor's office. Her son, Luis, has a sore throat. Her daughter, Rosa, has a stomachache. Her baby, Gabriel, has an earache. Maria doesn't have a sore throat. She doesn't have a stomachache. And she doesn't have an earache. But Maria has a very bad headache!

Page 51, Exercise 4A
CD1, Track 37

1. nose
2. teeth
3. finger
4. stomach
5. leg
6. hand
7. back
8. eye
9. toe
10. foot
11. knee
12. neck
13. ear
14. head
15. mouth
16. chin
17. shoulder

Review: Units 3 and 4

Page 56, Exercise 1
CD1, Track 38

Connie and her family are at home today. Connie has a headache. Her husband, Robert, has an earache. He's talking to the doctor on the phone. Connie's daughter is sleeping. Connie's son, Eddie, is in the living room. He's watching TV. Eddie has a stomachache.

Page 57, Exercise 3A
CD1, Track 39

happy
fever

Page 57, Exercise 3B
CD1, Track 40

son	husband
wife	daughter
head	yesterday
ear	grandmother
foot	grandfather
leg	newspaper
cooking	studying
homework	stomachache
toothache	tomorrow
headache	computer

Page 57, Exercise 3C
CD1, Track 41

1. father
2. earache
3. tired
4. birthday
5. thirsty
6. celebrate
7. finger
8. Brazil
9. repeat
10. elbow
11. reschedule
12. shoulder

Unit 5: Around town

Page 59, Exercises 2A and 2B
CD1, Track 42

Conversation A
A Excuse me. Where's the pharmacy?
B The pharmacy? It's on 5th Avenue.
A 5th Avenue? Is it far from here?
B No, just go straight about two blocks.
A Thank you very much.

Conversation B
A Excuse me. I'm looking for the museum.
B The museum? Hmmm. Oh yes. It's on C Street.
A C Street? Where is that?
B It's not far. Turn left at the next street.
A Thanks a lot.

Conversation C
A Excuse me. I can't find the post office.
B The post office? It's on 70th Street.
A 70th Street? That way?
B Yes, just go that way a block.
A Thanks for your help.

Conversation D
A Excuse me. Is the bus stop around here?
B The bus stop? Let's see . . . yes, it's on G Street.
A G Street? Is that far?
B No, it's across the street.
A Thank you. I appreciate it.

Conversation E
A Excuse me. I'm looking for the playground.
B The playground? It's on First Avenue.
A First Avenue? Where is that?
B Go to the corner and turn left.
A Thanks so much.

Conversation F
A Excuse me. Is there a restaurant near here?
B A restaurant? Oh yes! It's on Third Avenue.
A Third Avenue? Over there?
B Yes, it's not far. Go straight a few more blocks. It's on your right.
A Great! Thanks a lot.

Page 60, Exercise 2A
CD1, Track 43

1. **A** Where's the park?
   B It's next to the bank.
2. **A** Where's the library?
   B It's across from the bank.
3. **A** Where's the school?
   B It's on the corner of First Street and Grant Avenue.
4. **A** Where's the hospital?
   B It's on Grant Avenue.
5. **A** Where's the bank?
   B It's between the school and the park.
6. **A** Where's the post office?
   B It's next to the library.
7. **A** Where's the museum?
   B It's across from the park.
8. **A** Where's the car?
   B It's on Grant Avenue.

Page 61, Exercise 2B
CD1, Track 44

A Excuse me. Where's Kim's Coffee Shop?
B It's on Kent Street.
A Sorry. Could you repeat that, please?
B It's on Kent Street.
A Oh, OK. Thanks.

Page 62, Exercise 2A
CD1, Track 45

1. Go straight ahead.
2. Turn left.
3. Go three blocks.
4. Turn right.
5. Cross Union Street.
6. Go to Main Street.
7. Go two blocks.
8. Go to Union Street.

Page 63, Exercise 2B
CD1, Track 46

1. **A** Go two blocks. Turn left. It's across from the library.
   B The DMV.
2. **A** Go straight. Cross Grand Street. Turn right on Main Street. It's across from the post office.
   B The bank.
3. **A** Go to Grand Street. Turn left. It's next to the parking lot.
   B The train station.
4. **A** Go one block. Turn right on Grand Street. It's across from Ed's Restaurant.
   B The park.

Page 64, Exercise 2
CD1, Track 47

Hi Angela,

I love my new house. My neighborhood is great! Here are some pictures. There is a school on my street. My children go to the school. They like it a lot. There is a community center across from the school. My husband works at the community center. He walks to work. There is a grocery store next to my house. It's a small store, but we can buy a lot of things. There is a good Mexican restaurant on Second Street. It's right across from my house.

I like it here, but I miss you.
Please write.
Your friend,
Sandra

Page 65, Exercise 4A
CD1, Track 48

1. a shopping mall
2. a high school
3. a day-care center
4. a senior center
5. a playground
6. a police station
7. an apartment building
8. a hardware store
9. a courthouse

Page 66, Exercise 1A
CD1, Track 49

From the train station, turn right. Go straight on Pine Street. Turn right on Second Avenue. Go straight ahead. Cross Maple Street. Then turn left on Maple Street. Walk one block to the corner. The school is on the corner of Maple Street and Third Avenue. It's across from the apartment building.

Unit 6: Time

Page 71, Exercises 2A and 2B
CD2, Track 2

Conversation A
A Congratulations on your new job.
B Thanks.
A So when do you leave for work?
B I leave at ten-thirty.
A At night?
B Right.

Conversation B
A What time do you eat dinner?
B We eat dinner at six-thirty.
A And you don't go to work until ten-thirty?
B That's right.

Conversation C
A What time do you start work?
B I start work at eleven o'clock at night.
A So it takes you half an hour to get here?
B Yeah.

Conversation D
A What time do you catch the bus?
B I catch the bus at ten forty-five.
A Ten forty-five? Not ten-thirty?
B Right. Ten forty-five, not ten-thirty.

Conversation E
A What time do you take a break?
B I take a break at two forty-five in the morning.
A Two forty-five? Wow. I'm sleeping then!
B I know. So is my family.

Conversation F
A What time do you get home?
B I get home around seven-thirty.
A In the morning?
B Right. Just in time for breakfast!

Page 72, Exercise 2A
CD2, Track 3

1. **A** What do they do in the evening?
   B They watch TV.
2. **A** What does he do in the afternoon?
   B He studies.
3. **A** What does she do in the morning?
   B She exercises.

4. **A** What do they do on Sunday?
   B They go to the park.
5. **A** What does she do every evening?
   B She reads.
6. **A** What does he do in the afternoon?
   B He takes a nap.

Page 73, Exercise 2B – Part 1
CD2, Track 4

On Saturday morning, Jill watches TV. On Saturday afternoon, she plays soccer. On Saturday evening, she listens to music.

On Saturday morning, Mr. and Mrs. Wilder go shopping. On Saturday afternoon, they work in the garden. On Saturday evening, they pay bills.

On Saturday morning, Harry does his homework. On Saturday afternoon, he plays football. On Saturday evening, he goes to a movie.

Page 73, Exercise 2B – Part 2
CD2, Track 5

What does Jill do on Saturday morning? She usually watches TV.

Page 74, Exercise 2B
CD2, Track 6

1. **A** When do you go on vacation?
   B I usually go on vacation in July.
2. **A** When does your sister have class?
   B She usually has class on Saturday.
3. **A** When does your father catch the bus?
   B He always catches the bus at 8:45.
4. **A** When do you do homework?
   B I always do homework at night.
5. **A** When does your brother do his homework?
   B He usually does his homework in the evening.
6. **A** When does your mother exercise?
   B She usually exercises in the morning.

Page 75, Exercise 2C
CD2, Track 7

A When does Mrs. Wilder rest?
B She rests on Sunday.
A What time?
B From two to four p.m.

Page 76, Exercise 2
CD2, Track 8

Meet Our New Employee: Bob Green
Please welcome Bob. He is a new security guard. He works the night shift at the East End Factory. Bob starts work at 11:00 at night. He leaves work at 7:00 in the morning. Bob likes these hours because he can spend time with his family. Bob says, "I eat breakfast with my wife, Arlene, and my son, Brett, at 7:30 every morning. I help Brett with his homework in the afternoon. I eat dinner with my family at 6:30. Then we watch TV. At 10:30, I go to work."

Congratulations to Bob on his new job!

Page 77, Exercise 4A
CD2, Track 9

1. get up
2. eat breakfast
3. take a shower
4. get dressed
5. take the children to school
6. eat lunch
7. walk the dog
8. eat dinner
9. go to bed

Review: Units 5 and 6

Page 82, Exercise 1
CD2, Track 10

A Excuse me. Where is the DMV?
B It's at 515 Broadway. It's between the bank and the coffee shop.
A Oh, on Broadway. Across from the hospital?
B Yes, that's right.
A OK. Thank you.
B You're welcome. Good luck.

Page 83, Exercise 3A
CD2, Track 11

Where is the bank?
Is the bank on Broadway?
When is your class?
Is your class in the morning?

Page 83, Exercise 3B
CD2, Track 12

Wh- questions
1. **A** Where is the post office?
   B It's on First Street.
2. **A** What time do they eat dinner?
   B They eat dinner at 6:30.

Yes / No questions
3. **A** Are you from Mexico?
   B Yes, I am.
4. **A** Does he start work at 7:00?
   B No, he doesn't.

Unit 7: Shopping

Page 85, Exercises 2A and 2B
CD2, Track 13

Conversation A
A We need some milk. Is there any milk on sale?
B Yes. Milk is two sixty-nine.
A Two sixty-nine? That's cheap.
B How much do we need?
A A lot.

Conversation B
A Let's get some onions. Are there any good onions?
B Here are the onions. They're seventy-nine cents each.
A Whoa! Seventy-nine cents each! That's expensive.
B How many do we need?
A We just need one.
B OK.

Conversation C
A Are there any tomatoes on sale? We need some tomatoes.
B Oh look! They're one twenty-nine a pound.
A Really? That's cheap.
B How many do we need?
A Let's get a lot.

Conversation D
A Do we need any cheese? I see cheese is just six ninety-nine a pound.
B Six ninety-nine? Hey! That's good.
A How much do we need?
B Not much. Let's get half a pound.

Conversation E
A We need some potatoes. Are there any potatoes on sale this week?
B Yes. Potatoes are ninety-nine cents a pound.
A Wow! That's a good price.
B How many do we need?
A A lot!

Conversation F
A Is there any bread on sale?
B No, bread is three seventy-nine.
A What? That's not very good.
B Well, how much do we need?
A Not much.

Page 86, Exercise 2A
CD2, Track 14

Count nouns	Non-count nouns
1. carrots	2. water
4. peaches	3. bread
6. oranges	5. milk
7. eggs	8. meat
10. apples	9. coffee
12. pies	11. sugar

Page 87, Exercise 2C
CD2, Track 15

1. How many eggs do we need?
2. How much juice do we need?
3. How much milk do we need?
4. How many pies do we need?
5. How much bread do we need?
6. How many potatoes do we need?
7. How much rice do we need?
8. How much meat do we need?

Page 88, Exercise 2A
CD2, Track 16

1. There is sugar on the table.
2. There are six eggs in the refrigerator.
3. There is one apple on the table.
4. There are many peaches in the box.
5. There is bread on the shelf.
6. There is an orange on the table.
7. There are onions in the drawer.
8. There is meat in the refrigerator.

Page 88, Exercise 2B
CD2, Track 17

1. **A** Is there any meat in the refrigerator?
   B Yes, there is.
2. **A** Are there any oranges?
   B Yes, there are.
3. **A** Is there any cheese?
   B No, there isn't.
4. **A** Is there any sugar?
   B No, there isn't.
5. **A** Is there any milk in the refrigerator?
   B Yes, there is.
6. **A** Is there any coffee?
   B Yes, there is.
7. **A** Are there any apples?
   B No, there aren't.
8. **A** Are there any cherries?
   B Yes, there are.

Page 89, Exercise 2C
CD2, Track 18
1. There is one loaf of bread.
2. There are two cartons of apple juice.
3. There are three boxes of tea.
4. There are four bottles of water.
5. There is one package of ground meat.
6. There are six cans of soda.
7. There is one bag of flour.
8. There are two packages of cheese.

Page 90, Exercise 2
CD2, Track 19
Regular Customers
Shirley and Dan are regular customers at SaveMore Supermarket. They go to SaveMore three or four times a week. The cashiers and stock clerks at SaveMore know them and like them. There are fruit and vegetables, meat and fish, and cookies and cakes in the supermarket. But today, Shirley and Dan are buying apples, bananas, bread, and cheese. There is one problem. The total is $16.75. They only have a ten-dollar bill, five one-dollar bills, and three quarters!

Page 91, Exercise 4A
CD2, Track 20
1. a penny
2. a nickel
3. a dime
4. a quarter
5. a half-dollar
6. a one-dollar bill
7. a five-dollar bill
8. a ten-dollar bill
9. a twenty-dollar bill
10. a check
11. a credit card
12. a debit card

Unit 8: Work

Page 97, Exercises 2A and 2B
CD2, Track 21
Conversation A
A What does he do?
B He's a manager at a restaurant.
A Oh, really? What did he do before?
B He was a cashier.
A A cashier? When?
B For a while. I think from 2012 to 2016.

Conversation B
A What does Irene do?
B She's a nurse.
A Oh, that's nice. What did she do before?
B She was a cook.
A A cook? When?
B From 2016 to 2017.

Conversation C
A What does Brenda do?
B She's a teacher.
A Oh, that's great. What did she do before?
B She was a server.
A A server? When?
B Last year, from about May to August.

Conversation D
A What does he do?
B He's a busperson.
A Oh, really? What did he do before?
B He was a student.
A A student? When?
B For about six months, from January to June.

Conversation E
A What does he do?
B He's an electrician.
A Oh, yeah? What did he do before?
B He was a construction worker.
A A construction worker? When?
B I think it was in 2016.

Conversation F
A What does she do?
B She's a doctor.
A Oh, that's great. What did she do before?
B She was a medical student.
A A medical student? When?
B I'm not sure, but I think at least 15 years ago.

Page 98, Exercise 2A
CD2, Track 22
1. A She was a teacher before.
   B Now she is a nurse.
2. A She is a manager now.
   B She was a cashier before.
3. A They were students before.
   B Now they are electricians.
4. A He was a server before.
   B Now he is a construction worker.
5. A He was a server before.
   B Now he is a nursing assistant.
6. A Now they are managers.
   B They were cooks before.

Page 100, Exercise 2A
CD2, Track 23
1. A Can she speak Spanish?
   B Yes, she can.
2. A Can he drive a truck?
   B No, he can't.
3. A Can he fix a car?
   B Yes, he can.
4. A Can she paint a house?
   B No, she can't.
5. A Can they work with computers?
   B No, they can't.
6. A Can you cook?
   B Yes, I can.
7. A Can they build houses?
   B Yes, they can.
8. A Can she read a book?
   B No, she can't.
9. A Can you operate on someone?
   B Yes, I can.

Page 101, Exercise 2B
CD2, Track 24
1. A painter can paint.
2. A salesperson can sell things.
3. A carpenter can build things.
4. A gardener can take care of plants.
5. A child-care worker can take care of children.
6. An auto mechanic can fix cars.

Page 102, Exercise 2
CD2, Track 25
Dear Ms. Carter:
I am writing to recommend my student Mai Linh Lam.
Mai Linh was a teacher in Vietnam. She is looking for a new job in the United States. She is a certified nursing assistant now. She volunteers in a nursing home Monday through Friday from 12:00 to 4:30. She takes care of senior citizens.
Mai Linh has many good skills. She can write reports. She can help elderly people move around and sit down. She can help them eat. She can also speak English and Vietnamese. These skills are useful in her job, and she is very good at her work.
Sincerely,
Elaine Maxwell

Page 103, Exercise 4A
CD2, Track 26
1. housekeeper
2. custodian
3. pharmacy technician
4. factory worker
5. hairstylist
6. dental assistant

Review: Units 7 and 8

Page 108, Exercise 1
CD2, Track 27
Carlos was an office worker in his native country. Now, he is a construction worker. Every Thursday after work, Carlos buys groceries. Right now, he is shopping at SaveMore Supermarket. He is buying milk, cheese, bread, and a dozen eggs. His groceries cost $11.75. There is a ten-dollar bill and two quarters in his pocket. Good thing he has a credit card!

Page 109, Exercise 3A
CD2, Track 28
/s/: cakes, hairstylists
/z/: tomatoes, electricians
/ɪz/: peaches, nurses

Page 109, Exercise 3B
CD2, Track 29

/s/	/z/	/ɪz/
assistants	bananas	nurses
cooks	cashiers	oranges
students	drivers	packages
mechanics	cookies	boxes
receptionists	servers	peaches
books	teachers	sandwiches

Page 109, Exercise 3C
CD2, Track 30
1. bags
2. bottles
3. clerks
4. dimes
5. pages
6. carrots
7. desks
8. languages
9. glasses

Unit 9: Daily living

Page 111, Exercises 2A and 2B
CD2, Track 31

Conversation A
A Did you wash the clothes?
B No I didn't, but Rachel did.
A She did? When?
B She washed them last night.
A Good for her!

Conversation B
A Did you pay the bills?
B Yes, I did.
A Are you sure? When?
B I paid them yesterday morning.
A That's great! Thank you.

Conversation C
A Suzy, did you clean the bathroom?
B No, I didn't, but Rita did.
A Oh? When did she clean it?
B She cleaned it the day before yesterday.
A OK. Good.

Conversation D
A Frank, the rug is really clean. Did you vacuum it?
B Yes, I did.
A Did you do it last Friday?
B I vacuumed it every day last week.
A Every day? That's wonderful!

Conversation E
A Did Alice dust the bookshelves?
B Yes, she did.
A Oh, that's good.
B Yes, I told her yesterday.
A Well, I'll thank her.

Conversation F
A Ralph, did you mop the floor or did Victor do it?
B I mopped it.
A When?
B Last night.
A Well, it's dirty again!

Page 112, Exercise 2A
CD2, Track 32

1. Yousef cooked dinner.
2. He didn't clean the kitchen.
3. He dusted the shelves.
4. He mopped the floor.
5. He didn't wash the dishes.
6. He ironed the shirts.
7. He didn't empty the trash.
8. He didn't dry the dishes.

Page 113, Exercise 2B
CD2, Track 33

1. A Did Mr. Ramirez mop the floor?
   B Yes, he did.
2. A Did Mrs. Ramirez empty the trash?
   B Yes, she did.
3. A Did Monica mop the floor?
   B No, she didn't.
4. A Did Mr. and Mrs. Ramirez wash the dishes?
   B No, they didn't.
5. A Did Roberto dry the dishes?
   B Yes, he did.

6. A Did Luis vacuum the rug?
   B No, he didn't.
7. A Did Monica vacuum the rug?
   B Yes, she did.
8. A Did Luis wash the dishes?
   B Yes, he did.

Page 114, Exercise 2A
CD2, Track 34

Last night, Linda had to pay the bills. But first, she bought groceries after work. She paid $15. She got home, and she made dinner. She made soup and salad. She washed and dried the dishes. After dinner, she was very tired. She swept the kitchen floor, but she didn't pay the bills!

Page 115, Exercise 2B
CD2, Track 35

1. A Who bought the groceries?
   B Mom did.
2. A What else did mom do?
   B She did the laundry.
3. A Who got the mail?
   B Sasha did.
4. A What else did Sasha do?
   B She made the beds.
5. A Who vacuumed the rug?
   B Erica did.
6. A What else did Erica do?
   B She dusted the shelves.
7. A What did dad do?
   B Dad cut the grass.
8. A Where is the allowance for Sasha?
   B It's on the table.

Page 116, Exercise 2
CD2, Track 36

Dear Karen,

Welcome home! We were very busy today. Jeff ironed the clothes. Chris emptied the trash. Sharon mopped the floor. Ben vacuumed the rug and dusted the furniture. The house is clean for you! I cooked dinner. There is food on the stove.

Your tired husband,
Lucas

Page 117, Exercise 4A
CD2, Track 37

1. a sponge
2. a mop
3. a vacuum cleaner
4. a dustpan
5. an iron
6. a broom
7. a stove
8. a lawn mower
9. a bucket

Unit 10: Free time

Page 123, Exercises 2A and 2B
CD2, Track 38

Conversation A
A Hi, Diego!
B Oh! Hi, Carla. How are you? You look tired.

A Oh, no, I'm OK. I went hiking yesterday.
B Really, where?
A We went up to Bear Mountain.
B That's great. I'm going to go hiking next weekend.

Conversation B
A Hi, Nicholas. How are you?
B Oh, pretty good. What's new with you?
A Well, we went camping last weekend.
B Really? Did you have fun?
A Yes. When are you going to go camping?
B We're going to go camping next week.

Conversation C
A Hey, Bill. How are you?
B Terrific. I was on vacation all last week.
A Really? What did you do?
B Nothing. I just relaxed all day. When are you going to take a vacation?
A I'm going to take my vacation next month.

Conversation D
A Hi, Shawn. Where were you last Sunday?
B I went with my family to Lookout Park. We went on a picnic.
A Really? I'm going to have a picnic there next weekend.
B Well, watch out for the bees!
A I will. Thanks for telling me about them.

Conversation E
A Lidia, where were you yesterday?
B It was pretty hot, so we went swimming at the lake.
A Really? I'm going to go swimming next weekend.
B Great. Where?
A In the pool at my school.
B Have fun!

Conversation F
A Hey, Barbara, where did you get those fish?
B I went fishing today.
A Where did you go?
B We went to Lake Jenner.
A That sounds like fun. I'm going to go fishing there tomorrow.
B Good luck.

Page 124, Exercise 2A
CD2, Track 39

1. A What did Carl and Gina do last weekend?
   B They went to the zoo.
2. A What did Paul do yesterday?
   B He took a driving test.
3. A What did Diane do last night?
   B She wrote a letter.
4. A What did Mrs. Nelson do last weekend?
   B She saw the fireworks.
5. A What did Mr. Brown do last weekend?
   B He went fishing.
6. A What did Mr. and Mrs. Velez do last Saturday?
   B They went dancing.

7. **A** What did John do yesterday afternoon?
   B He rode his bicycle.
8. **A** What did Ana do last night?
   B She ate some pizza.
9. **A** What did Sophia and Alex do last weekend?
   B They drove to the mountains.

Page 126, Exercise 2A
CD2, Track 40

1. **A** What's Marta going to do next Monday?
   B She's going to take a test.
2. **A** What's Dad going to do next Monday?
   B He's going to pay the rent.
3. **A** What are Mom and Dad going to do next Thursday?
   B They're going to go dancing.
4. **A** What's Paco going to do next Tuesday?
   B He's going to play soccer.
5. **A** What's Alfredo going to do next Wednesday?
   B He's going to ride his bike.
6. **A** What's Mom going to do next Saturday?
   B She's going to do the laundry.
7. **A** What are Alfredo and Marta going to do next Friday?
   B They're going to go to a party.
8. **A** What's Paco going to do next Saturday?
   B He's going to wash the car.
9. **A** What are Mom and Dad going to do next Sunday?
   B They're going to go on a picnic.
10. **A** What's Alfredo going to do next Thursday?
    B He's going to take a guitar class.

Page 128, Exercise 2
CD2, Track 41

Dear Ming,

Last weekend, we went camping in the mountains. I went hiking. My husband and our sons went fishing. They also went swimming in the lake. We all had a great time!
Tonight we're going to eat fish for dinner. After dinner, we're going to watch a movie. Later tonight, we're going to be very busy. We are going to do the laundry. With three boys, we have a lot of dirty clothes!

See you soon,
Maria

Page 129, Exercise 4A
CD2, Track 42

1. football
2. baseball
3. basketball
4. ping-pong
5. ice hockey
6. soccer
7. surfing
8. ice skating
9. skiing

Review: Units 9 and 10

Page 134, Exercise 1
CD2, Track 43

A Hi, Melissa.
B Oh, hi, Ivan!
A How was your weekend?
B It was OK. On Sunday, we went on a picnic in the park.
A Really? That's great. What did you eat?
B Just hamburgers. What about you? How was your weekend?
A Well, on Saturday, we all did our chores at home. I cut the grass. My wife vacuumed the rugs. My son, Tommy, washed the clothes, and my daughter, Lisa, dusted the furniture.
B Wow! You were really busy!

Page 135, Exercise 3A
CD2, Track 44

/d/
cleaned: He cleaned his house.
dried: I dried all the dishes.
emptied: They emptied the trash.

/t/
cooked: They cooked dinner.
talked: She talked on the phone.
washed: She washed the car.

/ɪd/
dusted: I dusted the living room.
folded: He folded his clothes.
painted: They painted the house.

Page 135, Exercise 3B
CD2, Track 45

/d/
exercised
played
turned

/t/
camped
fished
walked

/ɪd/
celebrated
folded
visited

Page 135, Exercise 3C
CD2, Track 46

1. studied
2. ironed
3. mopped
4. rested
5. waited
6. hiked
7. vacuumed
8. worked

ACKNOWLEDGEMENTS

The authors and publishers acknowledge the following sources of copyright material and are grateful for the permissions granted. While every effort has been made, it has not always been possible to identify the sources of all the material used, or to trace all copyright holders. If any omissions are brought to our notice, we will be happy to include the appropriate acknowledgements on reprinting and in the next update to the digital edition, as applicable.

Key: Ex = Exercise, T = Top, B = Below.

Photos

All below images are sourced from GettyImages.

p. 4: Caiaimage/Robert Daly/OJO+; p. 5: izusek/iStock/Getty Images Plus; p. 8 (family): Lane Oatey/Blue Jean Images; p. 8 (photo 1): Ray Kachatorian/The Image Bank; p. 8 (photo 2): Kevin Dodge/Blend Images; p. 8 (photo 3): baileyguinness/Moment; p. 8 (photo 4): SensorSpot/E+; p. 8 (photo 5): RoBeDeRo/E+; p. 8 (photo 6): Katarina Premfors/arabianEye; p. 9: DGLimages/ iStock/Getty Images Plus; p. 13: Klaus Tiedge/Blend Images; p. 15: Ridofranz/iStock/Getty Images Plus; p. 19 (notebook): amnachphoto/iStock/Getty Images Plus; p. 19 (rulers): EugeneTomeev/iStock/Getty Images Plus; p. 19 and p. 22 (book): oboltus/iStock/Getty Images Plus; p. 19 (pens): Ilya_Starikov/ iStock/Getty Images Plus; p. 19 (calculator) and p. 101 (photo 1): Tetra Images; p. 19 (stapler): ScantyNebula/iStock/Getty Images Plus; p. 22 (pencil): Ivantsov/iStock/Getty Images Plus; p. 22 (pencils): seyfettinozel/iStock/Getty Images Plus; p. 22 (clock): PaulPaladin/iStock/Getty Images Plus; p. 22 (clocks): Anthony Bradshaw/Photolibrary; p. 22 (books): Zoonar/P.Malyshev/Getty Images Plus; p. 34 (photo 1): Glow Images, Inc/Glow; p. 34 (photo 2): George Doyle/Stockbyte; p. 34 (photo 3): Stockbyte; p. 34 (photo 4) and p. 129 (photo 8): Hero Images; p. 34 (photo 5) and p. 49 (photo 2): baona/iStock/Getty Images Plus; p. 34 (photo 6): AJ_Watt/iStock/Getty Images Plus; p. 34 (photo 7): Glow Images; p. 34 (photo 8): franckreporter/iStock/ Getty Images Plus; p. 34 (photo 9): Portland Press Herald; p. 35 (woman) and p. 101 (photo 6): kupicoo/E+; p. 35 (man): szefei/ iStock/Getty Images Plus; p. 36 (girl): Tomwang112/iStock/Getty Images Plus; p. 36 (man): laflor/E+; p. 45 (photo 1): klebercordeiro/iStock/Getty Images Plus; p. 45 (photo 2): ullstein bild; p. 45 (photo 3) and p. 49 (photo 4): Antonio_Diaz/iStock/ Getty Images Plus; p. 45 (photo 4): absolutimages/iStock/Getty Images Plus; p. 45 (photo 5): IAN HOOTON/SCIENCE PHOTO LIBRARY; p. 45 (photo 6), p. 46 (photo 1) and p. 103 (photo 2): AndreyPopov/iStock/Getty Images Plus; p. 46 (photo 2): JGI/ Jamie Grill/Blend Images; p. 46 (photo 3): KatarzynaBialasiewicz/ iStock/Getty Images Plus; p. 46 (photo 4): Sasha_Suzi/iStock/ Getty Images Plus; p. 46 (photo 5): chuckcollier/E+; p. 46 (photo 6): parinyabinsuk/iStock/Getty Images Plus; p. 46 (photo 7): BSIP/UIG/Universal Images Group; p. 46 (photo 8) and p. 99 (photo 2): Steve Debenport/E+; p. 46 (photo 9): Koldunov/ iStock/Getty Images Plus; p. 47 (photo 1, 3 and 9): subjug/ iStock/Getty Images Plus; p. 47 (photo 2): Diane Macdonald/ Photographer's Choice RF; p. 47 (photo 4): Fuse; p. 47 (photo 5): winterling/iStock/Getty Images Plus; p. 47 (photo 6): EdnaM/ iStock/Getty Images Plus; p. 47 (photo 7): GARO/PHANIE/ Canopy; p. 47 (photo 8): JoyTasa/iStock/Getty Images Plus; p. 49 (photo 1): PeopleImages/iStock/Getty Images Plus; p. 49 (photo 3): alvarez/iStock/Getty Images Plus; p. 49 (photo 5): Wavebreakmedia/iStock/Getty Images Plus; p. 49 (photo 7): kasinv/iStock/Getty Images Plus; p. 49 (John): Tomwang112/ iStock/Getty Images Plus; p. 49 (Jose): comzeal/iStock/Getty Images Plus; p. 49 (Dick): jjshaw14/iStock/Getty Images Plus;

p. 49 (Jane): philipimage/iStock/Getty Images Plus; p. 59 (photo 1): Juan Camilo Bernal/Moment Mobile; p. 59 (photo 2): Jeffrey Penalosa/EyeEm; p. 59 (photo 3): ClaudineVM/ iStock Editorial/Getty Images Plus; p. 59 (photo 4): Mario Gutiérrez/Moment; p. 59 (photo 5): Sylvain Sonnet/The Image Bank; p. 59 (photo 6): Dan Dalton/Caiaimage; p. 65 (photo 1): Ken Welsh/VisitBritain; p. 65 (photo 2): sshepard/E+; p. 65 (photo 3): Image Source; p. 65 (photo 4): Morsa Images/ DigitalVision; p. 65 (photo 5): Jeff Dunn/Photolibrary; p. 65 (photo 6): davidf/E+; p. 65 (photo 7): Richard Newstead/Moment; p. 65 (photo 8): IPGGutenbergUKLtd/iStock/Getty Images Plus; p. 65 (photo 9): Terry Carter/Dorling Kindersley; p. 69 (photo 1): jojoo64/iStock/Getty Images Plus; p. 69 (photo 2): GoodGnom/ DigitalVision Vectors; p. 69 (photo 3): TuelekZa/iStock/Getty Images Plus; p. 69 (photo 4): daizuoxin/iStock/Getty Images Plus; p. 69 (photo 5): arcady_31/iStock/Getty Images Plus; p. 69 (photo 6): alessandro0770/iStock/Getty Images Plus; p. 72 (photo 1): JGI/Tom Grill/Blend Images; p. 72 (photo 2): Portra/DigitalVision; p. 72 (photo 3): Peter Cade/The Image Bank; p. 72 (photo 4): Tang Ming Tung/Taxi; p. 72 (photo 5): SrdjanPav/ E+; p. 72 (photo 6) and p. 99 (photo 3): Westend61; p. 85 (photo 1): SvetlanaK/iStock/Getty Images Plus; p. 85 (photo 2): fcafotodigital/iStock/Getty Images Plus; p. 85 (photo 3): kuarmungadd/iStock/Getty Images Plus; p. 85 (photo 4): 4x6/ iStock/Getty Images Plus; p. 85 (photo 5): chictype/E+; p. 85 (photo 6): Topic Images Inc./Topic Images; p. 86 (photo 1): ClaudioVentrella/iStock/Getty Images Plus; p. 86 (photo 2): H. Armstrong Roberts/ClassicStock/Archive Photos; p. 86 (photo 3): nepstock/iStock/Getty Images Plus; p. 86 (photo 4): Jpecha/E+; p. 86 (photo 5): Garsya/iStock/Getty Images Plus; p. 86 (photo 6): anna1311/iStock/Getty Images Plus; p. 86 (photo 7): chengyuzheng/iStock/Getty Images Plus; p. 86 (photo 8): Lew Robertson/Photolibrary; p. 86 (photo 9): kyoshino/ iStock/Getty Images Plus; p. 86 (photo 10): bergamont/iStock/ Getty Images Plus; p. 86 (photo 11): pioneer111/iStock/Getty Images Plus; p. 86 (photo 12): jsmith/iStock/Getty Images Plus; p. 91 (photo 10): StockImages_AT/iStock/Getty Images Plus; p. 91 (photo 11): jauhari1/iStock/Getty Images Plus; p. 97 (photo 1): JPWALLET/iStock/Getty Images Plus; p. 97 (photo 2): Jose Luis Pelaez Inc/Blend Images; p. 97 (photo 3): Beau Lark/ Corbis/VCG/Corbis; p. 97 (photo 4): Andersen Ross/DigitalVision; p. 97 (photo 5): shapecharge/iStock/Getty Images Plus; p. 97 (photo 6): matthewennisphotography/iStock/Getty Images Plus; p. 99 (photo 1): Klaus Vedfelt/Taxi; p. 99 (photo 4): Reza Estakhrian/The Image Bank; p. 99 (photo 5): Hill Street Studios/ Blend Images; p. 99 (photo 6): Butch Martin/Photographer's Choice; p. 101 (photo 2): Gary John Norman/Taxi; p. 101 (photo 3): Monty Rakusen/Cultura; p. 101 (photo 4): Musketeer/ DigitalVision; p. 101 (photo 5): skynesher/E+; p. 103 (photo 1): Chris Ryan/OJO Images; p. 103 (photo 3):stevecoleimages/E+; p. 103 (photo 4): Philippe Roy/Cultura; p. 103 (photo 5): GoodLifeStudio/E+; p. 103 (photo 6): RapidEye/E+; p. 111 (photo 1): Lumina Images/Blend Images; p. 111 (photo 2): Andrew_Howe/E+; p. 111 (photo 3): SolStock/iStock/Getty Images Plus; p. 111 (photo 4), p. 123 (photo 1 and 2): kali9/E+; p. 111 (photo 5): Manfred Rutz/Photodisc; p. 111 (photo 6): MichalLudwiczak/iStock/Getty Images Plus; p. 117 (photo 1):

flubydust/E+; p. 117 (photo 2): EdnaM/iStock/Getty Images Plus; p. 117 (photo 3): DonNichols/iStock/Getty Images Plus; p. 117 (photo 4): GeniusKp/iStock/Getty Images Plus; p. 117 (photo 5): Floortje/E+; p. 117 (photo 6): Comstock/Stockbyte; p. 117 (photo 7): ppart/iStock/Getty Images Plus; p. 117 (photo 8): Travis Manley/Hemera/Getty Images Plus; p. 117 (photo 9): flyfloor/E+; p. 123 (photo 3): CO2/Stockbyte; p. 123 (photo 4): Aliyev Alexei Sergeevich/Cultura; p. 123 (photo 5): Trinette Reed/ Blend Images; p. 123 (photo 6): Atli Mar Hafsteinsson/Cultura; p. 124: Dear Blue/Moment; p. 129 (photo 1): YinYang/E+; p. 129 (photo 2): Tomasz Szymanski/Hemera/Getty Images Plus; p. 129 (photo 3): monkeybusinessimages/iStock/Getty Images Plus; p. 129 (photo 4): technotr/E+; p. 129 (photo 5): simonkr/E+; p. 129 (photo 6): Thomas Barwick/Taxi; p. 129 (photo 7): Specker/Vedfelt/Taxi; p. 129 (photo 9): Christoph Jorda/ LOOK-foto/LOOK; p. 130: dibrova/iStock/Getty Images Plus; p. 131 (T): Francisco Rama/EyeEm; p. 131 (B): greenicetea/E+; p. 135: -nelis-/iStock/Getty Images Plus; p. 137 (photo 1): Caiaimage/Sam Edwards; p. 137 (photo 2, photo 4): Stuart Paton/Photodisc; p. 137 (photo 3): NorioNakayama/iStock/Getty Images Plus; p. 138: karelnoppe/iStock/Getty Images Plus; p. 139 (photo 1): Jeffrey Coolidge/Iconica; p. 139 (photo 2): Hailshadow/iStock/Getty Images Plus; p. 139 (photo 3), p. 147 (photo 1): Jeffrey Coolidge/The Image Bank; p. 139 (photo 4): Raimund Koch/The Image Bank; p. 140: blue jean images; p. 141 (photo 1): jxfzsy/iStock/Getty Images Plus; p. 141 (photo 2): Studio Paggy; p. 141 (photo 3): Olivia Collins/EyeEm; p. 141 (photo 4): ABERRATION FILMS LTD/SCIENCE PHOTO LIBRARY; p. 142: Image Source; p. 143 (photo 1): Adrian Pope/ Photographer's Choice; p. 143 (photo 2): BSIP/UIG/Universal Images Group; p. 143 (photo 3): Gurpal Singh Datta/Canopy; p. 143 (photo 4): Science Photo Library - CDC/Brand X Pictures; p. 144: Guido Mieth/Taxi; p. 145 (photo 1): Image Source/ DigitalVision; p. 145 (photo 2): Maria Wachala/Moment; p. 145 (photo 3): 3D_generator/iStock/Getty Images Plus; p. 145 (photo 4): Richard Newstead/Moment; p. 146: PixelEmbargo/ iStock/Getty Images Plus; p. 147 (photo 2), p. 151 (photo 2): Dougal Waters/DigitalVision; p. 147 (photo 3): Maskot; p. 147 (photo 4): Jaimie Duplass/Hemera; p. 148: PhotoAlto/James Hardy/ PhotoAlto Agency RF Collections; p. 149 (photo 1): Dave and Les Jacobs/Lloyd Dobbie/Blend Images; p. 149 (photo 2, photo 3): Lucy Clark/Hemera/Getty Images Plus; p. 149 (photo 4): Tetra Images; p. 150: Dean Mitchell/Taxi; p. 151 (photo 1): Lucy Lambriex/Taxi; p. 151 (photo 3): deeepblue/ iStock/Getty Images Plus; p. 151 (photo 4): Echo/Juice Images; p. 152: Ariel Skelley/Blend Images; p. 153 (photo 1): Brand X Pictures/Stockbyte/Getty Images Plus; p. 153 (photo 2): Tetra Images; p. 153 (photo 3): Adam Gault/OJO Images; p. 153 (photo 4): Image Source/DigitalVision; p. 154: Hero Images; p. 155 (photo 1): Alexey Ivanov/EyeEm; p. 155 (photo 2): PeopleImages/DigitalVision; p. 155 (photo 3): Eva Moore/EyeEm; p. 155 (photo 4): Daniel Walls/EyeEm.

Below images are sourced from other libraries.

p. 49 (photo 6): Gabriel Blaj/Fotolia; p. 91 (photo 12): robertindiana/ Shutterstock; p. 91 (bank notes): Currency Images are courtesy of the Bureau of Engraving and Printing; p. 91 (coins): United States coin images from the United States Mint.

Illustrations

p. 2, p. 17, p. 19, p. 20, p. 23, p. 24, p. 25 (1, 4, 6), p. 29, p. 35, p. 37 (B), p. 38, p. 39, p. 43, p. 48, p. 55, p. 69, p. 74, p. 95, p. 96, p. 100, p. 105, p. 112, p. 113, p. 114 (3), p. 116, p. 121 and p. 133: QBS Learning; p. 11, p. 40 and p. 51 (T): Frank Montagna; p. 21, p. 107 and p. 127: Greg Paprocki; p. 22, p. 27, p. 73, p. 92 and p. 114 (1, 2, 4): Monika Roe; p. 25 (2, 3, 5, 7, 8, 9), p. 66 and p. 77: Jim Kopp; p. 37 (T), p. 87: Cybele; p. 60 (B), p. 61, p. 63: Maria Rabinky; p. 78: Travis Foster; p. 89: Kenneth Batelman; p. 100: Lucie Rice.

Back cover photography by PressureUA/iStock Getty Images Plus; Adidet Chaiwattanakul/EyeEm; pixelfit/E+.

Front cover photography by Kathrin Ziegler/Taxi/Getty Images.

Audio produced by CityVox.

AMERICAN
TIN-LITHO
TOYS

AMERICAN TIN-LITHO TOYS

By Lisa Kerr

Collectors Press
Portland, Oregon

DISCLAIMER

The vast information in this book has been compiled from the most reliable sources. Sincere efforts have been made to eliminate errors and questionable information. Nevertheless, errors are possible in a work of this scope. Neither the publisher nor the author will be held responsible for losses that may occur in either the purchase, sale or any other type of transaction because of information contained herein.

Design by Kim McLaughlin
Photography by Adam Griffith
Additional Photography by Robert Bruce Kerr

First Edition, 1995

Additional copies of this book may be ordered by sending
$29.95 plus $3.00 shipping to:

Collectors Press
P.O. Box 230986
Portland, Oregon 97281

ISBN #0-9635202-7-X
Printed in Singapore

Library of Congress Catalog Card Number : 95-69602

ACKNOWLEDGMENTS

IT is hard to know how to thank all of the people who have so generously helped me with this book. They have taken time out of busy schedules to share their knowledge and their collections with me. I would especially like to thank the following individuals:

Shirley and Jim Cox of Seattle; **Dorothy Ellen Masters** of Oregon
Dora C. Pohl and **Tom Frogge** of the Lily Pad in Tacoma, Washington
Heather Baker of Bakers Dozen Antiques in Vancouver, British Columbia
Connie and Robert Delaney of Nashville, Tennessee
Pat and Norma Weathersby of The Antique Colony in Aurora, Oregon
Jack and Barbara Craig of Craigs' Four Seasons Antiques in Aurora, Oregon
LaDonna Dolan, **Dorothea Sells** and **Claudette Job** of Old Town Antique Mall
    in Bellingham, Washington
Mike Milson of The Black Cat Antique Mall in Snohomish, Washington
Patty Cooper of Knoxville, Tennessee
Jim Gilcher of Ohio; **Laure St. Moritz** of Pennsylvania
Lisa and Carol of Rosa Mundi's Antiques in Edmonds, Washington
Margarie Bulett of WOLVERINE Company (now TODAY'S KIDS)
Carrie Killgallon of the OHIO ART Company
Bob McCumber, CHEIN expert and Connecticut author
Gaston Majeune, Toys in the Attic, Englewood, New Jersey

I would also like to thank my friends **Rita and John Griffith**, my dad, **Dr. Solomon Dworkin**, and my cousin **Sandra Dworkin** for their help.

I especially want to thank the photographer for this book, **Adam Griffith**, who never complained when I dragged him 120 miles without notice to photograph a few toys in some small town. I also thank my husband **Bruce** for contributing his significant photographic skills whenever needed.

CONTENTS

PREFACE

HAVE you ever noticed that addicted collectors cannot remember a time when they were not collecting *something?* I began collecting shells as a young child. Rocks, postcards, plastic purses and china figures followed. As I grew older, I graduated to beaded handbags, Bakelite and tin win-up toys. I clearly remember the summer day, a few years ago, when I was in a small antique store on the Oregon coast. I looked up high on a shelf and spotted two large tin-litho sandpails. One pictured chubby children playing at the seaside. I caught my breath. That sandpail brought back almost palpable childhood memories of sun-filled vacation days at the beach in Cape Cod with my family. I returned home to Seattle and thought about the sandpails. When I called back to the little store to buy them, they were gone!

No matter what the theme, all the toys share one predominant characteristic -- innocence. These toys were the product of a different world. Although it was far from perfect, it was a world in which neighborhoods were relatively safe, our streets were not a battleground, and children could play outside on summer nights until dark. Television did not dominate children's lives, nor did they spend hours immobile before a screen frenetically clicking a Nintendo control. Our children's world is no longer simple and innocent. It is partly the loss of this kind of world, and the memory of it, that makes these toys so appealing to me.

Regardless of one's reasons for collecting, however, it can really be fun. And the toys are beautiful! Only another collector can appreciate how thrilling it is to find an unusual toy and be able to identify its date and maker. I hope this book will contribute to the fun of collecting. Happy hunting, and don't be surprised when one day scientists announce that they've discovered a "collector's gene"!

INTRODUCTION

I COLLECTED much of the information in this book from researching books, magazine articles, and old catalogues and advertisements. I also amassed a great deal of information from talking to collectors, dealers, librarians, and authors from across the United States and Canada. When I was really fortunate, I spoke with people who either presently work for toy companies or worked for them in the past. It is amazing how generous people have been with their knowledge.

In several cases I was able to obtain beautiful copies of old catalogues issued by toy companies to advertise and promote their line of toys for a particular season. Some of these catalogues date back to the 1920s and are attractive enough to frame in their own right.

The toys pictured in this book represent only some of the toys of some of the major toy companies that existed from the 1920s through the 1960s. I tried to concentrate on companies that have been the subject of very little research, such as OHIO ART and WOLVERINE, rather than to present an in-depth study of the toys any one toy company produced. This book is meant to provide a general introduction and price guide for *some* of the toys. Moreover, each category of toys, such as wind-ups or banks, is far from complete. There is already a great deal of published information about certain categories of toys; for example, play sets, automotive toys and battery operated toys. I intentionally avoided these categories. Also available are excellent in-depth books on MARX toys, banks, and wind-ups of particular periods. See the Bibliography for more information.

All of the photographs in this book are either of toys from my own collection or those of other collectors and dealers who generously opened their doors to my photographer and let us take pictures, either in their homes or in their shops. Sometimes, if collectors lived too far away, they were kind enough to take the pictures themselves and send them. Thus, in a few cases, the quality of some of the photographs is a bit inconsistent.

WHAT IS TIN-LITHO?

MANY of the toys referred to as tin-litho are actually tin-plated steel. The colorful designs were applied through a process known as chromolithography. The term "lithography" comes from the Greek language and means "stone drawing" or "writing." This technique was originally used in print-making. A drawing was made on a specially prepared stone with a greasy crayon. The stone was wetted and then inked. The ink adhered to the drawn design and was repelled by the rest of the wet surface. Thus, the ink drawing itself printed the design onto paper and not the negative space as in a woodcut, for example.

In the late 1800s a process called "offset lithography" was used to print designs from a rubber composition roller onto tin-plated sheets. By the 1930s the process was further advanced and machines were developed that could lithograph over fifty tin-plated sheets per minute. Overlapping hues produced new hues, and varying applications of color density resulted in different shades as well. Thus, a wide palate of colors was available to the toy designer.

QUALITY AND PRICING

With a few exceptions, I have used two categories of toys for the purposes of pricing and the reader should extrapolate from there. The categories are "good" and "excellent." "Excellent" indicates no dents or rust and that the piece is clean and appears unused except for perhaps some minor scratches and/or other very minor signs of wear. "Good" indicates some wear in places, maybe some small scratches or small dents, but fairly clean. Although there may be a bit of rust, for example, on the underside of a sand pail or inside of a teacup, there is no rust on any of the lithography.

The one exception to this categorization is the addition of Mint in Box (MIB) for tin-litho tea sets. Because tea sets contain so many small parts, the box is often the only assurance that all the pieces came from the same dye-lot or year, or the same set. Moreover, there is something intrinsically charming about all the little pieces set out on cardboard in the box. Thus, the box is a big issue for tea sets, and I will include the MIB category, which basically means it is unused.

In general, the box can add anywhere from 25 percent to 100 percent to the value of a toy in excellent condition. It depends on the type and age of the toy and the charm of the box. For example, a dollhouse, MIB, usually means the dollhouse has never even been assembled. Thus, the metal tabs that hold the house together are fresh, and all the little extra parts, like doors and chimneys, are present. This can double the value of a dollhouse. Sand sets that include molds, shovels, and sand sieves will double in value if they are on their original card for the same reasons that the box increases the value of tea sets.

Similarly, a box in excellent condition can add 75 percent to the value of a wind-up toy. In other cases, however, the box is not a great issue. For example, some sand pails, noisemakers, tops, and drums were shipped in groups in cartons—there were no individual boxes.

Prices for purposes of this book were established by speaking with toy dealers across the nation and determining an average.

Regional Differences. Without a doubt, all of the dealers I spoke with agree on one thing—toys are becoming more expensive everywhere. Because toys are more plentiful in the mid-west and on the east coast, a buyer is more likely to find bargains in these regions than on the west coast where there are fewer toys. Many east coast dealers told me that much of their business comes from west coast buyers who find the prices on the east coast significantly lower. Moreover, I know quite a few west coast dealers who make regular trips to the southern United States in search of good buys on toys. In general, however, as toys become more popular, the prices become more uniform across the country.

IDENTIFICATION AND DATING

I have sometimes been frustrated by toy books that lack information on either the company that made the toy or the date it was made. Now, having undertaken my own book, I realize how difficult accurate dating can be. In part, this is because so many companies produced the same toy with the same lithography year after year—sometimes for decades.

For example, WOLVERINE manufactured the "Gee Wiz" Racing Game, No. 40, illustrated in Figure 1, from the mid-1920s through the 1950s.

WOLVERINE also produced a tin-litho carousel, No. 31, in 1936. It remained unchanged until 1950 when the lithography on the canopy and base was changed to include circus animals. It was renumbered 31a. (See Figures 2 and 3.) But the 1957 WOLVERINE catalogue advertises the old No. 31 with the old lithography; No. 31a is nowhere to be seen! A plausible explanation is that the company sold out of 31a and had some backstock of 31 to unload. However, this does not help the poor collector trying to determine a date for his or her toy.

CHEIN is another company that produced the same toy over a long time span while OHIO ART and MARX made more frequent changes in design, color, and lithography.

One of the best ways to get a ballpark date for a particular toy is to be familiar with the changes in the company's logo. Logos or factory locations often changed throughout the years, and the ability to recognize those changes facilitates dating. I will point out the changes in logos that I am familiar with when I discuss a particular toy company.

If I specified a year or years for a toy, it means that I found that toy listed in a catalogue for that year, but it does *not* mean that the toy was produced or sold in the listed years exclusively. As explained above, often a toy was produced for many years or decades with no changes. If I use the word "circa" and a date, it indicates that I did not find the toy in a catalogue but dated it by other means, such as logo style, and the date is approximate.

Fig. 1:
"Gee Wiz" Racing Game.

Fig. 2:
WOLVERINE carousel, No. 31, advertised in 1936 catalogue.

Fig. 3:
WOLVERINE carousel, No. 31a, advertised in 1950 catalogue.

Fig. 1

Fig. 2

Fig. 3

THE TOY COMPANIES

OHIO ART

IN many ways, OHIO ART is the quintessential American company. Dentist Henry Winzeler started the company in 1908 with the manufacture of oval picture frames in a loft in Archbold, Ohio. Winzeler chose the name OHIO ART to reflect his lifelong interest in art. Little did he know that he was laying the foundation for what would become one of the premiere producers of tin lithographed toys in the United States.

In 1917 OHIO ART bought Erie Toy Plant which produced "Zippo the Climbing Monkey" for Ferdinand Strauss. Louis Marx later purchased Erie from Winzeler, and it became the foundation for the MARX Toy Company.

In 1917 Winzeler purchased property in Bryan, Ohio. The first toy produced in Bryan was a lithographed metal tea set. In November of 1920 Winzeler displayed a line of tin-litho tea sets with the alphabet around the outer edge of the plates and saucers at the New York Toy Fair. In 1930 OHIO ART incorporated, and in 1931 the company paid its shareholders their first dividend of $6 per share.

OHIO ART not only produced lovely toys, but took its duties as a good citizen seriously. In 1926, Winzeler offered to donate $25,000 to Bryan for a hospital. From 1942 to 1944, the company stopped toy production and converted to war products such as tent pole ferrules, rocket parts, and celestial astrodomes for Flying Fortress navigation. In fact, in 1945 the OHIO ART Company was honored with the Army-Navy Production Award which was received by only four percent of U.S. companies.

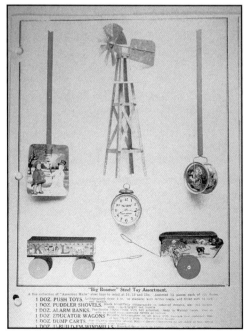

Fig. 4

Fig. 5

Fig. 6

Fig. 4:
Full-page color advertisement from 1929 to 1930 OHIO ART catalogue.

Figs. 5 and 6:
Early OHIO ART logos.

Toy production resumed in 1945, when the war restrictions on steel were lifted, and OHIO ART continued to grow. In 1948 the company exhibited its first item containing a plastic part, and in 1953 it produced its own internally manufactured plastics. In 1955, OHIO ART purchased Tacoma Metal Products Company, which made working toy electric stoves that bore the name "Little Chef." In 1960 the company began producing the well-known "Etch-a-Sketch." The year 1983 marked the 75th birthday of OHIO ART. The company is in operation to this day as a publicly held corporation in Bryan, Ohio.

OHIO ART logos have gone through a series of transformations making OHIO ART toys relatively easy for the collector to date. The earliest toys simply read:

> "Ohio Art Company, Bryan O. U.S.A." or
> "Ohio Art, U.S.A." or
> "Ohio Art Company, U.S.A."

Logos are pictured in Figures 5-10.

Often OHIO ART would use the designs of well-known illustrators for their colorful lithography. A striking example is the work of Fern Bisel Peat, an illustrator of children's books popular in the 1930s and 1940s. Because many collectors value her work, they are often willing to pay more for pieces lithographed with her designs.

Fig. 7:
The OHIO ART logo from 1945 to 1959.

Fig. 8:
The OHIO ART logo from 1959 to 1962.

Fig. 9:
The OHIO ART logo from 1963 to 1971.

Fig. 10:
The OHIO ART logo from 1972 to 1978.

Fig. 7

Fig. 9

Fig. 8

Fig. 10

WOLVERINE

The WOLVERINE Supply and Mfg. Co., founded in 1903 by Benjamin F. Bain, was named after the mascot for the University of Michigan, Bain's alma mater. The factory was located in Pittsburgh, Pennsylvania. The company originally made and repaired tools and dies for manufacturers. Not long after it began business, Wolverine was contracted to manufacture tools for a sand toy. The toy manufacturer went out of business and WOLVERINE decided to use the tools to enter the toy business, producing the "Sandy Andy," a gravity-action toy.

Three of WOLVERINE's early lines were "Sandy Andy," "Sunny Andy," and "Sunny Suzy." In addition to sand and action toys, WOLVERINE produced chime sets, pressure-lever operated merry-go-rounds, and a large variety of games, including shooting galleries, marble games, and pin-ball action type games. In 1926 WOLVERINE began making girls' housekeeping items, treasured by collectors today. These include cannister sets, sinks, stoves, and refrigerators with an array of food lithographed on the inside doors.

WOLVERINE prided itself on producing toys that combined "ingenious diversion with worthwhile instruction." Some of these toys included "The Little Gardener," introduced in 1931, which was an indoor/outdoor planting set including clay flower pots with saucers, packets of seeds, a sprinkling can, shovel, rake, hoe, pail, can of fertilizer and sieve. One of the most unusual educational toys was the Litho-Art Set, offered in 1936, which allowed children to reproduce ink and pencil drawings (see Figure 11). The set included an opal lithographing stone, rollers, inking plate, pencil, and various fluids, inks, and fixatives. All were packed in a "handsome wood box with metal clasp."

Other well-known toys included the company's "Delft Blue" tin-litho dish set and cannister sets produced from the early 1940s through the 1960s.

In 1968 Spang and Company acquired WOLVERINE. In 1971 the company moved to its new headquarters in Booneville, Arkansas, in the heart of the Ozark and Ouachita Mountains. Thus, if a toy is marked Booneville, Arkansas, you know it was made in the 1970s through the mid 1980s. Prior to the 1970s, pieces were made in Pittsburgh.

The WOLVERINE logo, pictured in Figure 12, remained essentially unchanged from the 1920s through the 1970s.

Fig. 11

Fig. 12

Fig. 13

Fig. 11:
Advertisement from WOLVERINE catalogue, 1936.

Fig. 12:
WOLVERINE logo.

Fig. 13:
WOLVERINE toy catalogue, 1955.

In 1986 the company's name was changed to TODAY'S KIDS. Today the company continues to manufacture many toys including the "Busy Center," an activity center for young children, and the "All Star Basketball Set."

MARX

The legendary Louis Marx began working in the toy industry when he was 16 years old. He started with Ferdinand Strauss in 1912, and by 1919 he incorporated his own company, Louis Marx and Company. His company was incredibly successful. MARX depended on large volume sales to keep costs down. MARX toys were carried in chain stores, such as Woolworth's, Sears, and J.C. Penney. By the 1950s, MARX had several overseas factories, including a Japanese company making toys under the name LINEMAR.

As one of the biggest toy manufacturers in the world, MARX produced a staggering variety of designs and lithography. The company continued to produce toys until 1972, when it was sold to the Quaker Oats Company. Quaker eventually sold to Dunbee-Combex, Ltd., which went bankrupt in 1980. An excellent source for information on older MARX toys is *Greenberg's Guide to Marx Toys*, Volume I, by Maxine A. Pinsky.

J. CHEIN & CO.

In 1903 Julius Chein founded J. CHEIN & CO. The company moved from its original New York location to Harrison, New Jersey, in 1907. In 1947, the company relocated to Burlington, New Jersey, where it produced toys until 1979.

J. CHEIN & CO. is well-known among today's collectors for its beautifully lithographed tops, banks, drums, and sand toys, as well as several outstanding wind-up toys, including its Ferris wheel and roller coaster. Much of the credit for these lovely toys goes to Gene Bosch, a designer and model maker who worked for J. CHEIN & CO. for 44 years. In the 1970s the government introduced new safety regulations, which made it difficult for CHEIN to remain competitive in the toy business.

CHEIN, like WOLVERINE, produced some of its toys year after year—sometimes over decades. Often the same molds were used but the lithography changed. A striking example is the little wind-up bear pictured in Figure 14.

Figures 15 through 22 illustrate a sequence of CHEIN logos.

Fig. 14:
CHEIN wind-up bear's evolution. The logos on the toys changed throughout the decades, which facilitates dating.

Fig. 15:
Circa 1920s or even earlier, name in a circular pattern with "Made in U.S.A."

Fig. 16:
Circa 1920s, printed circle added around the words.

Fig. 14

Fig. 15

Fig. 16

T. COHN, INC.

T. COHN, INC., is a lesser-known toy company that produced many charming lithographed toys. These include sand pails, noisemakers, and a fabulous line of dollhouses, as well as gas stations and airports. In the late 1930s T. COHN advertised a line of carnival and Halloween noisemakers as well as "Popeye" sand pails and other tin-litho items. In the 1940s T. COHN began producing metal dollhouses, and by 1960 the company advertised only "large" lithographed toys. The T. COHN factory was located in Brooklyn, New York, until 1970, when it appears to have gone out of business. Early T. COHN toys are marked with the symbol pictured in Figure 23. Figure 24 illustrates a subsequent logo. Later dollhouses are marked "T. COHN, Inc." or "Another Superior Toy by T. COHN."

KIRCHHOF PATENT CO., INC.

The KIRCHHOF PATENT CO., INC., was founded by German toymaker Charles Kirchhof in 1852. It produced, among other things, tin-litho banks, toys, novelties, and noisemakers. In the 1940s KIRCHHOF began producing the "Life of the Party" line from their plant in Newark, New Jersey. They touted the "new machinery" and "modern ideas" associated with this line. KIRCHHOF was still active under the KIRCHHOF name until 1965.

FERDINAND STRAUSS

Ferdinand Strauss began importing toys in the early 1900s. He started manufacturing his own toys in the early 1900s in his New Jersey factory. Two of his toys, "Zippo the Climbing Monkey" and a clockwork minstrel toy, were two of the first tin-litho mechanical toys to be produced in great numbers in the United States. "Zippo" was actually manufactured for STRAUSS in the Erie plant of C.E. Carter Company, which was purchased by OHIO ART in 1917. In the 1920s the Erie plant was sold to Louis Marx. Marx bought the dies for the monkey and the minstrel. Strauss sold his company in 1921 but continued to produce toys until the 1940s.

Fig. 17   Fig. 18   Fig. 19   Fig. 20

Fig. 17:
Tri-colored shield, circa 1930s.

Fig. 18:
Black and white or red and white shield, circa 1940s.

Fig. 19:
Plain shield, circa 1950s to 1967.

Fig. 20:
Clown logo, 1967.

U.S. METAL TOYS

U.S. METAL TOYS produced sand sets, snow shovels, trumpets, noisemakers, and horns from their factory in New York from the 1940s clear into the 1980s. They also produced metal tambourines with pictures of romantic Gypsies, Spanish dancers, and Halloween themes. U.S. METAL TOYS was still producing noisemakers in 1979. The wooden handles were replaced with plastic by 1965.

NASSAU PRODUCTS CORP.

NASSAU PRODUCTS CORP. produced strollers, walkers, and sulkies for dolls in Freeport, New York, until 1952, when it relocated to Troy, New York. It would appear that in 1965, NASSAU went out of business.

E. & L. MFG. CO.

E. & L. MFG. CO., located in New York, was known for producing carpet sweepers and nursery sets. In 1960 E. & L. added baseball, football, badminton, and croquet sets to its line. By 1965 E. & L. advertised only sports equipment and toys.

WYANDOTTE

WYANDOTTE, of Wyandotte, Michigan, produced toys from the 1920s through 1956. WYANDOTTE was best known for transportation toys, but also produced charming doll buggies, games, and mechanical toys like the incredible carnival pictured in Figure 528. WYANDOTTE was purchased by Louis Marx in the 1950s.

UNIQUE ARTS

UNIQUE ARTS MFG. CO. was in business from around 1916 until 1952. The company is best known for its wind-up toys including "Bombo the Monk," the "Kiddie Cyclist," and "Li'l Abner's Dogpatch Band." UNIQUE ARTS was located in Newark, New Jersey, until it was purchased in the 1950s by Louis Marx.

Fig. 21:
Spiral logo, 1969.

Fig. 22:
Spiral logo with smaller spiral and larger words, 1972.

Fig. 23:
T. COHN logo, 1920s and 1930s.

Fig. 24:
T. COHN logo, late 1930s and 1940s.

Fig. 21

Fig. 22

Fig. 23

Fig. 24

SAND PAILS AND SAND TOYS

PERHAPS it's because sand pails provide such a broad, uninterrupted canvas for design that they contain some of the most clever and charming lithography. OHIO ART produced many Disney sand pails in the 1930s and 1940s with fabulous pictures of Mickey, Minnie, and Donald engaged in a multitude of activities. Beach scenes and nursery rhymes were also popular themes.

Especially amusing is the "Butt Bucket" produced by OHIO ART and shown in Figure 53. This pail was handy at the beach to avoid throwing those burning cigarette butts in the sand where others might step on them.

The switch to plastic was more practical, as it solved the rust problem. However, plastic pails have very little personality when compared to the tin-litho sand pails of past decades. Sandpails make nice displays as well.

Prices are based on age, rarity, design, and size. For purposes of these photographs, small is 2-1/2 to 4-1/2 inches tall; medium is 5 to 6 inches tall; and large is 6 to 8 inches tall.

Fig. 25:
Full-page advertisement from J. CHEIN catalogue, 1958.

Fig. 26:
"Victorian Sand pail," circa early 1900s. (Courtesy of Tom Frogge.) This pail has an eagle embossed into the bottom.
Medium size, Excellent $175; Good $125.

Fig. 27:
Eagle embossed on the inside bottom of Victorian Sand pail.

Fig. 28:
"Victorian Sand pail," circa 1920s. (Courtesy of Jack and Barbara Craig.)
Medium size, Excellent $165; Good $115.

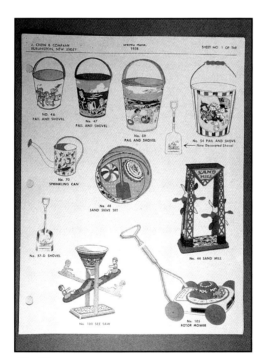

Fig. 25

Fig. 27

Fig. 26

Fig. 28

Fig. 29

Fig. 30

Fig. 31

Fig. 32

Fig. 33

Fig. 29:
"Mickey Mouse on Tropical Island," by OHIO ART, Walt Disney Enterprises, circa early 1930s. (Courtesy of Claudette Job.)
Small size, Excellent $250; Good $190.

Fig. 30:
"Mickey Mouse Lemonade Stand," by OHIO ART, 1937 to 1940, Walt Disney Enterprises. (Courtesy of Michael Milson.) This pail came as part of a fabulous sand set.
Small size, Excellent $235; Good $175.

Fig. 31:
"Donald Duck," by OHIO ART, Walt Disney Enterprises, 1938. (Courtesy of Michael Milson.)
Small size, Excellent $235; Good $175.

Fig. 32:
"Popeye," by T. COHN, circa 1930s. (Courtesy of Claudette Job.)
Large size, Excellent $250; Good $175.

Fig. 33:
"Three Little Pigs," by CHEIN, circa 1930s. (Courtesy of Claudette Job.)
Small size, Excellent $150; Good $100.

Fig. 34:
"Dutch Children," by
CHEIN, 1936. (Courtesy of
Claudette Job.)
*Large size, Excellent $135;
Good $100.*

Fig. 35:
"Carousel," by WOLVER-
INE, first issued in 1936
and still produced in 1959.
*Medium size, Excellent $75;
Good $60.*

Fig. 36:
"Nursery Rhymes," by
CHEIN, 1938 through
1960.
*Medium size, Excellent $85;
Good $55.*

Fig. 37:
"Donald Duck, Muscle
Beach," Walt Disney
Productions, by OHIO
ART, 1939. (Courtesy of
Shirley Cox.)
*Small size, Excellent $255;
Good $175.*

Fig. 38:
"Gulliver's Travels," by
CHEIN, 1939, copyright
Paramount Pictures.
*Small size, Excellent $100;
Good $65.*

Fig. 34

Fig. 36

Fig. 35

Fig. 37

Fig. 38

Fig. 39

Fig. 40

Fig. 41

Fig. 42

Fig. 43

Fig. 39:
"Barnacle Bill," circa 1930s.
(Courtesy of Claudette
Job.)
*Small size, Excellent $150;
Good $100.*

Fig. 40:
"Polar Bears," by OHIO
ART, 1942. (Courtesy of
Claudette Job.)
*Large size, Excellent $140;
Good $100.*

Fig. 41:
"Battleship Animals," by
OHIO ART, 1942.
(Courtesy of Claudette
Job.)
*Small size, Excellent $110;
Good $75.*

Fig. 42:
"Ducky Bath," by OHIO
ART, circa early 1940s,
designed by Fern Bisel
Peat. (Courtesy of
Claudette Job.)
*Small size, Excellent $150;
Good $95.*

Fig. 43:
"Geese on a Stroll," by
FBA, American company,
circa 1940s.
*Medium size, Excellent $65;
Good $35.*

Fig. 44:
"Piggies at the Beach," by
T. COHN, circa 1939 to
1940s.
*Large size, Excellent $100;
Good $75.*

Fig. 45:
"Bubble-Blowing Cow," by
T. COHN, circa 1930s to
1940s.
*Medium size, Excellent $85;
Good $60.*

Fig. 46:
"The Owl and the
Pussycat," by T. COHN,
circa 1939s to 1940s.
(Courtesy of Claudette
Job.)
*Medium size, Excellent $100;
Good $75.*

Fig. 47:
"Three Cheers for the Red,
White, and Blue," by T.
COHN, circa 1930s.
(Courtesy of Claudette
Job.)
*Large size, Excellent $125;
Good $90.*

Fig. 48:
"Beach and Boardwalk," by
T. COHN, circa 1920s.
*Large size, Excellent $125;
Good $100.*

Fig. 44

Fig. 45

Fig. 46

Fig. 47

Fig. 48

Fig. 49

Fig. 50

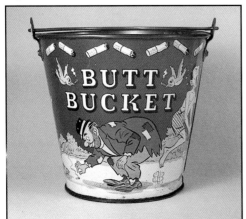

Fig. 53

Fig. 51

Fig. 52

Fig. 49:
Same as Figure 48, except some versions had lithography of a little girl and boy on the bottom, inside of the pail.
Add $25.

Fig. 50:
"Animal Bathtime," by T. COHN, circa 1930s.
Medium size, Excellent $75; Good $55.

Fig. 51:
"Three Pigs," by T. COHN, circa 1940s.
Medium size, Excellent $85; Good $65.

Fig. 52:
"Animal Picnic," by CHEIN, circa late 1940s to early 1950s.
Medium size, Excellent $60; Good $45.

Fig. 53:
"Butt Bucket," by OHIO ART, circa late 1940s to early 1950s.
Large size, Excellent $100; Good $75.

Fig. 54:
"Boy and Puppy," by
OHIO ART, circa late
1940s to early 1950s.
*Small size, Excellent $50;
Good $35.*

Fig. 55:
"Beach Kids on Plaid," by
OHIO ART, circa late
1940s to early 1950s.
*Medium size, Excellent $65;
Good $45.*

Fig. 56:
"Brick Wall," by OHIO
ART, circa late 1940s to
early 1950s. (Courtesy of
Dorothy Ellen Masters.)
*Medium size, Excellent $70;
Good $50.*

Fig. 57:
"Mexican Children," by
OHIO ART, circa late
1940s to early 1950s.
*Small size, Excellent $65;
Good $45.*

Fig. 58:
"Barnyard," by OHIO
ART, circa late 1940s to
early 1950s. (Courtesy of
Claudette Job.)
*Medium size, Excellent $75;
Good $50.*

Fig. 54

Fig. 55

Fig. 56

Fig. 57

Fig. 58

Fig. 59

Fig. 60

Fig. 61

Fig. 62

Fig. 63

Fig. 59:
"Circus Parade on Horizontal Stripes," by OHIO ART, circa late 1940s to early 1950s.
Medium size, Excellent $60; Good $45.

Fig. 60:
"Cowgirl," by OHIO ART, circa late 1940s to early 1950s.
Small size, Excellent $60; Good $45.

Fig. 61:
"Kids with Puppies," by OHIO ART, circa late 1940s to early 1950s. (Courtesy of Claudette Job.)
Small size, Excellent $50; Good $35.

Fig. 62:
"Roller Coaster," by CHEIN, 1950s through around 1960 in different sizes.
Medium size, Excellent $45; Good $30.

Fig. 63:
"Children at Beach," by OHIO ART, 1950.
Medium size, Excellent $70; Good $50.

Fig. 64:
"Children and Puppies at Beach," by OHIO ART, 1950.
Small size, Excellent $50; Good $40.

Fig. 65:
"Three Little Kittens," by CHEIN, circa 1950s.
Small size, Excellent $60; Good $45.

Fig. 66:
Advertisement that appeared in 1927 *Playthings* toy catalogue for New York Toy Show.

Fig. 67:
"Bunny in Airplane," by CHEIN, circa 1950s. (Courtesy of Dorothy Ellen Masters.)
Small size, Excellent $80; Good $60.

Fig. 68:
"Children Chasing Butterflies," by OHIO ART, 1953. (Courtesy of Claudette Job.)
Medium size, Excellent $70; Good $50.

Fig. 64

Fig. 66

Fig. 65

Fig. 67

Fig. 68

Fig. 69

Fig. 72

Fig. 70

Fig. 73

Fig. 71

Fig. 74

Fig. 69:
"Circus," by OHIO ART, 1953.
Large size, Excellent $75; Good $55.

Fig. 70:
"Cowboy," by OHIO ART, 1953 to 1955.
Small size, Excellent $65; Good $45.

Fig. 71:
"Clowns," by OHIO ART, 1953 to 1955.
Small size, Excellent $65; Good $45.

Fig. 72:
"Ark," by OHIO ART, 1956. (Courtesy of Shirley Cox.) The shovel fits through hole in the handle to make a sail.
Medium size, Excellent $135; Good $100.

Fig. 73:
"Small Easter Bunny Bucket," by CHEIN, circa 1950s. (Courtesy of Dorothy Ellen Masters.)
Small size, Excellent $65; Good $50.

Fig. 74:
"Square Bunny Airplane Pail," by CHEIN, circa 1950s. (Courtesy of Dorothy Ellen Masters.)
Medium size, Excellent $90; Good $65.

Fig. 75:
"Cowboys and Indians," by OHIO ART, circa early 1950s. (Courtesy of Claudette Job.)
Medium size, Excellent $75; Good $60.

Fig. 76:
"Balloon Man," by CHEIN, circa 1950s. (Courtesy of Claudette Job.)
Medium size, Excellent $75; Good $55.

Fig. 77:
"Pirate Hula," circa 1940s to 1950s. (Courtesy of Shirley Cox.)
Medium size, Excellent $65; Good $45.

Fig. 78:
"Kids with Lollipops," made for TASTY CANDY PRODUCTS INC., Yonkers, N.Y., circa 1940s to 1950s. (Courtesy of Claudette Job.)
Small size, Excellent $40; Good $25.

Fig. 79:
"Children in Boat with Anchor Border," by OHIO ART, circa 1950s. (Courtesy of Claudette Job.)
Large size, Excellent $70; Good $50.

Fig. 75

Fig. 76

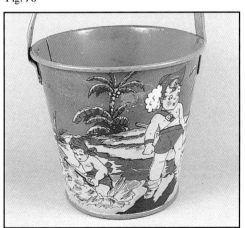
Fig. 77

Fig. 78

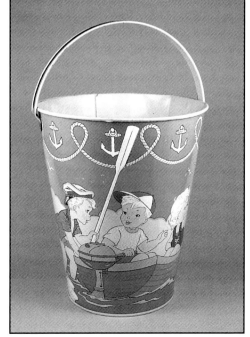
Fig. 79

Fig. 80

Fig. 81

Fig. 82

Fig. 83

Fig. 84

Fig. 80:
"Blue and Yellow Dutch Children," by U.S. METAL TOYS, circa 1950s. (Courtesy of Claudette Job.)
Medium size, Excellent $65; Good $45.

Fig. 81:
"Undersea," by CHEIN, circa 1950s. (Courtesy of Claudette Job.)
Large size, Excellent $65; Good $50.

Fig. 82:
"Beach Party/Wiener Roast," by OHIO ART, circa early 1960s. (Courtesy of Claudette Job.)
Medium size, Excellent $60; Good $45.

Fig. 83:
"Iridescent Swimmers," by OHIO ART, circa early 1960s. (Courtesy of Claudette Job.)
Medium size, Excellent $50; Good $35.

Fig. 84:
"Circus," by CHEIN, 1960.
Medium size, Excellent $45; Good $35.

Fig. 85:
"Undersea Swimmers," by
CHEIN, 1964. (Courtesy of
Dorothy Ellen Masters.)
*Medium size, Excellent $50;
Good $35.*

Fig. 86:
"Crowded Boat," by
CHEIN, 1965. (Courtesy of
Claudette Job.)
*Medium size, Excellent $45;
Good $30.*

Fig. 87:
"Iridescent Fish," by OHIO
ART, 1967.
*Large size, Excellent $45;
Good $30.*

Fig. 88:
"Ship in City," by CHEIN,
1967 to 1968. (Courtesy of
Claudette Job.)
*Medium size, Excellent $45;
Good $25.*

Fig. 89:
"Ship in City," by CHEIN,
1967 to 1968. (Courtesy of
Claudette Job.)
*Large size, Excellent $40;
Good $25.*

Fig. 85

Fig. 86

Fig. 87

Fig. 88

Fig. 89

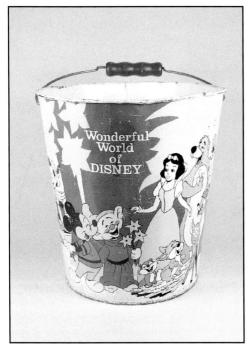

Fig. 90

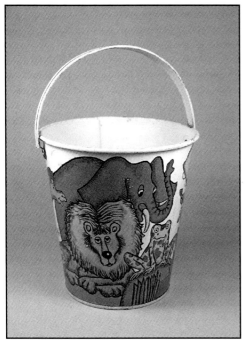

Fig. 91

Fig. 92

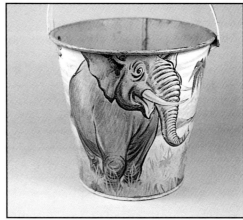

Fig. 93

Fig. 94

Fig. 90:
"Wonderful World of Disney," by CHEIN, 1969. (Courtesy of Claudette Job.)
Large size, Excellent $100; Good $75.

Fig. 91:
"Safari," by CHEIN, 1969 to 1970. (Courtesy of Claudette Job.)
Medium size, Excellent $40; Good $25.

Fig. 92:
"Tiger," by CHEIN, circa 1960s. (Courtesy of Dorothy Ellen Masters.)
Large size, Excellent $50; Good $30.

Fig. 93:
"Safari," by U.S. METAL TOYS, circa 1960s. (Courtesy of Claudette Job.)
Medium size, Excellent $35; Good $25.

Fig. 94:
"Safari," by U.S. METAL TOYS, circa 1960s to 1970s. (Courtesy of Claudette Job.)
Medium size, Excellent $35; Good $20.

Fig. 95:
"Iridescent Eagle," by OHIO ART, circa 1960s. (Courtesy of Claudette Job.)
Medium size, Excellent $60; Good $45.

Fig. 96:
"Iridescent Waterskiers," by U.S. METAL TOYS, circa 1960s to 1970s. (Courtesy of Claudette Job.)
Medium size, Excellent $40; Good $25.

Fig. 97:
"Iridescent Toucans," by OHIO ART, circa early 1960s. (Courtesy of Claudette Job.)
Large size, Excellent $65; Good $50.

Fig. 98:
"Tiger Pail," by OHIO ART, circa late 1960s.
Medium size, Excellent $45; Good $30.

Fig. 95

Fig. 97

Fig. 96

Fig. 98

Fig. 99

Fig. 101

Fig. 100

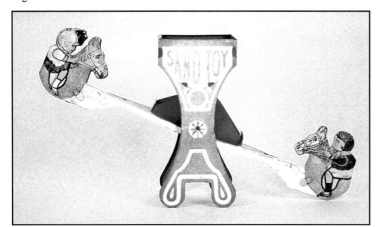

Fig. 102

Fig. 99:
"Iridescent Parrots," by OHIO ART, circa late 1960s.
Large size, Excellent $55; Good $40.

Fig. 100:
"Flowered Pail With Girl and Boy," by OHIO ART, circa 1959 to 1962.
Large size, Excellent $50; Good $35.

Fig. 101:
"Train," by CHEIN, 1965, circa late 1960s to early 1970s. (Courtesy of Dorothy Ellen Masters.)
Medium size, Excellent $45; Good $22.

Fig. 102:
"Children on Rocking Horses Sand Toy no. 49," by CHEIN, circa 1920s, circle logo. (Courtesy of Dorothy Ellen Masters.)
Excellent $225; Good $150.

Fig. 103:
"Sand Mill," by CHEIN, circa 1920s, circle logo. (Courtesy of Dorothy Ellen Masters.)
Excellent $225; Good $150.

Fig. 104:
"Busy Mike," by CHEIN, circa 1930s. (Courtesy of Dorothy Ellen Masters.)
Excellent $200; Good $125.

Fig. 105:
"See-Saw," by CHEIN, circa 1930s, tri-colored shield logo. (Courtesy of Dorothy Ellen Masters.)
Excellent $200; Good $125.

Fig. 106:
"Captain Sandy Andy, no. 63," by WOLVERINE, 1936 to 1950. (Courtesy of Connie and Robert Delaney.)
Excellent $160; Good $125.

Fig. 107:
"Mickey Mouse Sand Shovel," by OHIO ART, 1938 and 1940, Walt Disney Enterprises. (Courtesy of Dora C. Pohl.) This came as part of sand sets which included combinations of sand sieves, molds, sprinkling cans, and pails.
Excellent $125; Good $75.

Fig. 103

Fig. 104

Fig. 105

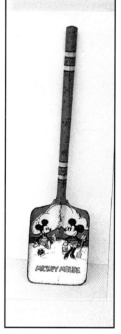

Fig. 107

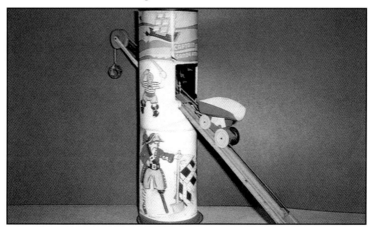

Fig. 106

Fig. 108

Fig. 110

Fig. 111

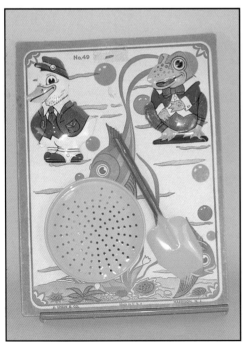

Fig. 109

Fig. 108:
"Sand Sieve Set no. 13," by
OHIO ART, 1942, 1943,
1949 and 1950.
Mint on card $50; Good $25.

Fig. 109:
"Sandset," by CHEIN,
circa mid 1940s. (Courtesy
of Dorothy Ellen Masters.)
Excellent $75; Good $45.

Fig. 110:
"Boy and Girl Shovel no.
29," by OHIO ART, 1949,
1950, 1951, and 1955.
Excellent $35; Good $20.

Fig. 111:
"Beach Kids Sand Sieve
Set," by OHIO ART, circa
late 1940s.
Excellent $75; Good $45.

Fig. 112:
"Sandy Andy no. 61," by
WOLVERINE. This toy
was first introduced in
1954. The cart, loaded with
sand "dashes" to the bottom, empties and returns
for reloads.
Excellent $100; Good $75.

Fig. 113:
"Sandmill no. 44," by
CHEIN, 1956. (Courtesy of
Dorothy Ellen Masters.)
Excellent $125; Good $85.

Fig. 114:
"Waterskiers Sand Sieve
Set," by OHIO ART, circa
1950s.
Excellent $75; Good $45.

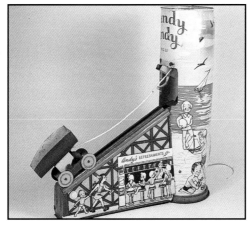

Fig. 112

Fig. 113

Fig. 114

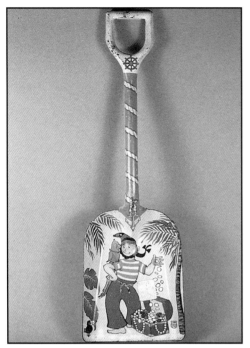

Fig. 115

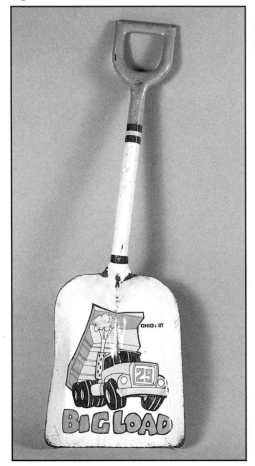

Fig. 117

Fig. 116

Fig. 115:
"Pirate Shovel," by
CHEIN, 1965. (Courtesy of
Dorothy Ellen Masters.)
Excellent $25; Good $18.

Fig. 116:
"Tiger Shovel," by CHEIN,
clown logo, 1967 and 1968.
Excellent $30; Good $20.

Fig. 117:
"Big Load Shovel," by
OHIO ART, circa 1979 to
1983.
Excellent $10; Good $7.

CHILDREN'S TEA SETS

OF all the tin-litho toys produced, the colorful tea sets are among the most charming. The emperor of the American-made tea sets was, without a doubt, the OHIO ART COMPANY. However, WOLVERINE produced some very nice sets as did CHEIN. Complete tea sets are difficult to come by, hence they tend to be expensive when compared to other tin-litho toys. One of the reasons they are expensive is that they are difficult to find in decent condition. When children played with tea sets, they used water; thus they are often found in very rusted condition. If you are lucky enough to find a set mint-in-box, you will be charmed by the packaging as well as the tea set.

Complete sets vary in size. Some of the most common sizes include:

Five-piece sets called "hummers" (one cup, one saucer, one pot with lid, and one plate to be used as tray);
Seven-piece sets (two cups, two saucers, a teapot with lid, and a tray);
Eight-piece sets (two cups, two saucers, two plates, teapot with lid);
Nine-piece set (two cups, two saucers, two plates, tray, teapot with lid);
Seventeen-piece sets (four plates, four cups, four saucers, sugar, creamer, teapot with lid, and tray);
Twenty-three-piece sets (six plates, six cups, six saucers, sugar, creamer, teapot with lid, and tray);
Thirty-one-piece sets (six dinner plates, six butter plates, six cups, six saucers, cake plate with lid, creamer, sugar bowl, teapot with lid, and tray).

Sets also came in three-place settings and six-place settings. When listing prices, I will note which size set I am referring to because the photograph, in most cases, will only show selected pieces from a complete set. Larger complete sets are, of course, more expensive. OHIO ART did not tend to produce the same sets for more than two to five years, while WOLVERINE and CHEIN produced the same set for up to twenty years.

The prices I have listed are for complete sets. In reality, however, collectors rarely find complete sets. It is far more likely that you will find a cup here, a plate there. How much should you pay for individual pieces? Obviously, you would not simply divide the list price for a set by the number of pieces because it's the fact that the set is complete that contributes to the overall price. Also, a teapot with a lid is worth a lot more than a plate or saucer because there were fewer made and they are harder to find. A rough guess is that a teapot with lid from the late 1920s through the early 1940s, in excellent condition, is worth anywhere from $35 to $60. A tray from one of these early sets can go from $35 to $60 , while a cup or a plate goes from $15 to $35. If the piece is marked Walt Disney, however, you can add at least 50 percent to 75 percent to the price depending on the pattern. Teapots from sets of the late 1940s through early 1950s are worth from $20 to $35 with trays going for $25 to $50 and plates and cups from $8 to $15.

While late 19th century and very early 20th century toys are beyond the purview of this book, as are European toys, I have included some early tea sets for no other reason than that they are beautiful. The first sixteen plates show various pieces of early American and European tin-litho dishes. Many of these early sets are not marked with a company name or country of manufacture. Some appear to be American while others appear to be English, French, or German. They are fine examples of the forerunners of the American sets produced in the 1920s.

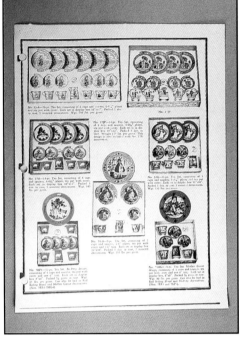

Fig. 118

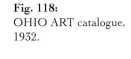

Fig. 118:
OHIO ART catalogue,
1932.

Fig. 119:
"Mother Goose," European,
circa early 1900s.
Plate, Excellent $28; Good $22.

Fig. 120:
"Squirrel," European, circa
early 1900s.
*Cup and saucer, Excellent $30;
Good $25.*
*Pitcher, Excellent $25;
Good $20.*

Fig. 121:
Bird Set, German, circa
1900.
Set, Excellent $350; Good $300.

Fig. 122:
"Children In Snow," circa
early 1900s. (Courtesy of
Shirley Cox.)
Excellent $60; Good $45.

Fig. 119

Fig. 120

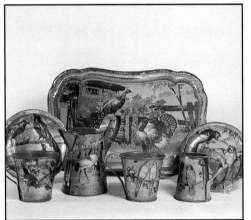

Fig. 121

Fig. 122

Fig. 123:
"Tennis Anyone?," circa
early 1900s. (Courtesy of
Shirley Cox.)
Set, Excellent $275; Good $200.

Fig. 124:
"Children with Snowman,"
1919. (Courtesy of Shirley
Cox.)
*Tray with three pieces,
Excellent $115; Good $85.*

Fig. 125:
"Dutch Scene," circa 1920s.
*Pieces shown, Excellent $150;
Good $95.*

Fig. 126:
"Hummingbird," circa early
1900s. (Courtesy of Shirley
Cox.)
*Pieces shown, Excellent $75;
Good $55.*

Fig. 127:
"Nursery Scenes," circa late
1800s to early 1900s.
*Cup and plate, Excellent $100;
Good $65.*

Fig. 123

Fig. 124

Fig. 125

Fig. 127

Fig. 126

Fig. 128

Fig. 129

Fig. 130

Fig. 131

Fig. 132

Fig. 128:
"Fantastic Floral Set,"
European, circa early
1900s. (Courtesy of Shirley
Cox.)
Excellent, $175; Good $120.

Fig. 129:
"Bear Plate," European,
circa 1920s.
Excellent $30; Good $20.

Fig. 130:
"Cat and Mouse,"
European, circa late 1800s
to early 1900s.
Excellent $35; Good $25.

Fig. 131:
"Serving Dish," European,
circa early 1900s.
Excellent $50; Good $55.

Fig. 132:
"Intricate Cup and Saucer,"
circa early 1900s.
Excellent $75; Good $50.

Fig. 133:
"Intricate Floral Pattern," circa early 1920s to 1930s. (Courtesy of Shirley Cox.) *Excellent $75; Good $50.*

Fig. 134:
"Children at Beach with Dolls," circa early 1900s. (Courtesy of Shirley Cox.) *Excellent $75; Good $60.*

Fig. 135:
"Early Indian Plate," circa late 1800s-early 1900s. (Courtesy of Dora C. Pohl.) *Excellent $75; Good $60.*

Fig. 136:
"Child's Play Pantry Cannister Set," by EMPECO, Metal Package Co., N.Y., 1926. (Courtesy of LaDonna Dolan.) *MIB $500; Excellent $225; Good $175.*

Fig. 137:
Box for EMPECO cannister set in Figure 136.

Fig. 133

Fig. 134

Fig. 135

Fig. 136

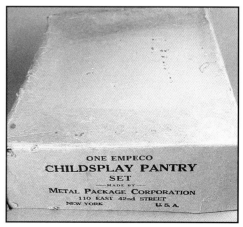

Fig. 137

Fig. 138

Fig. 138a

Fig. 140

Fig. 139

Figs. 138 and 138a:
"ABC Kitten Set." One of first tea sets produced by OHIO ART. H.S. Winzeler displayed this line at the New York Toy Fair on March 9, 1920. (ABC plate courtesy of Rosa Mundi's Antiques.)
Five-piece set with ABC tray, one cup, one saucer, one teapot with lid, MIB $250; Excellent $175; Good $150.

Fig. 139:
"Girl on Swing," by OHIO ART, circa 1920s, advertised in 1929-1930 catalogue. (Courtesy of Jack and Barbara Craig.) One of very first OHIO ART sets. This piece has the "Girl on Swing" lithography, but is a different dye-lot than the set advertised in the 1929-1930 catalogue.
Eight-piece set, MIB $300; Excellent $225; Good $150.

Fig. 140:
"Butterflies," by OHIO ART. This set was produced in the 1920s and advertised in the 1932 catalogue as a "Hummer" five-piece set. This early set has a different realistic and beautifully lithographed butterfly on each piece.
Nine-piece set, MIB $250; Excellent $200; Good $150.

Fig. 141:
"Little Red Riding Hood Blue Set," by OHIO ART. One of earlier sets produced in the 1920s and advertised in the 1929-1930 catalogue as a "Hummer" five-piece set. This particularly charming set has excellent lithography. Each piece depicts a different scene from the story. By 1932 this design was replaced by a new "Little Red Riding Hood" design.
Seven-piece set, MIB $525; Excellent $225; Good $150.

Fig. 142:
"Delft Blue," by OHIO ART. This sweet, soft blue set was issued in the 1920s and is advertised in catalogues from 1929 to 1931.
Seven-piece set, MIB $250; Excellent $175; Good $150.

Fig. 143:
"Mother Goose," by OHIO ART, 1931. The plate featured Mother Goose while the cups, teapot, saucers and tray featured characters from various nursery rhymes.
Seven-piece set, MIB $250; Excellent $175; Good $125.

Fig. 144:
"Bluebirds and Blossoms," by OHIO ART, produced in the 1920s and appeared in the 1929-1930 catalogue as a "Hummer" five-piece set.
Five-piece set, MIB $225; Excellent $150; Good $125.

Fig. 145:
"Japanese Design" or "Geisha Girls," by OHIO ART, 1931.
Eight-piece set, MIB $225; Excellent $175; Good $140.

Fig. 141

Fig. 142

Fig. 143

Fig. 144

Fig. 145

Fig. 146

Fig. 147

Fig. 146:
"Hansel and Gretel," by OHIO ART, 1933. *Fifteen-piece set, MIB $525; Excellent $225; Good $150.*

Fig. 147:
"Mickey's Helpmate," by OHIO ART, 1933, Copyright Walt Disney. *Seven-piece set, MIB $450; Excellent $300; Good $200. Twenty-three piece set with tray (service for six), MIB $1000; Excellent $650; Good $350.*

Fig. 147a:
"Mickey's Helpmate," by OHIO ART, 1933, Copyright Walt Disney. *Tray, Excellent $145; Good $100.*

Fig. 148:
"Three Little Pigs," by OHIO ART, 1934, Walt Disney Enterprises. *Twenty-three piece set, MIB $650; Excellent $350; Good $275.*

Fig. 149:
"Fairies," by OHIO ART, 1933 to 1935. This is one of the prettiest and most sought-after sets. *Eleven-piece set, MIB $300; Excellent $225; Good $175.*

Fig. 147a

Fig. 148

Fig. 149

Fig. 150:
A variation of "Fairies" tray in Figure 149, circa 1940s. (Courtesy of Shirley Cox.) *Excellent $50; Good $25.*

Fig. 151:
"Snow White and the Seven Dwarfs," by OHIO ART, 1938, Walt Disney Enterprises. This was the first Disney set connected to a full-length animated feature.
Seventeen-piece set, MIB $475; Excellent $350; Good $225.

Fig. 152:
"Pinocchio," by OHIO ART, 1939, Walt Disney Productions.
Twenty-three piece set, MIB $500; Excellent $385; Good $275.

Fig. 153:
"Clara Clack," by OHIO ART, 1939 and 1940, Walt Disney Enterprises. This charming older Disney set was issued in various sizes, including seven-, eleven-, seventeen-, and twenty-three piece sets.
Twenty-three piece set, MIB $800; Excellent $600; Good $400.
Seven-piece set, MIB $350; Excellent $250; Good $150.

Fig. 154:
"There Was an Old Woman," by OHIO ART, circa 1930s.
Tray, Excellent $75; Good $50.

Fig. 150

Fig. 151

Fig. 152

Fig. 153

Fig. 154

Fig. 155

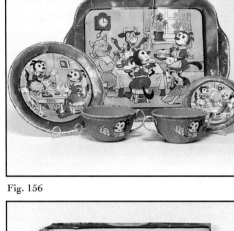

Fig. 156

Fig. 156a

Fig. 157

Fig. 158

Fig. 155:
"Mary Had a Little Lamb," by OHIO ART, circa 1920s.
Seven-piece set, MIB $250; Excellent $175; Good $135.

Figs. 156 and 156a:
"Crazy Cat," by CHEIN, tri-colored shield logo, circa 1930s. This set was also produced in the 1950s with either red or yellow borders. It had a plain shield logo.
Twenty-one piece set, MIB $350; Excellent $250; Good $175.

Fig. 157:
"Delft Blue," by WOLVERINE. Introduced in 1942 and produced through 1957. Pre-1950 picture was smaller in relation to border and did not have shading at children's feet. (Photo courtesy of Dora C. Pohl.)
Twenty-two piece set, MIB $325; Excellent $250; Good $175.

Fig. 158:
"Bunny Birthday," by OHIO ART, circa early 1940s.
Seven-piece set (two straight-sided cups, two saucers, plate/tray and straight-sided pot with lid), MIB $150; Excellent $110; Good $90.

Fig. 159:
"Humpty-Dumpty/Birdie,"
by OHIO ART, 1939 and
1940, designed by Fern
Bisel Peat. This set came in
a variety of combinations.
There were two versions of
the tray, one in which
Humpty falls off the wall,
and one in which he is
perched happily on the
wall. Humpty-Dumpty only
appears on the tray; all
other pieces have a little
birdie with a musical note
on a red gingham back-
ground. Some sets have
straight-sided cups, while
others have rounded cups.
*Eleven-piece set with two
rounded cups, two saucers, two
plates, sugar, creamer, pot with
lid and tray, MIB $175;
Excellent $125; Good $100.
Seven-piece set with no tray and
straight-sided cups, MIB $140;
Excellent $75; Good $50.*

Fig. 160:
"Little Maid," by OHIO
ART, circa 1940s. Designed
by Fern Bisel Peat.
Excellent $20; Good $12.

Fig. 161:
"Nursery Rhymes," by
ESSEX, U.S.A., circa
1940s.
Excellent $22; Good $15.

Fig. 159

Fig. 160

Fig. 161

Fig. 162

Fig. 163

Fig. 164

Fig. 165

Fig. 162:
"Elephant and Mouse," by CHEIN, circa 1930s to 1940s. This odd little set was advertised in the 1952 catalogue as a no. 220 tea set which included fifteen pieces. It was also advertised as a smaller seven-piece set, no. 215, which included two cups, two saucers, one plate/tray, and one teapot. In the late 1950s only the no. 215 set appeared in the catalogue. *Fifteen-piece set, MIB $175; Excellent $125; Good $90.*

Fig. 163:
"Delft Blue Cannister Set," by WOLVERINE. First produced in 1942 but with no writing on the cannisters. In 1950 the cannisters were labeled flour, sugar, etc. This set was still produced in 1957. *Four-piece set, MIB $200; Excellent $150; Good $100.*

Fig. 164:
"Donald Duck," by OHIO ART, 1942 and 1943, Walt Disney Productions. "Donald Duck" was issued in nine-, eleven-, and fourteen-piece sets. The plates show Donald with a steaming cup of coffee. The tray has Donald balancing a pile of plates and cups Dagwood-style, on the saucers, while the cups show just his face. *Seven-piece set, MIB $300; Excellent $225; Good $150.*

Fig. 165:
"Jack Be Nimble," by OHIO ART, 1942, 1943 and 1946. Designed by Fern Bisel Peat. *Seven-piece set, MIB $175; Excellent $125; Good $75.*

Fig. 166:
"Mexican Boy," by OHIO ART, 1942, 1943, 1946, and 1947.
Nine-piece set, MIB $175; Excellent $125; Good $90.

Fig. 167:
"Girl and Boy with Puppy," OHIO ART, 1942, 1943, and 1946. (Courtesy of Shirley Cox.)
Thirty-one piece set, MIB $275; Excellent $200; Good $175.

Fig. 168:
"She Loves Me, She Loves Me Not," by OHIO ART. The 1949 design was issued with straight-sided cups. In 1956, the set was reissued with rounded cups. This popular design shows a little boy and girl on the tray with a daisy. The other pieces feature the dark-haired girl and a cute gray kitten.
Seven-piece set, MIB $100; Excellent $70; Good $50.

Fig. 169:
Older, straight-sided "She Loves Me, She Loves Me Not" set, 1949.
Nine-piece set, MIB $150; Excellent $100; Good $75.

Fig. 170:
"Silhouette Set," by OHIO ART, circa 1930s. (Courtesy of Shirley Cox.)
Seven-piece set, MIB $175; Excellent $125; Good $75.

Fig. 166

Fig. 167

Fig. 168

Fig. 169

Fig. 170

Fig. 171

Fig. 172

Fig. 173

Fig. 174

Fig. 175

Fig. 171:
"Dutch Girl and Fairy," by OHIO ART, circa 1930s to early 1940s. Designed by Fern Bisel Peat.
Plate, Excellent $15; Good $10.

Fig. 172:
"Gingham Dog and Calico Cat," by OHIO ART, 1939 and 1940. Designed by Fern Bisel Peat. (Courtesy of Shirley Cox.)
Nine-piece set, MIB $200; Excellent $135; Good $100.

Fig. 173:
Illustration of "The Gingham Dog and Calico Cat," from book illustrated by Fern Bisel Peat, published in 1930.

Fig. 174:
"Silhouettes," by OHIO ART, 1939 to 1940, and 1942 to 1943. (Courtesy of Shirley Cox.)
Seven-piece set, MIB $175; Excellent $125; Good $75.

Fig. 175:
"Fiesta Ware," by OHIO ART. (Courtesy of Shirley Cox.) First introduced in 1939 to 1940. This multi-colored set came in assorted sizes from eight-piece to thirty-one-piece sets. The tray was green, the teapot was blue, the cake-plate was red, the creamer and sugar were green, and the plates, cups, and saucers came in red, yellow, dark blue, or green.
Thirty-one piece set, MIB $275; Excellent $175; Good $125.

Fig. 176:
"Girls as Kittens," by
OHIO ART. First issued in
early 1940s and reissued
after 1945. (Courtesy of
Shirley Cox.)
Fifteen-piece set, MIB $250;
Excellent $175; Good $140.

Fig. 177:
"Ducky Bathtime," by
OHIO ART, circa early
1940s. (Courtesy of Shirley
Cox.)
Thirty-one piece set, MIB $275;
Excellent $200; Good $150.

Fig. 178:
"Mary Had a Little Lamb,"
by OHIO ART, circa early
1940s. Design by Fern Bisel
Peat.
Seven-piece set, MIB $225;
Excellent $150; Good $100.

Fig. 179:
Box for tea set.

Fig. 180:
Tin-litho dishes on display
in old children's china cup-
board. (Courtesy of Shirley
Cox.)

Fig. 176

Fig. 177

Fig. 178

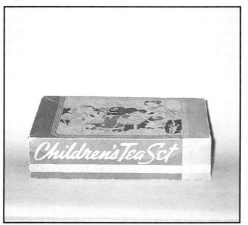

Fig. 179

Fig. 180

Fig. 181

Fig. 182

Fig. 183

Fig. 184

Fig. 185

Fig. 181:
"Circus," by OHIO ART, 1950 and 1954.
Thirty-one piece set (six dinner plates with elephant, six saucers with bare-back rider, six butter plates with monkey, creamer, cake plate with cover, teapot with lid, and two-handled sugar bowl), MIB $250; Excellent $175; Good $125.

Fig. 182:
"Girl with Dolly," by OHIO ART, 1954. (Courtesy of Shirley Cox.)
Nine-piece set, MIB $150; Excellent $115; Good $85.

Fig. 183:
"The Wedding," by OHIO ART. This was probably a special issue in the early 1950s. The set appears to represent a specific children's story.
Thirty-one piece set, MIB $250; Excellent $175; Good $125.

Fig. 184:
"Boy and Girl in Garden," by OHIO ART, 1956.
Fifteen-piece set (four place settings, teapot with lid and tray), MIB $175; Excellent $125; Good $90.

Fig. 185:
"Tea-party," with Donald, Daisy, and Mickey, circa 1950s to 1960s, Walt Disney Enterprises.
Plates - each, Excellent $20; Good $15.

Fig. 186:
"Red and Green Floral," by OHIO ART, circa late 1940s to early 1950s. This tastefully designed set came as a thirty-one piece set. *MIB $225; Excellent $150; Good $100.*

Fig. 187:
"Dutch Winter Wonderland," by OHIO ART, 1950.
Fifteen-piece set, MIB $200; Excellent $140; Good $100.

Fig. 188:
"Blue Willow," by OHIO ART, 1950.
Thirty-one piece set, MIB $250; Excellent $175; Good $125.

Fig. 189:
"Cinderella," by OHIO ART, circa 1952, Walt Disney Productions.
Seventeen-piece set, MIB $525; Excellent $225; Good $175.

Fig. 186

Fig. 187

Fig. 188

Fig. 189

Fig. 190

Fig. 191

Fig. 192

Fig. 193

Fig. 190:
"Mickey Mouse Set," by CHEIN, 1954, Walt Disney Productions. (Courtesy of Dorothy Ellen Masters.) *Fifteen-piece set, MIB $350; Excellent $225; Good $175.*

Fig. 191:
"Swanset," by OHIO ART, 1956. This charming, somewhat campy set is a very 1950s example of the pink and black rage. The twenty-one-piece set consisted of 4 dinner plates, 4 salad plates, 4 cups, 4 saucers, a footed creamer and sugar bowl, a pot with lid and a large 9" x 13" heavy tray. *MIB $175; Excellent $140; Good $100.*

Fig. 192:
"Cherry Cannister Set, no. 193," by OHIO ART, 1956. (Courtesy of Shirley Cox.) Total sixteen-piece set (three cannisters with lids, three mixing bowls, pastry board, two pie-pans, rolling pin, cookie sheet, shell mold and large mixing spoon). This set also came in a twenty-three piece set, no. 93, advertised in 1954. The larger set had four cannisters and more molds. *Sixteen-piece set, MIB $300; Excellent $200; Good $150.*

Fig. 193:
"Farm Set," by OHIO ART. This set was first introduced in 1954 in yellow and green and reissued in the early 1960s. *Twenty-one piece set from 1960s, MIB $140; Excellent $100; Good $65.*

Fig. 194:
"Red Plaid," by OHIO ART, 1956.
Twenty-three piece set, MIB $225; Excellent $160; Good $125.

Fig. 195:
"Alice in Wonderland," by BANNER PLASTIC, 1956. Tin-litho plates and saucers, and hard plastic teapot, sugar, creamer, cups and silverware. Set also came with tray.
MIB $400; Excellent $325; Good $225.

Fig. 196:
"Pink Floral," by OHIO ART, circa 1950s.
Four-place set, MIB $150; Excellent $100; Good $50.

Fig. 197:
"Flower Cart," by OHIO ART, circa 1950s.
Seventeen-piece set, MIB $150; Excellent $100; Good $75.

Fig. 198:
"Leaves," by OHIO ART, circa 1950s.
Twenty-three piece set, MIB $150; Excellent $100; Good $65.

Fig. 199:
"Blue Heaven," by OHIO ART, circa 1950s.
Fifteen-piece set, MIB $135; Excellent $75; Good $45.

Fig. 194

Fig. 195

Fig. 196

Fig. 197

Fig. 198

Fig. 199

Fig. 200

Fig. 202

Fig. 203

Fig. 204

Fig. 200:
"Blue Dresden," by CHEIN, 1958. Combination of soft poly and metal. Flatware and pitcher in poly.
Thirty-one piece set, MIB $175; Excellent $125; Good $90.

Fig. 201:
"Star Cannisters," by WOLVERINE, 1959. (Courtesy of Patty Cooper.)
Complete set of four, Mint In Package $155; Excellent $125; Good $100.

Fig. 202:
"Strawberries," by CHEIN, 1960.
Eighteen-piece set (service for five), MIB $175; Excellent $100; Good $60.

Fig. 203:
"Pink floral mint," by OHIO ART, circa 1959 to 1962.
Seventeen-piece-set, MIB $150; Excellent $100; Good $75.

Fig. 204:
"Ms. Poodle," by OHIO ART, circa 1959 to 1962.
Thirteen-piece set, MIB $125; Excellent $85; Good $55.

Fig. 205:
"Rooster," by WOLVER-INE, circa 1960s.
Thirteen-piece set, MIB $85; Excellent $60; Good $40.

Fig. 206:
"Bunnies," by CHEIN, 1964.
Thirteen-piece set (four cups, four plates, four saucers, one tray), MIB $140; Excellent $95; Good $50.

Fig. 207:
"Delft Blue," by WOLVERINE, circa 1940s to 1950s. Mix of cannisters and dishes. (Courtesy of Shirley Cox.)

Fig. 208:
"Little Red Riding Hood," by OHIO ART. This "Storytime" set was issued in the early 1960s. It was all metal with a floral design on the bottom of each cup. In 1967 it was issued with plastic cups.
Fourteen-piece set, MIB $145; Excellent $85; Good $50.

Fig. 205

Fig. 206

Fig. 207

Fig. 208

Fig. 209

Fig. 210

Fig. 211

Fig. 209:
"Old English," by CHEIN, 1965. (Courtesy of LaDonna Dolan.) Flatware and handle of teapot made of styrene. It came in a "Mylar Window Box."
MIB $145; Excellent $90; Good $65.

Fig. 210:
"Swiss Miss," by OHIO ART, 1967.
Thirteen-piece set, MIB $135; Excellent $100; Good $75.

Fig. 211:
"Three Little Pigs," by OHIO ART, circa 1960s to 1970s. Each plate had a different pig.
Single plates, Excellent $10; Good $7.

TOPS AND DRUMS

I REALIZE that tops and drums are not intrinsically superior to Nintendo and Game Boy, but they are undeniably simpler. The fanciful designs and bright colors make them a pleasure to look at. Many of the drums have military or patriotic themes featuring soldiers or battle scenes. Many are not marked with a manufacturer but appear to be American based in their themes and symbols. Tops have definitely survived the test of time. Spinners are still sold today, although the materials and designs have changed radically from the old tin-litho tops.

Fig. 213:
Page from CHEIN catalogue, 1952.

Fig. 214:
"Large Circus Top," by CHEIN. CHEIN produced this design from the 1930s through the 1950s. The one pictured has the older tricolored shield.
Excellent $75; Good $50.

Fig. 215:
"Mickey Mouse Top," by OHIO ART, Walt Disney Enterprises, circa 1930s with long-billed Donald Duck. (Courtesy of Dora C. Pohl.)
Excellent $525; Good $275.

Fig. 216:
"Musical Children Top," by CHEIN, circa 1930s. (Courtesy of Dora C. Pohl.) CHEIN reissued this litho design in 1956 and 1960, but with different colors. The newer version has a red stripe around the perimeter and a yellow top. The beauty shown here is advertised in the 1935 catalogue.
Excellent $155; Good $100.

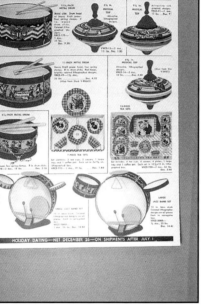

Fig. 213

Fig. 214

Fig. 215

Fig. 216

Fig. 217

Fig. 219

Fig. 221

Fig. 218

Fig. 220

Fig. 222

Fig. 217:
"Snow White Top," circa 1930s to 1940s. (Courtesy of Dora C. Pohl.) This is not a Disney "Snow White."
Excellent $175; Good $150.

Fig. 218:
"Old Fashioned Games Top," circa 1920s to 1930s.
Excellent $60; Good $45.

Fig. 219:
"Cat Top," by OHIO ART, circa late 1930s to early 1940s. (Courtesy of Shirley Cox.)
Excellent $75; Good $55.

Fig. 220:
"Children Top," by WYAN-DOTTE, circa 1930s.
Excellent $100; Good $75.

Fig. 221:
"Pirates Top," by OHIO ART, circa early 1940s. Designed by Fern Bisel Peat.
Excellent $85; Good $60.

Fig. 222:
"Geometric Top with Wooden Spinner," CHEIN, circa 1930s. (Courtesy of Dorothy Ellen Masters.) I have not been able to find this style of top in any CHEIN catalogue. It is possible it was made for another company or for promotion.
Excellent $30; Good $20.

Fig. 223:
"Zebra Top," by OHIO ART, 1956.
Excellent $50; Good $35.

Fig. 224:
"Children and Stars Top," by OHIO ART, 1956.
Excellent $50; Good $35.

Fig. 225:
"Boy, Girl, Teddy, and Rocking-Horse Humming Top," by CHEIN, circa 1960s. (Courtesy of Dorothy Ellen Masters.)
Excellent $45; Good $50.

Fig. 226:
"Circus Cars Top," by CHEIN, circa 1960s.
Excellent $55; Good $25.

Fig. 227:
"Here We Go Round the Mulberry Bush," by OHIO ART, circa late 1960s.
Excellent $55; Good $25.

Fig. 223

Fig. 224

Fig. 225

Fig. 226

Fig. 227

Fig. 228

Fig. 230

Fig. 229

Fig. 231

Fig. 228:
"Mickey Mouse Top," by CHEIN, circa 1970s, spiral logo, Walt Disney Productions. (Courtesy of Dorothy Ellen Masters.) *Excellent $100; Good $75.*

Fig. 229:
"Giant Musical Top," by CHEIN, 1962. (Courtesy of Connie and Bob Delaney.) *MIB $75; Good $30.*

Fig. 230:
"Animal Top," by OHIO ART, circa 1963 to 1971. *Excellent $25; Good $18.*

Fig. 231:
"Eagle Drum," by NON-PAREIL TOY AND NOVELTY CO. INC., Newark, New Jersey, circa 1920s. (Courtesy of Heather Baker.) *Excellent $100; Good $55.*

Fig. 232:
"Large Children Marching Drum," by CHEIN, circa 1930s. This drum was also issued in different sizes in 1952. *Excellent $125; Good $75.*

Fig. 232

Fig. 233:
"Mickey Mouse Parade Drum," by OHIO ART, 1938, Walt Disney Enterprises.
Excellent $275; Good $225.

Fig. 234:
"Gulliver's Travels," by CHEIN, 1939, Paramount Pictures. This drum had a cloth head and a tri-colored shield logo.
Excellent $150; Good $125.

Fig. 235:
"Air Battle Drum," circa 1940s. (Courtesy of Michael Milson.) This drum shows various war scenes using air power.
Excellent $100; Good $75.

Fig. 236:
"Spanish-American War Drum," circa early 1900s. (Courtesy of Heather Baker.)
Excellent $150; Good $115.

Fig. 237:
"Boy Banging Drum and Girl Holding Ears," by OHIO ART, 1942, 1943 and 1946. Designed by Beatrice H.C. Benjamin.
Excellent $60; Good $45.

Fig. 233

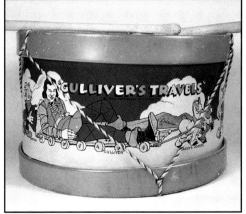

Fig. 234

Fig. 236

Fig. 235

Fig. 237

Fig. 238

Fig. 239

Fig. 241

Fig. 242

Fig. 240

Fig. 238:
"Two Wars Drum," circa 1920s. This drum is lithographed on pressed steel. It shows the Revolutionary War and George Washington on one side and General Pershing on the other.
Excellent $100; Good $70.

Fig. 239:
The Pershing side of the "Two Wars Drum" in Figure 238.

Fig. 240:
"Nursery Rhyme Drum," by OHIO ART, late 1940s.
Excellent $55; Good $45.

Fig. 241:
"Children's Parade on Diagonal Stripes," by OHIO ART, circa 1950s.
Excellent $50; Good $35.

Fig. 242:
"Presidential Drum," by CHEIN, 1952, 1956 and 1958. This drum had parchment heads.
Excellent $75; Good $50.

Fig. 243:
"Children Marching on Vertical Stripes," by OHIO ART, 1954.
Excellent $50; Good $35.

Fig. 244:
"On the Farm Drum," by OHIO ART, circa 1963 to 1971.
Excellent $35; Good $25.

Fig. 245:
"Circus Animals Drum," by CHEIN, 1965. (Courtesy of Dorothy Ellen Masters.)
Excellent $35; Good $25.

Fig. 246:
"Parade Drum," by CHEIN, 1976. (Courtesy of Dorothy Masters.)
Excellent $30; Good $20.

Fig. 243

Fig. 244

Fig. 245

Fig. 246

Fig. 247

Fig. 247:
"Bombers and Warships Drum," circa WWII. (Courtesy of Heather Baker.)
Excellent $125; Good $100.

Fig. 248:
Another view of "Bombers and Warships Drum" in Figure 247.

Fig. 248

HOUSEKEEPING TOYS

WHILE this category may seem incredibly sexist to some of us, the fact is, that from the 1920s through the 1960s, housekeeping was considered the exclusive domain of females and these toys were considered, for the most part, "girl toys."

Especially appealing are the refrigerators, particularly the older ones produced by WOLVERINE with the fabulous array of lithographed food on the inside door. Appliances modernized with the times. Washboards evolved into wringer washers, which in turn became automatic washing machines over the decades. During World War II some companies appeared to have relied on their backstock of materials and toys because of the shortage of metal. A stunning example is this refrigerator, produced by WOLVERINE out of Upson board, a "non-critical" material in 1943 to 1944.

Fig. 249:
WOLVERINE catalogue, 1938.

Fig. 250:
WOLVERINE catalogue, 1943 to 1944.

Fig. 251:
"Empire Stove," 1924. (Courtesy of La Donna Dolan.) Although this stove is not tin-lithographed, it is a good example of the older forerunners of the tin-litho kitchen appliances. This model and size is difficult to find.
Excellent $475; Good $325.

Fig. 252:
"Little Orphan Annie Stove," circa 1930s to 1940s. These stoves are found marked "MARX," "GIRARD TOYS," and unmarked. Some of them were electric and others were not. Some had an upper oven or upper and lower ovens. These stoves are most commonly found in a cream and light green combination, but they can also be found in red. The lithographed plates on all are the same, showing Annie serving cake to her dog or a name plate picturing Annie holding up the cake.
In electrical working condition, Excellent $185; Good $150. Without electricity, Excellent $160; Good $135.

Fig. 249

Fig. 251

Fig. 250

Fig. 252

Fig. 253

Fig. 255

Fig. 254

Fig. 256

Fig. 253:
"Dolly Washer," by CHEIN, 1930s, tri-colored shield.
Excellent $200; Good $150.

Fig. 254:
"Sunny Suzy Deluxe Washing Machine, no. 79," by WOLVERINE, 1936 to 1939. (Courtesy of Tom Frogge.) In 1940 no. 79 was produced with the "Delft Blue" design. This washing machine actually worked. According to the ad, the lithography is "richly done in good taste."
Excellent $225; Good $140.

Fig. 255:
Ad showing interior workings of washing machine from WOLVERINE catalogue, 1936.

Fig. 256:
"Washtub with Scrub Board, Clothesline, and Clothespins," by WOLVERINE. WOLVERINE produced this style clothesline with the coiled wire base all the way through the 1940s and 1950s.
Excellent $100; Good $80.

Fig. 257:
Refrigerator, no. 182, by
WOLVERINE, 1942 and
1947.
Excellent $125; Good $90.

Fig. 258:
Close-up of lithographed
inner door in Figure 257.

Fig. 259:
Sink, no. 198, by
WOLVERINE, 1943 and
1947. This sink had a reservoir in back that could be
filled with water and the
faucet would work!
Excellent $100; Good $75.

Fig. 260:
Refrigerator, no. 184, by
WOLVERINE, 1955.
Touted for its replication of
the newest design—sepa-
rate freezer and fridge
doors. It came with ice-
cube trays and miniature
packages of well-known
products.
Excellent $95; Good $60.

Fig. 261:
Close-up of lithographed
inner door, no. 184.

Fig. 257

Fig. 258

Fig. 259

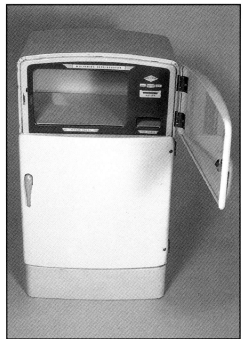

Fig. 260

Fig. 261

Fig. 262

Fig. 264

Fig. 265

Fig. 263

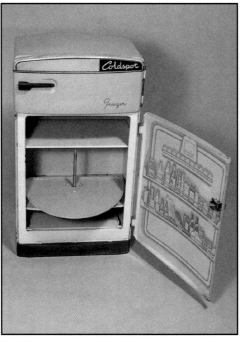

Fig. 266

Fig. 262:
Stove, no. 188, by WOLVERINE. Also new in 1950. This stove came with plastic accessories. *Excellent $65; Good $45.*

Fig. 263:
Sink, no. 197, by WOLVERINE, 1950. This sink had working faucets and water reservoir in back. *Excellent $75; Good $55.*

Fig. 264:
Wolverine catalogue, 1955, advertisement for whole set. "For Volume Selling," no. 265 includes: Refrigerator, no. 184; Stove, no. 188; and Sink, no. 197. *Excellent $255; Good $160.*

Fig. 265:
Pink Stove, no. 189, by WOLVERINE, 1957. This is essentially the same stove as no. 188, but in "New Pink Colors." *Excellent $65; Good $45.*

Fig. 266:
Green Refrigerator Deluxe, no. 187, by WOLVERINE, 1957. This refrigerator featured a revolving lower shelf. It came with ice-cube trays and imitation foods. *Excellent $65; Good $45.*

Fig. 267:
Snow White Disney Stove, by WOLVERINE, Walt Disney Productions, circa late 1960s to early 1970s. *Excellent $55; Good $40.*

Fig. 268:
Snow White Disney Refrigerator, by WOLVER-INE, Walt Disney Productions, late 1960s to early 1970s, part of set. *Excellent $55; Good $40.*

Fig. 269:
Refrigerator, by MARX, circa 1950s. *Excellent $45; Good $30.*

Fig. 270:
Interior of MARX refrigerator.

Fig. 267

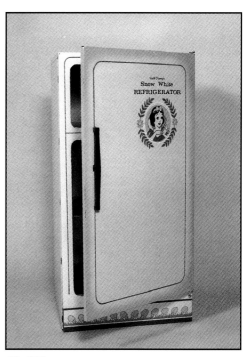

Fig. 268

Fig. 269

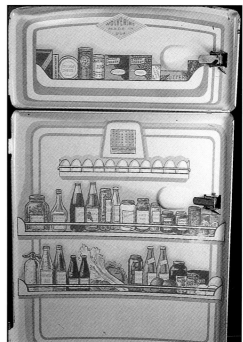

Fig. 270

Fig. 270a

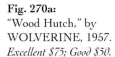

Fig. 270a:
"Wood Hutch," by
WOLVERINE, 1957.
Excellent $75; Good $50.

Fig. 271:
"Donald Duck Carpet
Sweeper," by OHIO ART,
Walt Disney Productions,
1941 to 1943.
Excellent $225; Good $175.

Fig. 272:
"Johnny and Mary Carpet
Sweeper," by E & L
MANUFACTURING CO.,
New York, circa 1950s.
Excellent $75; Good $45.

Fig. 271

Fig. 272

Fig. 273:
"Suzy Goose Carpet Sweeper," by KIDDIE BRUSH AND TOY CO., Jonesville, Michigan, circa 1950s.
Excellent $60; Good $35.

Fig. 274:
"Alice-in-Wonderland Roller," circa late 1940s to early 1950s.
Excellent $60; Good $35.

Fig. 275:
"Blondie Stroller," by NASSAU PRODUCTS CORP., Freeport, N.Y., 1949.
Excellent $350; Good $200.

Fig. 276:
Close-up of lithography on "Blondie Stroller."

Fig. 273

Fig. 275

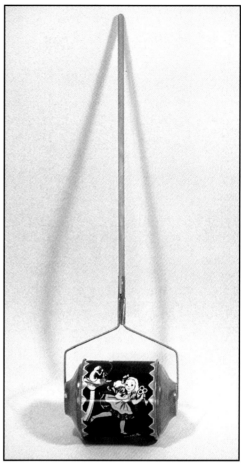

Fig. 274

Fig. 276

Fig. 277

Fig. 278

Fig. 277:
"Teddy-Bear Pink Stroller,"
by OHIO ART, circa early
to mid 1950s.
Excellent $65; Good $40.

Fig. 278:
"Bear Red Stroller," by
OHIO ART, early to mid
1950s.
Excellent $65; Good $40.

ARCHITECTURE

TIN-LITHO dollhouses are one of the toys most likely to produce a gasp of recognition from women over 30 years old. Many of us remember these dollhouses that came flat and unassembled in the box, and were put together by inserting metal tabs into slots. What is particularly stunning about dollhouses is the detail of both the exterior and interior design. From the pea-green sculpted carpets, and the huge swans on the bathroom walls, to the rifle hanging over the fireplace, we get a peek at the decorating style and aesthetic values of middle America from the 1940s into the 1960s.

Many of the dollhouses came with plastic furniture made by RENWALL, SUPERIOR, PLASCO, or MARX. Others included cars, playsets, and swimming pools. The biggest producers of dollhouses were PLAYSTEEL, T. COHN, and the well-known MARX. The prices reflected here are without the furniture, cars, or people.

In addition to dollhouses, toy companies manufactured tin-litho gas stations, barns, forts, ranches, and train stations, to name only a few. The following pictures represent a very small sampling of the huge variety of tin-litho places to live, work, and play produced by American toy companies.

Fig. 279:
"Spanish Two-Story With One Patio," by T. COHN INC., 1948.
Excellent $175; Good $125.

Fig. 280:
Fabulous swan bathroom in Figure 279.

Fig. 281:
Living room with green sculpted carpet in Figure 279.

Fig. 282:
Colonial Dollhouse, by PLAYSTEEL, 1948.
MIB $250; Excellent $185; Good $140.

Fig. 279

Fig. 281

Fig. 280

Fig. 282

Fig. 283

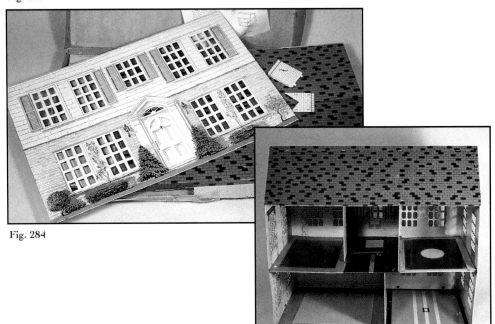

Fig. 284

Fig. 286

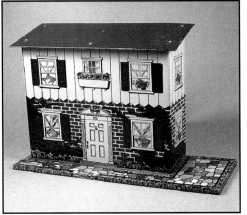

Fig. 287

Fig. 283:
The box for the PLAYSTEEL dollhouse, in Figure 282, was designed to provide landscaping for the house.

Fig. 284:
PLAYSTEEL dollhouse unassembled in box.

Fig. 285:
Interior PLAYSTEEL dollhouse.

Fig. 286:
The nursery of the PLAYSTEEL dollhouse.

Fig. 287:
Miniature Dollhouse, no. 95, with 28 Pieces of Plastic Furniture, by OHIO ART, 1949. (Courtesy of Tom Frogge.) This dollhouse measures 3" x 8-1/2" x 5-1/4." By 1953, OHIO ART had changed no. 95 to a miniature metal barn.
Excellent with furniture $75; Good $40.

Fig. 285

Fig. 288:
Interior of miniature doll-house in Figure 287.

Fig. 289:
"Spanish Two-Story With One Patio," by T. COHN, marked "Another Superior Toy, mfg. by T. COHN Inc. NYC.," 1950.
Excellent $155; Good $110.

Fig. 290:
Tiled bathroom from doll-house in Figure 289.

Fig. 291:
Sundeck from dollhouse in Figure 289.

Fig. 292:
Carpeted living room from dollhouse in Figure 289.

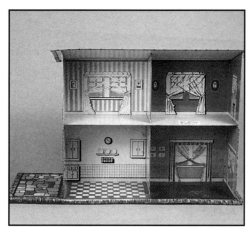

Fig. 288

Fig. 289

Fig. 290

Fig. 291

Fig. 292

Fig. 293

Fig. 293:
"Two-Story With Disney Nursery," by MARX, 1950. *Excellent $150; Good $120.*

Fig. 294:
Interior of two-story nursery in Figure 293.

Fig. 295:
Close-up of Disney nursery in Figure 293.

Fig. 296:
Two-Story Colonial, by MARX, circa early 1950s. *Excellent $100; Good $70.*

Fig. 297:
Close-up of Colonial in Figure 296.

Fig. 294

Fig. 296

Fig. 295

Fig. 297

Fig. 298:
"Stylish Pink and Turquoise Kitchen," by T. COHN, circa late 1940s to early 1950s. (Courtesy of Shirley Cox.)
Excellent $125; Good $95.

Fig. 299:
"Kitchen," by MARX, circa late 1950s to early 1960s. (Courtesy of Jack and Barbara Craig.)
Excellent $100; Good $75.

Fig. 300:
"Kitchen," by T. COHN, Another Superior Toy by T. COHN Inc., circa 1940s. (Courtesy of Jack and Barbara Craig.)
Excellent $150; Good $115.

Fig. 301:
Two-story colonial, by MARX, circa 1950s. (Courtesy of Connie and Robert Delaney.)
Excellent $120; Good $85.

Fig. 298

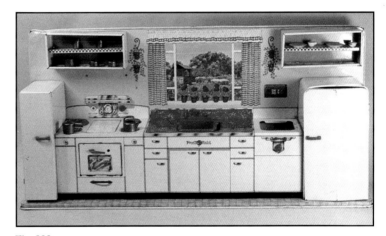

Fig. 299

Fig. 300

Fig. 301

Fig. 302

Fig. 303

Fig. 304

Fig. 305

Fig. 306

Fig. 302:
Two-story with Breezeway, by MARX, circa 1950s. (Courtesy of Connie and Robert Delaney.) *Excellent $120; Good $85.*

Fig. 303:
"Suburban," by MARX, 1958. (Courtesy of Connie and Robert Delaney.) *Excellent $100; Good $65.*

Fig. 304:
House with Carport, Patio and Pool, by MARX, 1953. (Courtesy of Connie and Robert Delaney.) *Excellent $125; Good $85.*

Fig. 305:
Two-story with Shed Dormer, by MARX, circa 1950s. (Courtesy of Connie and Robert Delaney.) *Excellent $115; Good $75.*

Fig. 306:
Yellow and Green with Corner Window, by MARX, circa early 1950s. (Courtesy of Connie and Robert Delaney.) *Excellent $115; Good $75.*

Fig. 307:
Ranch House, by MARX, circa 1950s. (Courtesy of Connie and Robert Delaney.)
Excellent $80; Good $60.

Fig. 308:
Ranch House #623, by T. COHN, circa 1950s. (Courtesy of Connie and Robert Delaney.)
Excellent $80; Good $60.

Fig. 309:
Ranch House with Side Porch, by MARX, circa early 1960s. (Courtesy of Connie and Robert Delaney.) This house came in pink, yellow ochre, grey, and orange.
Excellent $70; Good $50.

Fig. 310:
"Bungalow," by MARX, circa 1950s. (Courtesy of Connie and Robert Delaney.)
Excellent $80; Good $60.

Fig. 311:
In the 1920s, MARX produced a series of six wonderful miniature rooms. the "Newlyweds" series. (Courtesy of Gaston Majeune.) Each room was approximately 5 inches wide, 3 inches high, and 2-1/2 inches deep. The inside of the rooms was lithographed in the 1920s style, and all the furniture was lithographed, shaped tin. They were sold separately or stacked and enclosed in the cardboard dollhouse shown.
Four rooms and dollhouse box, MIB $525; Excellent $225; Good with some pieces missing $125.

Fig. 307

Fig. 308

Fig. 309

Fig. 311

Fig. 310

Fig. 312

Fig. 313

Fig. 314

Fig. 315

Fig. 316

Fig. 312:
Box in Figure 311 opened to reveal rooms.

Fig. 313:
"Newlyweds Living Room," by MARX, no. 193, circa 1920s. (Courtesy of Gaston Majeune.)
MIB with furniture, $325; Excellent $225; Good with some pieces missing $125.

Fig. 314:
"Newlyweds Bedroom," by MARX, no. 191, circa 1920s. (Courtesy of Gaston Majeune.)
MIB with furniture, $325; Excellent $225; Good with some pieces missing $125.

Fig. 315:
"Newlyweds Kitchen," by MARX, no. 190, circa 1920s. (Courtesy of Gaston Majeune.) The furniture includes a table with plates of bread and butter. The kitchen cabinet has drawers labeled with names of food. The floor is red and white tile.
MIB with furniture $325; Excellent $225; Good with some pieces missing $125.

Fig. 316:
"Newlyweds Dining Room," by MARX, no. 192, circa 1920s. (Courtesy of Gaston Majeune.) Note the wonderful yellow and green "tiled" floor.
MIB with furniture $325; Excellent $225; Good with some pieces missing $125.

Fig. 317:
"Home Town Drug Store,"
by MARX, no. 184, circa
1920s. (Courtesy of Gaston
Majeune.) The pieces in the
"Home Town" series, num-
bered 180-187, are not
marked with the MARX
logo, but their boxes are.
The tiny businesses say
"Home Town" in a circle on
the inside back wall.
*MIB $275; Excellent $225; Good
with some pieces missing $125.*

Fig. 317a:
"Home Town Police
Station," by MARX, no.
185, circa 1920s. (Courtesy
of Gaston Majeune.)
*MIB $275; Excellent $225, Good
with some pieces missing $125.*

Fig. 318:
"Service Station, BlueBird
Garage," by MARX, 1937.
(Courtesy of Jim Cox.)
This was one of MARX's
fabulous deco-style pieces.
Excellent $550; Good $225.

Fig. 319:
"Roadside Rest Service
Station," by MARX, 1935.
(Courtesy of Jim Cox.)
This set is usually found
with the oil can and trolley
missing. Some believe the
two attendants at the snack
bar are meant to look like
Laurel and Hardy.
Excellent $1500; Good $1200.

Fig. 320:
"Auto-Laundry," possibly
Firestone or Sears, circa
1950s. (Courtesy of Jim Cox.)
Excellent $100; Good $75.

Fig. 321:
"Britelite Filling Station,"
by MARX, circa 1930s.
(Courtesy of Jim Cox.)
Batteries go in the standing
case which feeds the pump
and lights.
Excellent $525; Good $250.

Fig. 317

Fig. 317a

Fig. 318

Fig. 319

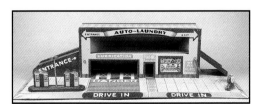
Fig. 320

Fig. 321

Fig. 322

Fig. 323

Fig. 324

Fig. 325

Fig. 326

Fig. 322:
"The Corner Grocer," by WOLVERINE, no. 182., circa 1932 to 1940s. (Courtesy of Jim Cox.) This wonderful toy included a roll of butcher paper, a telephone, boxes of grocery products, and a scale. In 1942 the colors changed and WOLVERINE added no. 188, the "Playtown Drugstore." By the late 1940s the grocery store was no longer produced. *Excellent and Complete $600; Good and not quite Complete $350.*

Fig. 323:
Advertisement of "Corner Grocer" from 1936 Wolverine catalogue.

Fig. 324:
Advertisement of "Corner Grocer" from 1942 Wolverine catalogue.

Fig. 325:
"Lazy Days Farms," by MARX, circa 1950s. *Excellent with all pieces, $175; Good $135.*

Fig. 326:
"Roy Rogers Rodeo Ranch," by MARX, circa 1950s. *MIB $140; Good $95.*

Fig. 327:
Interior of ranch house in Figure 326.

Fig. 328:
Close-up of exterior of Roy Rogers ranch house in Figure 326.

Fig. 329:
"Log Cabin," by MARX, circa 1950s.
Excellent with all pieces, $145; Good $110; As pictured, no accoutrements, $45.

Fig. 330:
Interior of cabin in Figure 329.

Fig. 331:
"Sears Service Station," by MARX, circa 1950s.
(Courtesy of Dorothy Ellen Masters.)
Excellent $160; Good $120.

Fig. 327

Fig. 328

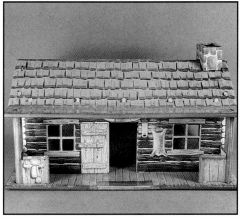

Fig. 329

Fig. 330

Fig. 331

Fig. 332

Fig. 333

Fig. 334

Fig. 332:
"Babyland Nursery," by
MARX, circa 1950s.
(Courtesy of Patty Cooper.)
This rather hard-to-find
nursery came complete with
seven figures, little cribs,
covers, baby bottles, steril-
izer, bath, scale, cupboards,
high chair, and other accessories.
Excellent with all pieces $275;
Good with some pieces missing
$150.

Fig. 333:
"Friendly Folks Toy Motel,"
by KIDDIE BRUSH CO.,
1954. (Courtesy of Patty
Cooper.) This very hard-to-
find motel came with hard
plastic furniture and both
hard and soft plastic accessories.
Excellent with all pieces $500;
Good with some pieces missing
$200.

Fig. 334:
Interior of motel in Figure
333.

WIND-UP TOYS

OF all the tin-litho toys, wind-ups are the most sought after and the most expensive. The clever mechanics are as irresistible to adults as they are to children. Moreover, wind-ups don't just picture a bear, or a cowboy, or a clown —they are the bear, cowboy or clown. Many American toy companies produced wind-ups, but MARX was, by far, the most prolific. However, there are some terrific wind-ups by CHEIN, UNIQUE ARTS, WOLVERINE, STRAUSS, and WYANDOTTE as well. Following is a sampling of the many wind-ups produced in America.

Fig. 335:
"Santee Claus," by FERDI-NAND STRAUSS, circa 1920s. (Courtesy of Jack and Barbara Craig.) Note the magnificent lithography covering the sleigh.
Excellent $1200; Good $800.

Fig. 336:
"Zilotone," by WOLVER-INE, 1920s and 1931, no. 48. (Courtesy of Jack and Barbara Craig.) This ingenious toy duplicates a xylophonist by using little metal records. The "gay" tunes include "My Old Kentucky Home," "Sidewalks of New York," and "Farmer in the Dell."
Excellent $850; Good $600.

Fig. 337:
"Luck O' Wheel," by DURABLE TOY AND NOVELTY CORP., circa 1920s. (Courtesy of Jack and Barbara Craig.)
Excellent $475; Good $325.

Fig. 338:
"Rabbit on Cart," circa 1920s. (Courtesy of Dora C. Pohl.) Lithography on pressed steel.
Excellent $165; Good $100.

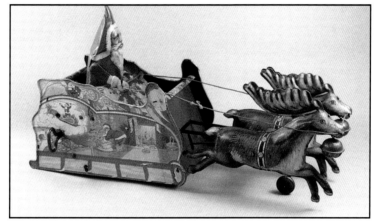

Fig. 335

Fig. 337

Fig. 336

Fig. 338

Fig. 339

Fig. 340

Fig. 341

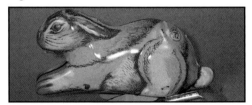

Fig. 342

Fig. 343

Fig. 339:
"Aeroplane," by CHEIN, 1929, no. 65. (Courtesy of Dora C. Pohl.)
Excellent $350; Good $275.

Fig. 340:
"Li'l Abner and His Dogpatch Band," by UNIQUE ART, 1930. (Courtesy of Heather Baker.) When wound, all of the different characters on this incredible toy would play instruments or dance. This toy was issued in several different combinations of Dogpatch characters.
MIB $1050; Excellent $800; Good $550.

Fig. 341:
Box for the band in Figure 340.

Fig. 342:
"Hopping Rabbit, no. 79," by CHEIN, 1931. (Courtesy of Heather Baker.)
Excellent $200; Good $150.

Fig. 343:
"Tidy Tim," by MARX, 1935. (Courtesy of Pat and Norma Weathersby.)
Excellent $700; Good $500.

Fig. 344:
"Native Boy on Alligator,"
by CHEIN, no. 140.
(Courtesy of Pat and
Norma Weathersby.)
Produced in the 1930s and
again in 1958 and 1960.
The older version is pic-
tured.
Excellent $300; Good $250.
Newer version, Excellent $200;
Good $150.

Fig. 344

Fig. 345:
"Popeye Roll-Over
Airplane," by MARX, 1936.
(Courtesy of Pat and
Norma Weathersby.) This
plane also came in red,
white, and blue.
Excellent $1000; Good $750.

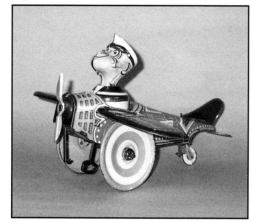
Fig. 345

Fig. 346:
"Carousel," by WOLVER-
INE, no. 31, circa 1936 to
1950, when a new design
was introduced, no. 31a.
(See Figures 2 and 3 for
comparison.) Older version
shown. (Courtesy of Jack
and Barbara Craig.)
Excellent $660; Good $550.
No. 31a, Excellent $575;
Good $275.

Fig. 346

Fig. 347:
"Clucking Chicken,"
Possibly BALDWIN, 1936.
(Courtesy of Heather
Baker.)
Excellent $175; Good $125.

Fig. 348:
"Roll-Over Rabbit," by
CHEIN, no. 89, 1938.
(Courtesy of Dorothy Ellen
Masters.)
Excellent $225; Good $175.

Fig. 347

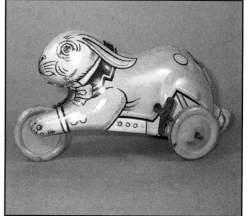
Fig. 348

Fig. 349

Fig. 350

Fig. 351

Fig. 352

Fig. 353

Fig. 354

Fig. 349:
"Ducky," by CHEIN, 1938, no. 72. (Courtesy of Dorothy Ellen Masters.) This duck looks a lot like the long-billed Donald, but CHEIN did not have Disney rights at the time. *Excellent $175; Good $125.*

Fig. 350:
"Trapeze Artist," by WYANDOTTE, circa 1930s. (Courtesy of Jack and Barbara Craig.) *Excellent $300; Good $225.*

Fig. 351:
"Motorcycle Man," by MARX, 1938. (Courtesy of Tom Frogge.) *Excellent $450; Good $300.*

Fig. 352:
"Penguin," by CHEIN, circa 1930s. (Courtesy of Dorothy Ellen Masters.) *Excellent $225; Good $150.*

Fig. 353:
"Racetrack Carousel," by WOLVERINE, no. 30, 1930s through 1940. (Courtesy of Connie and Robert Delaney.) Pressure-lever action. *Excellent $650; Good $350.*

Fig. 354:
"Snare Drummer," by CHEIN, 1930s through 1956, no. 109. (Courtesy of Dorothy Ellen Masters.) In 1960, a mechanical bass drummer, no. 110, was introduced. *With tri-colored shield, Excellent $250; Good $175.*

Fig. 356:
"Ferris Wheel," by CHEIN, circa 1930s through 1960s. This intricately lithographed Ferris wheel had six gondolas until the 1960s, when it was produced with only four gondolas. It has a bell and a large motor.
With six gondolas, Excellent $400; Good $275.
With four gondolas, Excellent $250; Good $165.

Fig. 357:
"Roller Coaster," by CHEIN, circa 1950s. (Courtesy of Jack and Barbara Craig.)
Excellent $400; Good $275.

Fig. 358:
"Hokey-Pokey," by WYANDOTTE, circa 1930s. (Courtesy of Tom Frogge.)
Excellent $325; Good $225.

Fig. 359:
"Race Car," by MARX, circa 1940s. (Courtesy of Heather Baker.) This toy has the same mold as the MARX zeppelin. Right after the Hindenberg crashed, MARX used the zeppelin mold to make this race-car.
Excellent $350; Good $250.

Fig. 360:
"Airplane Carousel," probably WYANDOTTE, circa 1930s. (Courtesy of Dora C. Pohl.)
Excellent $400; Good $275.

Fig. 356

Fig. 357

Fig. 359

Fig. 358

Fig. 360

Fig. 361

Fig. 362

Fig. 365

Fig. 366

Fig. 364

Fig. 363

Fig. 361:
"Jo Penner and His Duck Goo-Goo," by MARX, 1934. (Courtesy of Jack and Barbara Craig.) Jo Penner was a comedian of the burlesque theatre, radio, and films.
MIB $850; Good $475.

Fig. 362:
"B.O. Plenty," by MARX, circa 1930s. (Courtesy of Heather Baker.) "Bo Plenty" was a character from Dick Tracy comic books.
Excellent $400; Good $300.

Fig. 363:
"Mortimer Snerd," by MARX, circa 1930s. (Courtesy of Heather Baker.)
Excellent $450; Good $350.

Fig. 364:
Back of "Mortimer Snerd," Figure 363, and "B.O. Plenty," Figure 362.

Fig. 365:
"Drum Major," by WOLVERINE, circa mid 1930s through the 1950s. (Courtesy of Heather Baker.) In 1936, WOLVERINE advertised this toy, no. 27, as playing "stirring march rhythms." The 1936 version had one vertical stripe across the front of the jacket and a square base. In 1950, WOLVERINE introduced no. 27a which had crossed stripes on the jacket front and a round base.
With crossed stripes, Excellent $525; Good $225.

Fig. 366:
Back of drummer in Figure 365.

Fig. 367:
"Hillbilly Express," by
UNIQUE ART, circa
1930s. (Courtesy of
Heather Baker.)
Excellent $225; Good $175.

Fig. 368:
Close-up of lithography in
Figure 367.

Fig. 369:
"Giant Scottie," by MARX,
circa late 1930s. (Courtesy
of Heather Baker.) This
Scottie was produced in a
variety of colors and sizes.
The very early ones had
wooden paws.
Excellent $525; Good $275.

Fig. 370:
"Capitol Hill Race," by
UNIQUE ART, circa
1930s. (Courtesy of
Heather Baker.)
Excellent $225; Good $175.

Fig. 371:
Close-up of race game in
Figure 370.

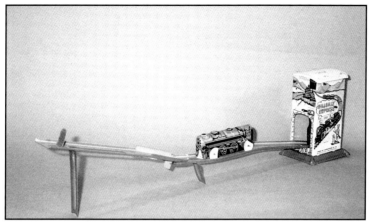

Fig. 367

Fig. 368

Fig. 369

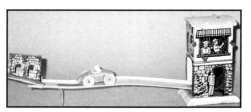

Fig. 370

Fig. 371

Fig. 372

Fig. 373

Fig. 374

Fig. 375

Fig. 376

Fig. 372:
"Seal with Ball," by CHEIN, circa early 1930s, no. 72. (Courtesy of Dorothy Ellen Masters.) *Excellent $225; Good $175.*

Fig. 373:
"Mickey Mouse Express," by MARX, 1952. (Courtesy of Dora C. Pohl.) *Excellent $550; Good $300.*

Fig. 374:
"Mechanical Fish," by CHEIN, 1956 and 1964, no. 55. (Courtesy of Dorothy Ellen Masters.) *Excellent $125; Good $75.*

Fig. 375:
"Minnie Mouse Knitting," by LINE MAR (MARX'S Japanese company), circa 1950s. (Courtesy of Pat and Norma Weathersby.) *Excellent $950; Good $600.*

Fig. 376:
"Aquaplane," by CHEIN, no. 39. (Courtesy of Jack and Barbara Craig.) This toy was produced in the early 1930s with crossed stripes on the wings. In 1956 and 1960 it appears in catalogues with stars on the wings. The colors varied from year to year. In 1956 the plane had red pontoons, red nose, yellow body and blue stars. In 1960 it had blue pontoons, yellow body, blue nose, and red stars. The one pictured is different yet.
Plane from the 1950s or 1960s, Excellent $150; Good $100.
Aquaplane from the 1930s, Excellent $300; Good $200.

Fig. 377:
"Handstand Clown," by CHEIN, circa 1950s. (Courtesy of Dorothy Ellen Masters.) In the 1960s this same clown was reissued with purple pants and a green shirt.
Excellent $150; Good $100. Clown with purple pants, Excellent $125; Good $60.

Fig. 378:
"Pelican," by CHEIN, circa 1950s. (Courtesy of Dorothy Ellen Masters.)
Excellent $150; Good $125.

Fig. 379:
"Indian Chief," often attributed to CHEIN, circa 1950s.(Courtesy of Dorothy Ellen Masters.)
Excellent $175; Good $135.

Fig. 380:
"Greyhound Bus," by CHEIN, circa 1950s. (Courtesy of Dorothy Ellen Masters.) This bus, no. 219, was first produced in the early 1930s. It has evolved significantly over the years.
1930s Greyhound bus, Excellent $240; Good $125.

Fig. 381:
"Chick," by CHEIN, circa 1950s. (Courtesy of Dorothy Ellen Masters.)
Excellent $125; Good $75.

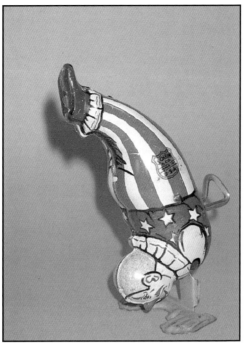
Fig. 377

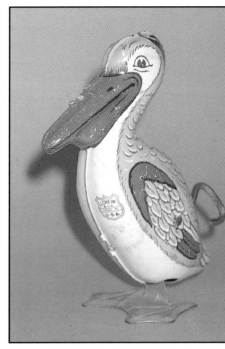
Fig. 378

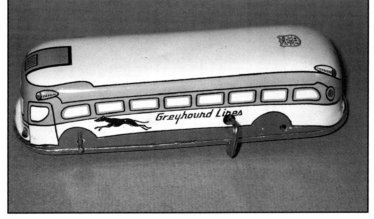
Fig. 380

Fig. 381

Fig. 379

Fig. 382

Fig. 383

Fig. 386

Fig. 385

Fig. 384

Fig. 382:
"Bunny With Hands in Pockets," by CHEIN, circa 1950s. (Courtesy of Dorothy Ellen Masters.) *Excellent $125; Good $95.*

Fig. 383:
"Policeman," by CHEIN, circa 1950s. (Courtesy of Dorothy Ellen Masters.) *Excellent $125; Good $100.*

Fig. 384:
"Piggy," by CHEIN, circa 1950s. (Courtesy of Dorothy Ellen Masters.) *Excellent $150; Good $100.*

Fig. 385:
"Motor Boat with People," by LINDSTROM TOOL AND TOY COMPANY, circa 1930s. (Courtesy of Heather Baker.) *Excellent $150; Good $100.*

Fig. 386:
"Mother Duck and Babies," by WYANDOTTE, circa 1950s. (Courtesy of Jack and Barbara Craig.) *Excellent $125; Good $75.*

Fig. 387:
"Big and Little Ducks," by CHEIN. (See Figure 349 for "Big Duck.") Little duck, circa 1950s.
Excellent $85; Good $50.

Fig. 388:
"Handstand Clown, Newer Version," by CHEIN, 1965. (Courtesy of Dorothy Ellen Masters.)
Excellent $125; Good $60.

Fig. 389:
"Boat with Prop and Man," by CHEIN, 1956 to 1960, no. 56. (Courtesy of Dorothy Ellen Masters.)
Excellent $150; Good $85.

Fig. 390:
"Sea Plane," by OHIO ART, 1959 to 1962. (Courtesy of Tom Frogge.)
Excellent $120; Good $80.

Fig. 391:
"Frogman," by CHEIN, 1964, no. 122. (Courtesy of Dorothy Ellen Masters.)
Excellent $100; Good $65.

Fig. 387

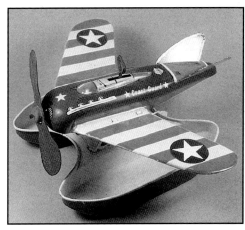

Fig. 390

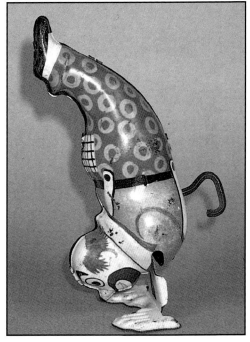

Fig. 388

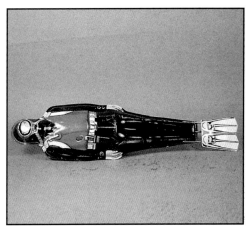

Fig. 391

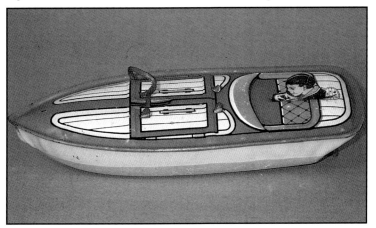

Fig. 389

Fig. 392

Fig. 394

Fig. 392:
"Speed Cruiser in Package," by CHEIN, 1964, no. 306. (Courtesy of Dorothy Ellen Masters.)
Excellent $95; Good $45.

Fig. 393:
"Chicken with Blue Bow," by CHEIN, 1964 to 1965. (Courtesy of Dorothy Ellen Masters.)
Excellent $90; Good $50.

Fig. 394:
"Bear," by CHEIN, 1965. (Courtesy of Dorothy Ellen Masters.) This bear features the newer lithography on the same body as the older bears.
Excellent $75; Good $50.

Fig. 393

BANKS

MANY collectors specialize in banks, including cast-iron, mechanical, still, safe and dime banks. Tin-litho banks are generally still affordable and are just becoming highly collectible. CHEIN produced a huge variety of these banks from the early 1920s on. A good source for information on CHEIN banks is Bob McCumber's *CHEIN Toys and Bank Catalogs*.

Fig. 395:
"Lucky Savings Bank," by SHANK WORKS, AMERICAN CAN COMPANY, MAYWOOD, ILL., 1913 and 1916. (Courtesy of Dorothy Ellen Masters.) *Excellent $275; Good $200.*

Fig. 396:
Back of bank in Figure 395. Note the complex directions.

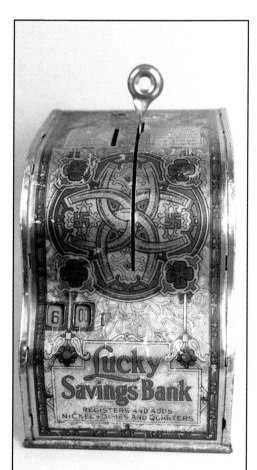

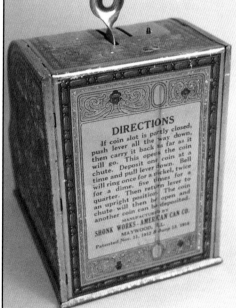

Fig. 396

Fig. 395

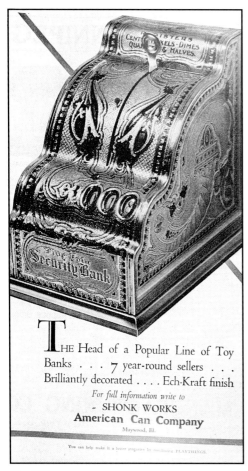

Fig. 397

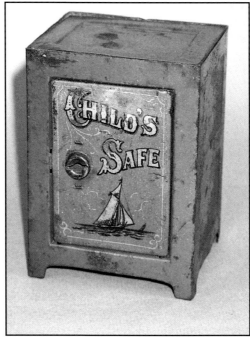

Fig. 398

Fig. 399

Fig. 400

Fig. 397:
Advertisement that appeared in 1927 *Playthings* toy catalogue for the New York Toy Show.

Fig. 398:
"Child's Safe," by CHEIN, 1910 to 1921. Round logo or no logo. (Courtesy of Dorothy Ellen Masters.) *Excellent $200; Good $140.*

Fig. 399:
"Child's Safe," by CHEIN, 1910 to 1921. No logo. (Courtesy of Dorothy Ellen Masters.) *Excellent $200; Good $140.*

Fig. 400:
"Small Mascot Safe," by CHEIN, 1914. (Courtesy of Dorothy Ellen Masters.) *Excellent $200; Good $140.*

Fig. 401:
"Popeye Dime Register Bank," by KING FEATURE SYND., 1929. (Courtesy of Dorothy Ellen Masters.)
Excellent $140; Good $115.

Fig. 402:
"Popeye Dime Register Bank," by KING FEATURE SYND., 1956. (Courtesy of Dorothy Ellen Masters.)
Excellent $125; Good $100.

Fig. 403:
"Little Cowboy Dime Register Bank," by KALON MFG. CORP., circa 1950s. (Courtesy of Dorothy Ellen Masters.)
Excellent $100; Good $85.

Fig. 404:
"Circus Dime Register Bank," circa 1950s. (Courtesy of Dorothy Ellen Masters.)
Excellent $75; Good $50.

Fig. 405:
"New York World's Fair Dime Register Bank," presented by U.S. STEEL, 1939.
Excellent $125; Good $90.

Fig. 406:
"Astronaut Dime Register Bank," by KALON MFG. CORP., circa 1960s. (Courtesy of Dorothy Ellen Masters.)
Excellent $100; Good $85.

Fig. 401

Fig. 402

Fig. 403

Fig. 404

Fig. 405

Fig. 406

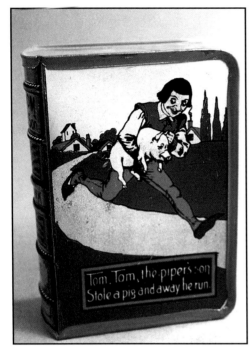

Fig. 407

Fig. 408

Fig. 409

Fig. 410

Fig. 407:
"Tom, Tom the Piper's Son, Book Bank," by KIRCH-HOF, circa 1930s or 1940s, Volume I. One of series of four book banks, each listed by volume. (Courtesy of Dorothy Ellen Masters.) *Excellent $90; Good $65.*

Fig. 408:
"Simple Simon, Book Bank," by KIRCHHOF, Volume II, circa 1930s to 1940s. Another in the book series. *Excellent $90; Good $75.*

Fig. 409:
"Old Mother Hubbard," by KIRCHHOF, Volume III, circa 1930s to 1940s. Another in the book series. *Excellent $90; Good $75.*

Fig. 410:
"Old King Cole," by KIRCHHOF, Volume IV, circa 1930s to 1940s. Another in the book series. *Excellent $90; Good $75.*

Fig. 411:
The complete four-volume set in Figures 407-410. (Courtesy of Dorothy Ellen Masters.) *Complete set, Excellent $375; Good $275.*

Fig. 411

Fig. 412:
"Humpty-Dumpty Head Bank," by CHEIN, 1934 to 1941. (Courtesy of Dorothy Ellen Masters.)
Excellent $135; Good $95.

Fig. 413:
"Mechanical Monkey Bank," by CHEIN, 1941 to 1960, no. 11. (Courtesy of Ellen Dorothy Masters.) This bank was very likely introduced before 1941. The year 1941 is listed because it was the earliest catalogue find. The one shown has a key and is an earlier bank.
Square trap, Excellent $140; Good $100.
Later version, Excellent $95; Good $60.

Fig. 414:
"Uncle Wiggly Mechanical Bank, no. 22," by CHEIN, circa early 1950s to 1960s. (Courtesy of Ellen Dorothy Masters.)
"C" keyed bottom, Excellent $125; Good $90.

Fig. 415:
"Clown Head Mechanical Bank," by CHEIN, 1931 through the mid-1940s. (Courtesy of Dorothy Ellen Masters.)
Square key lock coin trap, Excellent $225; Good $175.

Fig. 412

Fig. 413

Fig. 414

Fig. 415

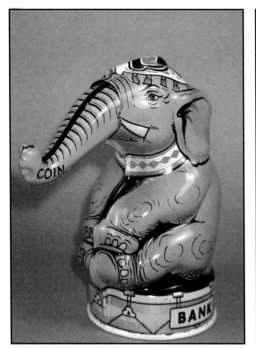

Fig. 416

Fig. 417

Fig. 418

Fig. 419

Fig. 420

Fig. 416:
"Mechanical Elephant," by
CHEIN, circa 1950s to
1960s. (Courtesy of
Dorothy Ellen Masters.)
*Round coin trap, Excellent $95;
Good $65.*

Fig. 417:
"Roly-Poly Monkey Bank,"
by CHEIN, circa 1930s.
(Courtesy of Dorothy Ellen
Masters.)
Excellent $225; Good $175.

Fig. 418:
"Happy Days Register
Bank," by CHEIN.
(Courtesy of Dorothy Ellen
Masters.) This bank was
introduced in the mid 1930s
and produced through the
1950s.
Excellent $75; Good $45.

Fig. 419:
"Register Dime-Bank with
Floral Scroll," by CHEIN,
1948 to 1969. (Courtesy of
Dorothy Ellen Masters.)
*Slide opening, Excellent $50;
Good $35.*

Fig. 420:
"Register Bank," by
CHEIN, 1939 to 1969, no. 5.
(Courtesy of Dorothy Ellen
Masters.)
*Round trap, MIB $65;
Good $35.*

Fig. 421:
"Thrifty Elf Dime-A-Day
Register Bank," by
CHEIN, circa mid-1950s,
no. 2. (Courtesy of Dorothy
Ellen Masters.)
Excellent $45; Good $35.

Fig. 422:
Back of bank in Figure 421.

Fig. 423:
"Mercury Bank," by
CHEIN, 1945 through the
mid-1960s. (Courtesy of
Dorothy Ellen Masters.)
Excellent $45; Good $55.

Fig. 424:
"Happy Days Barrel Bank,"
by CHEIN, 1933 to 1955.
(Courtesy of Dorothy Ellen
Masters.) This bank was
introduced after repeal of
liquor prohibition. The ver-
sion with the square trap is
older than that with the
round trap.
*Square trap, Excellent $50;
Good $35.*
*Round trap, Excellent $35;
Good $25.*

Fig. 425:
"Happy Days Barrel Bank
Promotional," by CHEIN.
(Courtesy of Dorothy Ellen
Masters.) These banks were
produced for special orders
for promotions. The one
pictured is from the mid
1930s and advertised a
Detroit-area car dealer.
*Excellent $75;
Good (as shown) $60.*

Fig. 421

Fig. 423

Fig. 422

Fig. 424

Fig. 425

Fig. 426

Fig. 427

Fig. 426:
Examples of different coin traps on banks over a twenty-year period. The oldest is on the left. Left: circa late 1920s to early 1930s; Center: circa 1930s; Right: circa 1940s to 1950s.

Fig. 427:
In the 1970s, CHEIN produced prototypes of reproductions of four of its older mechanical banks. They only produced six of each of these four banks which included: 1) Mechanical Elephant, 2) Clown Head, 3) Mechanical Monkey, and 4) Uncle Wiggly. The prototypes had the spiral logo. Pictured here is a comparison of the original bank and the reproduction. Note the logos near the bottom. Because they are so rare, these banks can sometimes sell for as much as $400.

Fig. 428:
"Three Little Pigs Bank," by CHEIN, circa early 1930s. (Courtesy of Dorothy Ellen Masters.) *Excellent $175; Good $135.*

Fig. 429:
"Log Cabin and Singers Bank," by CHEIN, circa mid 1930s. (Courtesy of Dorothy Ellen Masters.) *Excellent $185; Good $140.*

Fig. 428

Fig. 429

Fig. 430:
"New Deal Bank," by
CHEIN, 1937. (Courtesy of
Dorothy Ellen Masters.)
Excellent $150; Good $115.

Fig. 431:
"Boy Scout Bank," by
CHEIN, 1939, no. 180.
(Courtesy of Dorothy Ellen
Masters.) Extremely rare.
Excellent $250; Good $200.

Fig. 432:
"Cash Register Bank," circa
early 1920s. (Courtesy of
Connie and Bob Delaney.)
Excellent $150; Good $85.

Fig. 433:
"Drum Bank," by OHIO
ART, 1941 and 1950.
Designed by Fern Bisel
Peat.
Excellent $60; Good $35.

Fig. 434:
"Snow White Disney
Bank," Walt Disney
Enterprises, 1938.
(Courtesy of Heather
Baker.)
Excellent $135; Good $90.

Fig. 430

Fig. 431

Fig. 432

Fig. 433

Fig. 434

Fig. 435

NOISEMAKERS

PEOPLE have a universal affinity for noisemakers. In America, we associate them with New Year's Eve or with loud and wild parties. However, noisemakers have a far deeper significance than simple fun. The custom of making noise goes back to the ancient practice of driving away evil spirits. In fact, the use of noisemakers in connection with the New Year is one of the earliest and longest continued customs known to humankind. The custom was said to have originated in Babylon and India, but noisemakers in some form are synonymous with New Year's celebrations the world over.

On the Jewish holiday Purim, noisemakers are sounded whenever the name of the Jew's nemesis, Haman, is said aloud in the telling of the ancient story. Since the 13th century in France and Germany, the "gragger," a noisemaker which is a combination of a "bullroarer" and a "scraper," has been used.

Many tin lithographed noisemakers were produced in the United States. They were decorated with lithography depicting musicians, dancers, clowns, and holiday themes — especially Halloween and New Years. The main producers were KIRCHHOF, U. S. METAL TOYS, T. COHN, CHEIN, and GOTHAM STEEL.

Noisemakers are still an affordably priced collectible with some terrific lithography. Good condition Halloween noisemakers are one of the best finds.

Fig. 438:
Old style wooden gragger noisemaker, American, circa 1920s.
Excellent $35; Good $20.

Fig. 438

Fig. 439

Fig. 440

Fig. 441

Fig. 442

Fig. 443

Fig. 444

Fig. 439:
"Asian Dancer," old German noisemaker, circa 1920s.
Excellent $80; Good $65.

Fig. 440:
"Boxers," old German noisemaker, circa 1920s.
Excellent $90; Good $75.

Fig. 441:
"Gotham Rattler," by GOTHAM STAMPING AND DIE CORP, New York City, circa 1920s.
Excellent $24; Good $20.

Fig. 442:
"Butterfly Dancers," by KIRCHHOF, circa 1940s.
Excellent $20; Good $16.

Fig. 443:
"Mardi Gras Couple," by U. S. METAL TOYS, circa 1950s.
Excellent $15; Good $10.

Fig. 444:
"Jitterbug," by T. COHN, circa late 1940s to 1950s.
Excellent $20; Good $14.

Fig. 445:
"Copacabana," by KIRCH-
HOF, circa 1940s.
Excellent $24; Good $20.

Fig. 446:
"Conga-Line," by T.
COHN, circa 1930s.
Excellent $22; Good $18.

Fig. 447:
"At the Ball," by T. COHN,
circa 1930s.
Excellent $25; Good $20.

Fig. 448:
"Mexican Guitarist," by
U. S. METAL TOYS, circa
1950s.
Excellent $18; Good $14.

Fig. 449:
"Carnival Dancer," by T.
COHN, circa 1940s to
1950s.
Excellent $20; Good $15.

Fig. 445

Fig. 446

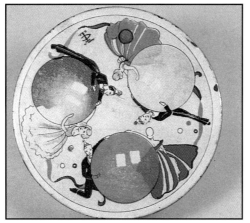

Fig. 447

Fig. 448

Fig. 449

Fig. 450

Fig. 451

Fig. 453

Fig. 452

Fig. 454

Fig. 450:
"Many Faces of Dance," by
U. S. METAL TOYS, circa
1950s.
Excellent $22; Good $18.

Fig. 451:
"Rock n' Roll," circa 1950s
to 1960s.
Excellent $18; Good $14.

Fig. 452:
"Flamenco Dancer," by
U. S. METAL TOYS, circa
1940s to 1950s.
Excellent $22; Good $18.

Fig. 453:
"Tap Dancers," by KIRCH-
HOF, circa 1940s to 1950s.
Excellent $18; Good $12.

Fig. 454:
"Carmen Miranda," by T.
COHN, circa 1940s to
1950s.
Excellent $22; Good $18.

Fig. 455:
"Tap Dancers," by KIRCH-HOF, circa 1940s to 1950s.
Excellent $15; Good $10.

Fig. 456:
"Conga Drummer," circa 1950s.
Excellent $20; Good $15.

Fig. 457:
"Spanish Dancer," by KIRCHHOF, "Life of the Party" line. Circa 1940s.
Excellent $22; Good $18.

Fig. 458:
"Gypsy Dancers, by KIRCHHOF, "Life of the Party" line. Circa 1950s.
Excellent $20; Good $16.

Fig. 459:
"Softshoe," by U. S. METAL TOYS, circa 1940s to 1950s.
Excellent $25; Good $21.

Fig. 455

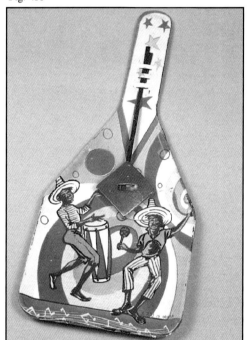

Fig. 456

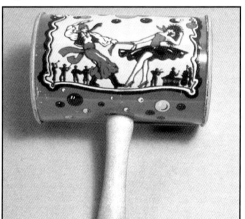

Fig. 458

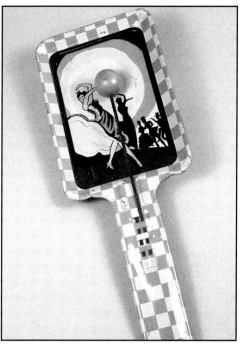

Fig. 457

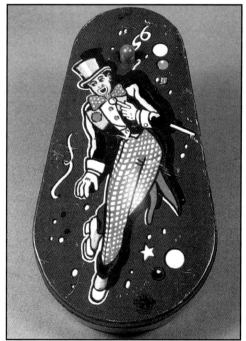

Fig. 459

Fig. 460

Fig. 463

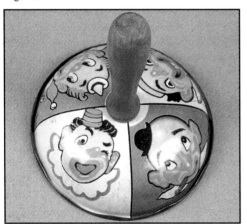

Fig. 461

Fig. 464

Fig. 462

Fig. 460:
"Harmonica Player," by
U. S. METAL TOYS, circa
1930s or 1940s.
Excellent $25; Good $21.

Fig. 461:
"Four Clowns," by T.
COHN, circa 1930s.
Excellent $20; Good $16.

Fig. 462:
"Clown Face," by KIRCH-
HOF, circa 1930s or 1940s.
Excellent $25; Good $20.

Fig. 463:
"Two Clowns Pulling
Ducks on Leashes," by T.
COHN, circa 1930s.
Excellent $25; Good $20.

Fig. 464:
"Clown Faces," by KIRCH-
HOF, circa 1950s.
Excellent $16; Good $11.

Fig. 465:
"Clowns and Balloons," by
T. COHN, circa 1920s to
early 1930s.
Excellent $28; Good $24.

Fig. 466:
"Clowns," by KIRCHHOF,
circa 1950s.
Excellent $15; Good $11.

Fig. 467:
"Clown Face," by KIRCH-
HOF, "Life of the Party"
line.
Excellent $15; Good $12.

Fig. 468:
"Clown Face," by U. S.
METAL TOYS, circa
1940s.
Excellent $15; Good $11.

Fig. 469:
"Clown Face," by T.
COHN.
Excellent $20; Good $15.

Fig. 465

Fig. 467

Fig. 466

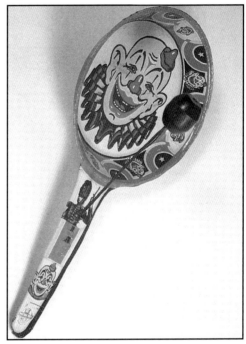

Fig. 468

Fig. 469

Fig. 470

Fig. 471

Fig. 473

Fig. 472

Fig. 474

Fig. 470:
"Clown Face," by KIRCH-
HOF, "Life of the Party"
line, circa 1940s.
Excellent $20; Good $15.

Fig. 471:
"Clown Face," by KIRCH-
HOF, "Life of the Party"
line, circa 1950s.
Excellent $15; Good $12.

Fig. 472:
"Three Clowns," by T.
COHN, circa 1940s.
Excellent $28; Good $24.

Fig. 473:
"Clowns," by BUBLE
TOY, made in U.S.A., circa
1940s to 1950s.
Excellent $25; Good $20.

Fig. 474:
"Balloons," by T. COHN,
circa 1930s to 1940s.
Excellent $18; Good $12.

Fig. 475:
"Party Scene," possibly
CHEIN, circa 1930s to
1940s.
Excellent $25; Good $20.

Fig. 476:
"Pierrot," by KIRCHHOF,
"Life of the Party" line,
circa 1920s to 1950s. This is
an example of what
KIRCHHOF termed the
"twirly-click" style noisemaker introduced in 1927.
Excellent $18; Good $15.

Fig. 477:
"Man With Balloon," by T.
COHN, circa 1930s.
Excellent $22; Good $18.

Fig. 478:
"Pierrot and Party," by
U. S. METAL TOYS, circa
1940s to 1950s.
Excellent $18; Good $15.

Fig. 479:
"Party with Clown," by
U. S. METAL TOYS, circa
1960s to 1970s.
Excellent $15; Good $10.

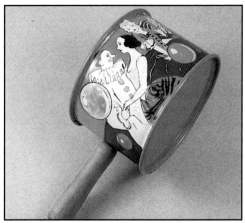

Fig. 475

Fig. 477

Fig. 476

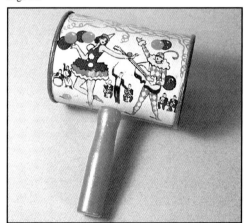

Fig. 478

Fig. 479

Fig. 480

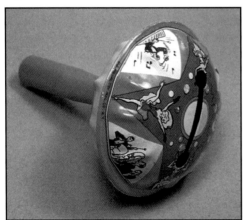

Fig. 481

Fig. 482

Fig. 483

Fig. 484

Fig. 485

Fig. 480:
"Party and Man with Horn," by U. S. METAL TOYS, circa 1950s.
Excellent $20; Good $16.

Fig. 481:
"Musicians and Dancers," by U. S. METAL TOYS, circa 1950s.
Excellent $16; Good $12.

Fig. 482:
"Bat, Witches, and Cat," by KIRCHHOF, circa late 1940s to early 1950s.
Excellent $26; Good $20.

Fig. 483:
"Halloween Cast of Characters," by U. S. METAL TOYS, circa 1940s.
Excellent $22; Good $18.

Fig. 484:
"Pumpkins," by T. COHN, circa 1930s.
Excellent $24; Good $20.

Fig. 485:
"Witch's Head," by KIRCHHOF, "Life of the Party" line, circa late 1940s to 1950s.
Excellent $26; Good $22.

Fig. 486:
"Witch's Brew," by U. S. METAL TOYS, circa 1940s.
Excellent $26; Good $22.

Fig. 487:
"Witch, Cat, and Owl," by U. S. METAL TOYS, circa 1950s.
Excellent $20; Good $18.

Fig. 488:
"Flight Over City," by T. COHN, circa 1930s to 1940s.
Excellent $40; Good $34.

Fig. 489:
"Owl," by KIRCHHOF, circa 1950s.
Excellent $25; Good $22.

Fig. 490:
"Witch Over Fire," by KIRCHHOF, circa 1940s to 1950s.
Excellent $24; Good $20.

Fig. 486

Fig. 487

Fig. 488

Fig. 489

Fig. 490

Fig. 491

Fig. 492

Fig. 493

Fig. 495

Fig. 494

Fig. 491:
"Witch and Broom," by
U. S. METAL TOYS, circa
1950s.
Excellent $30; Good $25.

Fig. 492:
"Skeletons and Witch," by
U. S. METAL TOYS, circa
1950s to 1960s.
Excellent $16; Good $14.

Fig. 493:
"Witches and Ghosts," by
U. S. METAL TOYS, circa
1960s to 1970s.
*With plastic handle, Excellent
$14; Good $10.*

Fig. 494:
"Scary Witch," by U. S.
METAL TOYS, circa
1940s to 1950s.
Excellent $35; Good $30.

Fig. 495:
"Cat's Head," by KIRCH-
HOF, circa 1940s to 1950s.
Excellent $26; Good $22.

Fig. 496:
"Black Cats," by KIRCH-HOF, circa 1940s to 1950s.
Excellent $26; Good $22.

Fig. 497:
"Circle of Stereotypes," by T. COHN, circa 1930s.
Excellent $35; Good $30.

Fig. 498:
"Geometric Design," by T. COHN, circa 1930s.
Excellent $25; Good $20.

Fig. 499:
"Minstrel Singer," by U. S. METAL TOYS, circa 1940s to 1950s. This is an unfortunate example of what was acceptable just a few decades ago.
Excellent $25; Good $21.

Fig. 500:
"Geometric Design," by KIRCHHOF, circa 1930s to 1940s.
Excellent $25; Good $22.

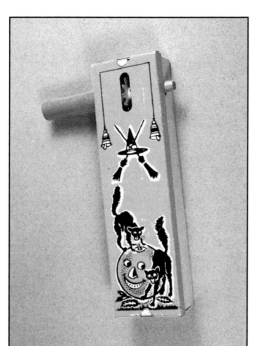

Fig. 496

Fig. 497

Fig. 498

Fig. 499

Fig. 500

Fig. 501

Fig. 502

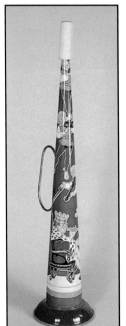

Fig. 503

Fig. 504

Fig. 505

Fig. 506

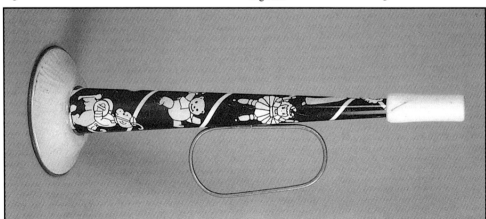

Fig. 507

Fig. 501:
"Around the World," by
KIRCHHOF, circa 1950s.
Excellent $20; Good $15.

Fig. 502:
"Circus," by KIRCHHOF,
circa 1950s.
Excellent $20; Good $15.

Fig. 503:
"Old King Cole Horn," by
T. COHN, circa 1930s to
1940s.
Excellent $30; Good $24.

Fig. 504:
"Nursery Rhymes Horn,"
by U. S. METAL TOYS,
circa 1940s to 1950s.
Excellent $18; Good $14.

Fig. 505:
"Nursery Rhymes Whistle,"
by KIRCHHOF, circa
1930s to 1940s.
Excellent $25; Good $30.

Fig. 506:
"Abraham Lincoln
Whistle," by KIRCHHOF,
circa 1940s to 1950s. A por-
tion of the Gettysburg
Address is lithographed on
this whistle.
Excellent $30; Good $25.

Fig. 507:
"Children and Animals
Playing Horns," by T.
COHN, circa 1930s.
Excellent $26; Good $22.

Fig. 508:
"Soldier Horn," by T. COHN, circa 1930s.
Excellent $50; Good $24.

Fig. 509:
"Halloween Horn," by T. COHN, circa 1940s to 1950s.
Excellent $50; Good $26.

Fig. 510:
"Party Horn," by U. S. METAL TOYS, circa 1950s to 1960s.
Excellent $14; Good $10.

Fig. 511:
"Decorative Horn," by GOTHAM PRESSED STEEL, circa late 1920s.
Excellent $58; Good $55.

Fig. 512:
"Gypsy Tambourine," by CHEIN, circa 1920s.
Excellent $85; Good $60.

Fig. 513:
"Halloween Pumpkin Tambourine," by U. S. METAL TOYS, circa 1950s.
Excellent $40; Good $55.

Fig. 514:
"Spanish Dancers Tambourine," by U. S. METAL TOYS, circa 1950s.
Excellent $25; Good $20.

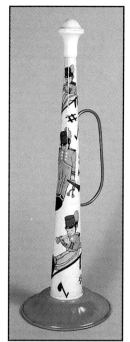

Fig. 508

Fig. 509

Fig. 510

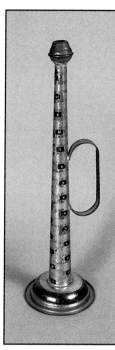

Fig. 511

Fig. 512

Fig. 513

Fig. 514

Fig. 515

Fig. 516

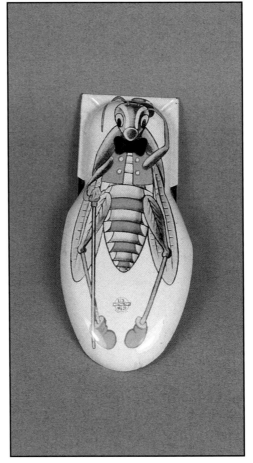

Fig. 517

Fig. 515:
"Gypsy Caravan Tambourine," by U. S. METAL TOYS, circa 1950s.
Excellent $25; Good $20.

Fig. 516:
"Clown Tambourine," made in U.S.A., circa 1950s.
Excellent $20; Good $15.

Fig. 517:
"Grasshopper Clicker," by U. S. METAL TOYS, circa 1950s.
Excellent $15; Good $12.

Fig. 518:
"Pierrot and Woman," by
KIRCHHOF, circa 1940s
to 1950s. This clicker is 2-1/2
inches long.
Excellent $10; Good $6.

Fig. 519:
"Halloween Owl Clicker,"
unmarked, circa 1950s.
Excellent $22; Good $18.

Fig. 520:
"Jester and Flapper," by
KIRCHHOF, circa 1950s.
Excellent $18; Good $15.

Fig. 521:
"Hopalong Cassidy
Clicker," by KIRCHHOF,
circa 1950s.
Excellent $30; Good $25.

Fig. 518

Fig. 520

Fig. 519

Fig. 521

Fig. 521a

Fig. 521b

Fig. 521a:
"Genie Clicker," unknown,
U.S.A., circa 1930s.
Excellent $35; Good $20.

Fig. 521b:
"Frog Clicker," unknown,
U.S.A., circa 1940s.
Excellent $18; Good $14.

Fig. 521c:
"Bucking Bronco Clicker,"
by KIRCHHOF, circa
1950s.
Excellent $22; Good $16.

(All clickers courtesy of
Ariel Kerr.)

Fig. 521c

MISCELLANEOUS

Fig. 522:
"Pull Toy," by HUSTLER
TOY CORP., circa 1920s,
pressed steel litho bed.
(Courtesy of Dora C.
Pohl.)
Excellent $185; Good $150.

Fig. 523:
"Dump-Truck," by
CHEIN, 1920s. (Courtesy
of Dorothy Ellen Masters.)
Excellent $300; Good $200.

Fig. 524:
"Toytown Ticket Office," by
CHEIN, no. 91, circa
1920s. (Courtesy of Pat and
Norma Weathersby.)
Excellent $125; Good $90.

Fig. 522

Fig. 524

Fig. 523

Fig. 525

Fig. 526

Fig. 527

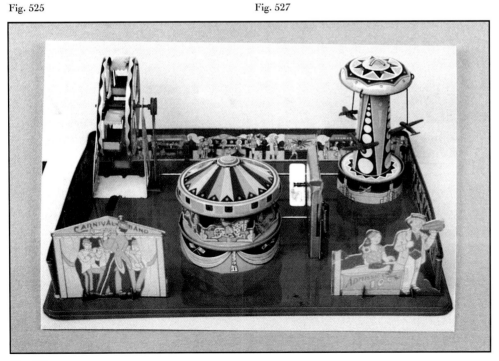

Fig. 528

Fig. 525:
"Windmill," date unknown, made in U.S.A.
Excellent $75; Good $50.

Fig. 526:
"Sunny Andy Cable Car," by WOLVERINE, 1931 and 1936, no. 53. (Courtesy of Shirley and Jim Cox.) This top notch marble game included action in which one car, loaded with a marble, would speed down the tracks while another would race up. The action was continuous as long as a supply of marbles kept coming.
Excellent $375; Good $225.

Fig. 527:
"Bunny with Egg-Shaped Cart, no. 161," by CHEIN, circa 1930s through 1950s. CHEIN produced several different egg carts throughout the decades, changing the lithography but keeping the same shapes.
Excellent $95; Good $50.

Fig. 528:
"Carnival," by WYANDOTTE, probably 1930s, crank-operated. (Courtesy of Dora C. Pohl.) Base is around 11-1/2" x 16".
Excellent $1200; Good $900.

Fig. 529:
"Bunny Cart," by CHEIN, circa 1930s. (Courtesy of Dorothy Ellen Masters.)
Excellent $225; Good $150.

Fig. 530:
"Sparkler on Card," by CHEIN, no. 95, 1932 through the early 1970s. (Courtesy of Dorothy Ellen Masters.) The logo and design on the box or card changed and makes it easier to date. The one pictured is most likely from the 1940s.
Excellent $55; Good $40.

Fig. 531:
"Sparkler with Box," by CHEIN, no. 95 with its box, circa 1930s. (Courtesy of Dorothy Ellen Masters.)
Excellent $75; Good $55.

Fig. 532:
"Music Box," by OHIO ART, 1939 to 1940, 4-1/2" high. (Courtesy of Michael Milson.)
Excellent $85; Good $60.

Fig. 533:
"Carousel Watering Can," by WOLVERINE, 1936 to 1959. (Courtesy of Dora C. Pohl.)
Excellent $75; Good $45.

Fig. 529

Fig. 532

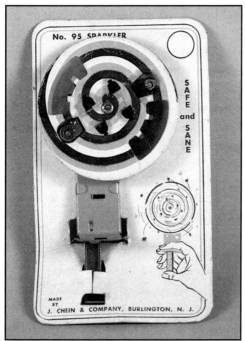

Fig. 530

Fig. 533

Fig. 531

Fig. 535

Fig. 536

Fig. 537

Fig. 538

Fig. 535:
"Shooting Gallery," by WYANDOTTE, circa 1930s. (Courtesy of Tom Frogge.)
Excellent $225; Good $150.

Fig. 536:
"Motorcycle Bunny," by WYANDOTTE, circa 1930s.
Excellent $225; Good $160.

Fig. 537:
"Sprinkling Can," by OHIO ART, circa late 1930s. Designed by Fern Bisel Peat.
Excellent $125; Good $75.

Fig. 538:
"Typewriter, Junior Dial," by MARX, circa 1930s. (Courtesy of Tom Frogge.)
Excellent $150; Good $100.

Figs. 539 and 539a:
"Donald Duck Watering Can," by OHIO ART, Walt Disney Enterprises, no. 29, 1940, 5-1/2" high. This amusing can shows Donald walking blithely along on one side, and on the other, an angry Donald after he trips over a brick.
Excellent $175; Good $100.

Fig. 540:
"Music Box," by OHIO ART, circa late 1940s. (Courtesy of Dora C. Pohl.)
Excellent $75; Good $45.

Fig. 541:
"Bunny with Egg-Shaped Cart," CHEIN, 1957. (Courtesy of Dorothy Ellen Masters.) This is another version of no. 161.
Excellent $95; Good $50.

Fig. 542:
"Chick Pushing Cart," by CHEIN, no. 82, 1953. (Courtesy of Jack and Barbara Craig.)
Excellent $75; Good $45.

Fig. 539

Fig. 541

Fig. 539a

Fig. 542

Fig. 540

Fig. 543

Fig. 544

Fig. 545

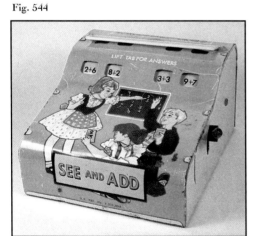

Fig. 546

Fig. 547

Fig. 543:
"Sprinkling Can," by CHEIN, no. 74, circa 1950s to 1960. (Courtesy of Dorothy Ellen Masters.) This sprinkling can has particularly graceful lines. It was produced with several different litho designs. *Excellent $75; Good $45.*

Fig. 544:
"Money Box," by OHIO ART, no. 121, 1956. (Courtesy of Jacob Kerr.) *Excellent $40; Good $25.*

Fig. 545:
"Roy Rogers Lantern," by OHIO ART, 1956. *Excellent $150; Good $100.*

Fig. 546:
"See and Add," by WOLVERINE, circa late 1950s through 1960s. This is one of several educational arithmetic, spelling, and geography toys produced by WOLVERINE. *Excellent $65; Good $45.*

Fig. 547:
"Church Organ Music Box," by CHEIN, 1952 and 1958. (Courtesy of Dorothy Ellen Masters.) *Excellent $75; Good $50.*

Fig. 548:
"Sparkler with Box, no. 95," by CHEIN, circa early 1960s. (Courtesy of Dorothy Ellen Masters.)
Excellent $40; Good $20.

Fig. 549:
"Music Box with Angels on Musical Notes," by OHIO ART, circa late 1940s to early 1950s.
Excellent $65; Good $40.

Fig. 550:
"Musical Ka-Yo," by CAYO MFG. CO., Benton Harbor, Michigan, circa 1950s. (Courtesy of Jack and Barbara Craig.)
Excellent $55; Good $20.

Fig. 551:
"Circus Shooting Gallery," by OHIO ART, 1960 to 1966. (Courtesy of Connie and Robert Delaney.)
Excellent $125; Good $60.

Fig. 548

Fig. 549

Fig. 550

Fig. 551

Fig. 552

Fig. 552:
"Union Station Train Station," circa 1950s. (Courtesy of Connie and Robert Delaney.)
Excellent $225; Good $180.

Fig. 553:
"Jungle Eyes Shooting Gallery," by OHIO ART, circa 1960s. (Courtesy of Connie and Robert Delaney.)
Excellent $125; Good $60.

Fig. 554:
"Watering Can," by OHIO ART, circa early 1940s. (Courtesy of Shirley Cox.) Designed by Fern Bisel Peat.
Excellent $100; Good $65.

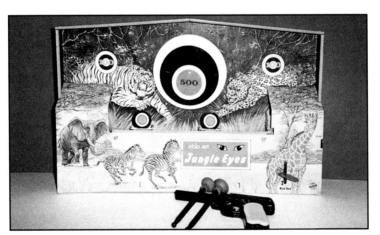

Fig. 553

Fig. 554

Fig. 555:
"Automatic Target Range,"
by MARX, 1957. (Courtesy
of Tom Frogge.)
Excellent $125; Good $75.

Fig. 556:
"Knock Down Target
Game," by MARX, circa
late 1950s to early 1960s.
(Courtesy of Tom Frogge.)
Excellent $125; Good $75.

Fig. 557:
Box for game in Figure 556.

Fig. 558:
"State Fair Bagatelle
Game," by MARX, circa
1960s.
Excellent $125; Good $85.

Fig. 555

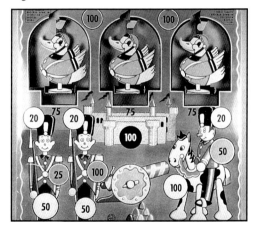

Fig. 556

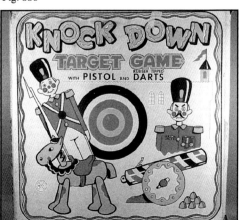

Fig. 557

Fig. 558

Fig. 559

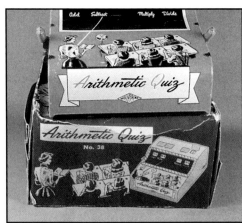

Fig. 560

Fig. 561

Fig. 562

Fig. 559:
"Watering Can," by OHIO ART, circa early 1960s. (Courtesy of Tom Frogge.) *Excellent $50; Good $35.*

Fig. 560:
"Arithmetic Quiz," by WOLVERINE, no. 38, circa 1950s to 1960s. (Courtesy of Tom Frogge.) In 1969 a new game was issued called "Modern Math." *Excellent $65; Good $45.*

Fig. 561:
"See and Spell," by WOLVERINE, no. 41, 1957 to 1960s. *Excellent $65; Good $45.*

Fig. 562:
OHIO ART catalogue cover, 1927.

ABOUT THE AUTHOR

LISA KERR has a master's degree in education. She worked as a professional choreographer and dance teacher for twenty years, choreographing original works and musical theater productions for theater companies, light opera, and universities. As artistic director of a modern dance company, Lisa was the recipient of two National Endowment for the Arts grants for choreography.

In 1989, Lisa returned to school in Oregon to get her law degree in order to pursue her interests in environmental protection and wildlife preservation issues. She currently lives in Seattle, Washington, with her husband and two children, where she researches and writes legal briefs and studies flamenco dance.

Lisa collects tin-lithographed toys—especially wind-ups, dishes, and sand pails. She and her partner, Rita Griffith, buy and sell the toys under the name "Windmill Productions."

BIBLIOGRAPHY

Baker, *Modern Toys 1950 - 1980*, 1991.

CHEIN Toy Catalogues, 1929 to 1960s.

Ebert, John and Katherine, *Old American Prints for Collectors*, Charles Scribner's and Sons, New York, 1974.

Field, Eugene, *The Sugar Plum Tree*, The Saalfield Publishing Company, Ohio, New York, 1930.

Ickis, Marguerite, *The Book of Festivals and Holidays the World Over*, Dodd, Mead & Company, New York, 1970.

Longest, David and Stern, Michael, *Disneyana, A Value and Identification Guide*, Collector Books, Kentucky, 1992.

Longest, David, *Toys: Antique to Modern 1870-1950 — ID and Values*, 1994.

McCumber, Bob, *Chein Toys and Bank Catalogues*, Robert McCumber, Connecticut, 1993.

OHIO ART Toy Catalogues, 1929 to 1960s.

Pinsky, Maxine A., *Greenberg's Guide to Marx Toys*, Greenberg Publishing Company, Inc., Maryland, 1988.

Playthings Directories, 1927 through 1960s.

Punchard, *Playtime Kitchen Items and Table Accessories*, 1993.

Sommer, *I Had One of Those, Toys of the Baby Boom Years*, 1992.

Tempest, Jack, *Collector's Guide to Postwar Tin Toys*, 1991.

Whitmyer, *Collector's Encyclopedia of Children's Dishes*, 1993.

WOLVERINE Toy Catalogues, 1931 to 1960s.